INSTRUCTOR'S MANUAL
AND TEST BANK

TO ACCOMPANY

America: A Narrative History

Sixth Edition

George Brown Tindall
University of North Carolina
and
David E. Shi
Furman University

PREPARED BY
Mark S. Goldman, Tallahassee Community College
David B. Parker, Kennesaw State University

W. W. Norton & Company
New York / London

ISBN 0-393-92423-8 (pbk.)

W. W. Norton & Company, Inc.
500 Fifth Avenue, New York, NY 10110

www.wwnorton.com

W. W. Norton & Company, Ltd.
Castle House, 75/76 Wells Street, London W1T 3QT

1 2 3 4 5 6 7 8 9 0

CONTENTS

Preface iv

Bibliography of Selected Reference Works in American History v

1. The Collision of Cultures 1
2. England and Its Colonies 12
3. Colonial Ways of Life 22
4. The Imperial Perspective 33
5. From Empire to Independence 43
6. The American Revolution 55
7. Shaping a Federal Union 66
8. The Federalist Era 76
9. The Early Republic 87
10. Nationalism and Sectionalism 98
11. The Jacksonian Impulse 109
12. The Dynamics of Growth 120
13. An American Renaissance: Religion, Romanticism, and Reform 130
14. Manifest Destiny 140
15. The Old South 150
16. The Crisis of Union 161
17. The War of the Union 172
18. Reconstruction: North and South 184
19. New Frontiers: South and West 196
20. Big Business and Organized Labor 208
21. The Emergence of Urban America 220
22. Gilded-Age Politics and Agrarian Revolt 231
23. An American Empire 243
24. The Progressive Era 254
25. America and the Great War 266
26. The Modern Temper 279
27. Republican Resurgence and Decline 290
28. New Deal America 303
29. From Isolation to Global War 315
30. The Second World War 327
31. The Fair Deal and Containment 339
32. Through the Picture Window: Society and Culture, 1945–1960 351
33. Conflict and Deadlock: The Eisenhower Years 361
34. New Frontiers: Politics and Social Change in the 1960s 373
35. Rebellion and Reaction in the 1960s and 1970s 385
36. A Conservative Insurgency 397
37. Triumph and Tragedy: America at the Turn of the Century 407

Appendix: Sample Final Examinations 417

PREFACE

This *Instructor's Manual and Test Bank* is meant to assist novice instructors in developing a course around the sixth edition of *America: A Narrative History*, by George Brown Tindall and David E. Shi, and to aid more experienced instructors with nearly 2,500 questions for examinations and an outline of each chapter of the text.

This sixth edition of the *Instructor's Manual and Test Bank* is keyed to the sixth edition of *America: A Narrative History*. Each chapter provides several suggested lecture topics, closely related to the text itself, with a brief list of possible sources for the lectures. The manual also includes a Test Bank of nearly 2,500 questions: multiple choice, matching, true/false, chronology, and essay.

A computerized version of the test-item file is available separately for use on Macintosh and IBM-compatible systems. A test-creation system (Norton TestMaker) is provided with the test-item file diskettes, allowing instructors to create tests easily, choosing those questions from the Test Bank that they wish to use and allowing them to write questions if they wish. Norton TestMaker is available at no charge to instructors who adopt a minimum number of copies of *America: A Narrative History*.

Instructors who wish their students to use a self-administered guide for assistance in studying the text are urged to consider the *Study Guide* written by Charles Eagles. That guide contains carefully selected documents and readings, and some instructors will want to use it as a required supplement to the course. Others may wish only to request that the campus bookstore order copies to ensure its availability to students. Instructors who adopt Tindall's text may request a set of selected map transparencies for use on overhead projectors.

Thank yous need to go to Thomas S. Morgan, coauthor of the first edition of this *Instructor's Manual*, who died in April 1996, and David Parker who authored the next four editions of this guide.

Special thanks go to my loving wife, Carol Chenoweth, who besides putting up with me every day is my best friend and has been my biggest supporter in all my pursuits, especially concerning my academic career; and to my children, Leben and Sarah, who have brought me nothing but joy throughout their lives. I continue to appreciate all my family's love and support. Special thanks also to the folks at W. W. Norton—Matthew Arnold, Sarah England, and others—who, as always, have been great. I must give a special thumbs-up to George Tindall for writing a superb textbook, and to David Shi for maintaining that standard of excellence in his revisions.

Mark S. Goldman
Tallahassee Community College

iv

BIBLIOGRAPHY OF SELECTED REFERENCE WORKS IN AMERICAN HISTORY

The following list is intended for the beginning instructor as a convenient guide to the wealth of reference materials available for teachers of American history. The usual disclaimer that one finds on such a list—that it is suggestive rather than exhaustive—certainly applies here.

Perhaps the single most useful reference book for historians is the *Harvard Guide to American History* (2 vols.; rev. ed., 1979), edited by Frank B. Freidel. Besides several stimulating essays on the art and methodology of history, the *Harvard Guide* contains a lengthy bibliography. For biographical information, turn first to the multivolume *Dictionary of American Biography* (1928–1987), edited by Allen Johnson, Dumas Malone, and others, and kept up-to-date with periodic supplements. Richard B. Morris's *Encyclopedia of American History* (7th ed., 1996) contains general and topical chronologies, several hundred biographical sketches, and other useful material. The value of Scribner's *Dictionary of American History* (8 vols.; rev. ed., 1976–1978) is greatly enhanced by its comprehensive index. Other useful books include *Documents of American History* (10th ed., 1988), edited by Henry Steele Commager; the *Atlas of American History* (2nd rev. ed., 1985), edited by James T. Adams; the *Album of American History* (6 vols.; 1981), edited by James Truslow Adams. The last-mentioned book is mainly a pictorial work that includes thousands of illustrations covering American history through the early 1960s; a supplement (1985) brings it up to 1982.

Besides the *Harvard Guide*, two bibliographical guides stand out. *America: History and Life* is regularly updated, and is therefore useful for finding more recent materials. *Goldentree Bibliographies in American History*, under the general editorship of Arthur S. Link, are more specialized guides for various topics; examples include John Shy's volume on the American Revolution, Vincent P. De Santis's on the Gilded Age, and Paul M. Gaston's on the New South.

Historical surveys (some more interpretative than others) of various important topics include Thomas A. Bailey's *A Diplomatic History of the American People* (10th ed., 1980), Winthrop S. Hudson's *Religion in America: An Historical Account of the Development of American Religious Life* (5th ed., 1992), Stanley Lebergott's *The Americans: An Economic Record* (1984), Alfred H. Kelly, Winfred Harbison, and Herman Belz's *The American Constitution: Its Origins and Development* (7th ed., 1991), Mary P. Ryan's *Womanhood in America: From Colonial Times to the Present* (3rd ed., 1983), and John Hope Franklin's *From Slavery to Freedom: A History of Negro Americans* (7th ed., 1991).

For ideas concerning lecture topics, instructors might turn to Carl Degler's *Out of Our Past: The Forces That Shaped Modern America* (3rd ed., 1984). *The Comparative Approach to American History* (1968), edited by C. Vann Woodward, compares various aspects of American history to that of other nations. Also useful are *Myth and the American Experience* (3rd ed., 1990), edited by Nicholas Cords and Patrick Gerster; and Daniel Boorstin's *The Americans* (3 vols., 1958–1973). Three series of volumes—the American Historical Association's *AHA Pamphlets*, D. C. Heath's *Problems in American Civilization*, and Little, Brown's *Critical Issues in American History*—offer historical and historiographical introductions to a number of topics. Harold S. Sharp's *Footnotes to American History: A Bibliographic Source Book* (1977) is a handy guide for information on such "footnotes" as the Norse discovery of America, the Lost Colony, the trial of Anne Hutchinson, on down to the Manson family murders, William Calley, and Patty Hearst.

There are a number of books that discuss history itself and the teaching of history. Lester D. Stephens's *Probing the Past: A Guide to the Study and Teaching of History* (1974) offers a good introduction to both topics. For the students' side, see Norman F. Cantor and Richard I. Schneider's *How to Study History* (1967) and Jules R. Benjamin's *A Student's Guide to History* (7th ed., 1997). While meant for students, these last two books have much to offer instructors as well. Some teachers may wish to assign portions of these books to their students at the beginning of the term.

Instructors designing their first course, or changing an existing one, might look at *American History* (3 vols.; 2nd ed., 1987), a set in the series *Selected Reading Lists and Course Outlines from American Colleges and Universities*; volume 1 contains materials from survey courses in American history. Finally, instructors should consult *The History Teacher*, a quarterly journal that features reviews of textbooks and reference aids, articles on teaching history, and historiographical essays.

Chapter 1

THE COLLISION OF CULTURES

This chapter covers the origins of Indian civilizations in the New World, the motivations for European exploration and colonization, the Spanish conquest, and developments in other European countries prior to the first permanent English settlements.

Chapter Outline

I. Pre-Columbian Indian civilizations
   A. Possible origins of the American Indian
      1. Siberia
      2. Southwestern Europe
   B. Basic stages of development in Middle America
      1. Early stages
      2. Permanent towns emerged about 2000 B.C. in Mexico
      3. Flowering of classical Middle American culture (Mayans) from A.D. 300 to 900
      4. Aztecs followed and developed the culture that was present when the Spanish arrived
      5. South American cultures: Chibchas and Incas
   C. Indians in the present United States reached three minor cultural climaxes
      1. Adena-Hopewell peoples of the Ohio Valley (800 B.C.–A.D. 600) had great earthworks
      2. Mississippian culture of the Mississippi Valley (A.D. 600–1500) climaxed about the time of the European discovery and influenced many tribes
      3. Pueblo-Hohokam-Anasazi cultures of the Southwest (400 B.C.–present) had looser class structure
   D. Ill-equipped to resist European invasion
      1. Europeans were more technologically advanced than the Indians
      2. Political disunity and tribal wars
   E. Indian adaptations to Europeans

II. Early European contacts with the New World
    A. European mythological visions of the New World
    B. Norse explorations

III. European development prior to Columbus
    A. The Renaissance brought an intense interest in knowledge of the world
       1. Knowledge that the earth was round
       2. Improved navigational aids: compass and astrolabe
       3. Development of trade among towns
          a. Merchant class
          b. Corporations that shared risk
       4. Barriers to trade with the Orient
       5. Rise of the nation states
       6. Contributions of the merchant class, professionals, gunpowder, and Crusades

IV. Christopher Columbus and the discovery
    A. Explorations of the Portuguese
    B. Early life and efforts to gain support for a voyage west
    C. First voyage
    D. Later voyages
    E. America named for Amerigo Vespucci

V. The great biological exchange
    A. Animals
    B. Plants
    C. Devices
    D. Diseases

VI. Other early explorers
    A. John Cabot gave England claim in 1497
    B. Portuguese efforts of Vasco da Gama and Ferdinand Magellan

VII. Spanish conquest and settlement of the new lands
    A. Cultural clash
    B. Hernando Cortés and conquest of the Aztecs
    C. Patterns of Spanish conquest
       1. *Encomienda* system
       2. Introduction of African slavery
       3. Catholic missionary opposition to Spanish conquest
    D. Differences between the cultures of Spanish America and North America
       1. Existing Indian cultures less nomadic
       2. Influences of Catholicism
       3. Spanish-American culture

    E. Spanish exploration of North America
       1. Ponce de León
       2. Narváez and de Vaca
       3. de Soto
       4. Coronado
    F. Early Spanish settlements
       1. Nature of Spanish settlements
       2. St. Augustine, first European town in United States
       3. The Spanish Southwest
          a. Importance of Catholic missions
          b. *Encomenderos*
          c. Popé's rebellion
          d. Spain regained control of New Mexico

VIII. Impact of Protestant Reformation in Europe
    A. Early causes and spread of the movement
    B. Martin Luther
    C. Impact of Calvin
    D. Reformation in England
       1. An initial political revolt
       2. Periods of conflict
       3. Elizabethan settlement

IX. Other early European efforts at colonization
    A. French efforts
       1. Verrazano explored coast in 1524
       2. Cartier led three voyages
    B. Dutch opposition to Spain
       1. Rebellion of the Netherlands against Spanish rule, 1567–1648
       2. Dutch "Sea Beggars" plunder Spanish ships
    C. English effort
       1. Elizabethan "Sea Dogges": John Hawkins and Francis Drake
       2. Defeat of the Spanish Armada, 1588
       3. Promotion of English colonization
       4. Sir Walter Raleigh's unsuccessful efforts and fate of the Lost Colony

Lecture Ideas

1. A lecture on Pre-Columbian America is very appropriate. Give a general overview of the Hemisphere including the Inca, Maya, and Aztec. Then focus in on the rest of North America, especially the contiguous forty-eight states. Describe the wide variety of cultures

that existed as well as the various philosophies concerning shared land, governance, and so forth. A good source would be Alvin M. Josephy and Frederick E. Hoxie, eds., *America in 1492* (1993) and Thomas D. Dillehay's *The Settlement of the Americas* (2001).

2. Depending on the size of your class, divide them up into groups and assign each group a European country that planted colonies in the Western Hemisphere (Britain, France, Spain, Portugal, the Netherlands, Russia, and so forth). Have them research their motivation, destination, and successes or failures. Each group can also assess the long-term impact each country had on America. Use Samuel Eliot Morison's *The European Discovery of America: The Northern Voyages* (1993) and *The Southern Voyages* (1974) and John H. Parry's *The Age of Reconnaissance: Discovery, Exploration and Settlement 1450–1650* (1988).

3. The subject of Columbus will be of great interest to your students. You can discuss the impact his voyages and claims had on America. Such issues as: did he discover America, what impact did he have on native populations, and what impact did he have on the European community are good topics for discussion. This lecture will invariably lead you to a discussion on the "Columbia Exchange." See William D. Phillips, Jr. and Carla Rahn Phillips's *The Worlds of Christopher Columbus* (1992), Kirkpatrick Sales's *The Conquest of Paradise: Christopher Columbus and the Columbian Legacy* (1990), and Alfred W. Crosby's *The Columbian Exchange* (1972).

4. After the Europeans arrived, a very useful lecture on Native American/ European relations would be recommended. This will allow you to establish a great comparison of native to European cultures and beliefs. Take your students on a journey. Have some of them research the European mindset on land ownership, communal responsibilities, power, religion, values, and any other issues they may encounter. Then compare these to that of the various Native American beliefs, and a great group discussion should follow. You might write the major points of their arguments on the board/overhead and use that as a stimulus for the discussion. See Gary B. Nash's *Red, White, and Black* (3rd ed., 1992), and John Axtell's *The Invasion Within* (1986).

True/False Questions

T   1. Many of the New World's early explorers were looking for a shorter and safer route to the Orient.

F   2. Christopher Columbus had to convince his sponsors that the earth is round.

T 3. The New World was named for the Italian explorer Amerigo Vespucci.

F 4. The horse was the only domestic four-legged animal in the New World before the arrival of the Europeans.

F 5. England's glorious age of discovery came during the reign of Henry VIII.

F 6. Mary Scot was the first English child born in the New World.

T 7. Ferdinand Magellan's ship was the first to sail around the world.

F 8. Calvinism stressed tolerance and liberal theology rather than a strict moral code.

T 9. Those who wanted to purify the Church of England were called "Puritans."

T 10. Francis Drake was one of the most famous of the English "Sea Dogges."

Multiple-Choice Questions

1. From A.D. 300 to 900, which group in Middle America (Mesoamerica) developed a great city, including gigantic pyramids and temple complexes:
   A. Aztecs.
   B. Inca.
   * C. Mayas.
   D. Pueblos.

2. When Columbus first reached the New World, the population of what is now the United States was about:
   A. 100,000.
   B. 500,000.
   C. 2,000,000.
   * D. 4,000,000.

3. The culture known for its elaborate earthworks and burial mounds in the Northeast was the:
   * A. Adena-Hopewell.
   B. Chibchas.
   C. Hohokam.
   D. Mayan.

4. The Aztecs:
    A. were the most advanced example of the Adena-Hopewell culture.
  * B. had an empire of perhaps five million people in Mexico.
    C. absorbed the Mayas around 1425.
    D. succumbed to the Toltecs around A.D. 900.

5. Montezuma ruled the:
  * A. Aztecs.
    B. Inca.
    C. Mayas.
    D. Toltecs.

6. The Anasazis:
    A. lacked a rigid class structure.
    B. engaged in warfare only for self-defense.
    C. lived in the Southwest.
  * D. are correctly described by all the above statements.

7. The Norse settlements in the New World:
  * A. were made about A.D. 1000.
    B. were located on the coast of what is now Florida.
    C. led directly to later Spanish explorations.
    D. are correctly described by all the above statements.

8. Which of the following was *not* one of the developments of the late Middle Ages that helped to promote exploration?
    A. the rise of the nation states and monarchs
    B. the rise of towns and trade
  * C. the development of the power of feudal lords
    D. the invention of new instruments that permitted navigation far from shore

9. Prince Henry the Navigator:
  * A. began a systematic exploration of the coast of Africa.
    B. financed Columbus's first expedition.
    C. explored the Hudson River.
    D. reached the Philippine Islands by sailing around Africa.

10. Christopher Columbus first landed in the New World in:
    A. 1451.
    B. 1487.
  * C. the Bahamas.
    D. Florida.

11. Christopher Columbus:
    A. was supported in his voyages to the New World by Portugal.
    B. forced the first natives he encountered to sign the Treaty of Tordesillas.
    * C. made a total of four voyages to the New World.
    D. is correctly described by all the above statements.

12. Which of the following animals were *not* found in the New World before the Europeans came?
    A. flying squirrels and catfish
    B. bison and opposums
    * C. sheep and pigs
    D. turkeys and rattlesnakes

13. Which of the following plants did the Europeans introduce into the New World?
    A. cacao (for chocolate) and sweet potatoes
    B. peanuts and tobacco
    C. pumpkins and tomatoes
    * D. rice and oats

14. The explorer who landed at Newfoundland in 1497 and thus gave England the basis for a claim to North America was:
    A. John White.
    * B. John Cabot.
    C. Arthur Barlowe.
    D. Sir Humphrey Gilbert.

15. Bartolomé de las Casas:
    A. led the first voyage around the world.
    B. was the first governor of the Spanish territory in the New World.
    * C. gave rise to the "Black Legend" of Spanish cruelty to the Indians.
    D. urged Spanish conquest of the Indians in order to improve civilization.

16. Tenochtitlán:
    * A. was the Aztec capital (now Mexico City).
    B. was the bloodthirsty Mayan sun god, symbolized by the hummingbird.
    C. was the Portuguese name for Cuba.
    D. organized the most successful resistance against the Spanish in Florida.

17. The Aztecs were conquered:
    A. by Hernando Cortés.
    B. in the 1520s.
    C. in part to satisfy the Spanish desire for gold.
    * D. all the above statements are true.

18. The *encomiendo* system:
    A. kept the Portuguese out of Mexico.
    * B. allowed Spanish landowners to control Indian villages.
    C. benefited the Native American populations of Spanish America.
    D. allowed Mayan and Incan leaders to become very wealthy through the labor of their people.

19. By the seventeenth century, the Indian population in Spain's New World empire had decreased by about:
    A. 10 percent.
    B. 25 percent.
    C. 50 percent.
    * D. 90 percent.

20. By 1600 Spain's New World empire included all the following *except*:
    * A. Brazil.
    B. Florida.
    C. Mexico.
    D. New Mexico.

21. The government of Spain in the New World differed from that of the later English colonies in that:
    A. Spain permitted a greater degree of self-government in its colonies.
    B. there was less bureaucracy associated with the government of the Spanish colonies.
    * C. every detail of colonial administration was closely regulated by the Spanish king.
    D. Spain completely uprooted the native cultures it encountered.

22. The Indian leader Popé organized a massive rebellion against the Spanish in:
    A. Florida.
    B. Hispaniola.
    * C. New Mexico.
    D. Peru.

23. The first permanent European city in the present-day United States was:
    * A. St. Augustine, in what is now Florida.
    B. Sante Fe, in what is now New Mexico.
    C. Port Royal, in what is now South Carolina.
    D. New Orleans, in what is now Louisiana.

24. Who wrote the "Ninety-Five Theses"?
    A. Catherine of Aragon
    B. John Hawkins
    * C. Martin Luther
    D. Moses

25. The Protestant Reformation in England:
    * A. occurred more for political reasons than because of disagreement about religious doctrine.
    B. was almost undone when Elizabeth tried to reimpose Catholicism.
    C. was led by John Calvin.
    D. occurred prior to the Reformation in Germany.

26. The earliest major attempts at colonization by the French in the New World were in what is now:
    A. Florida.
    * B. Canada.
    C. Cuba.
    D. Virginia.

27. The defeat of the Spanish Armada:
    * A. led to English naval supremacy.
    B. led to the execution of Christopher Columbus.
    C. gave France virtual control of Brazil.
    D. was King Henry VIII's greatest military achievement.

28. Sir Walter Raleigh argued that which country should establish colonies in the New World?
    * A. England
    B. France
    C. Holland
    D. Spain

29. The colony planted in 1587 at Roanoke:
    A. grew to become the present state of North Carolina.
    B. was the first permanent English colony in the New World.
    C. was established to mine the gold that Indians claimed was there.
    * D. was left on its own for three years because of England's war with Spain.

30. About how many English colonists were in the New World in 1600?
    * A. fewer than 5,000
    B. 20,000
    C. 250,000
    D. 1 million

Essay Questions

1. Describe the development of Spanish rule over its territory in America.

2. In 1600, which European nation seemed to have the best chance at eventually controlling what is now the United States? Why?

3. Explain the origins of the American Indians and compare the general cultures that they developed in South, North, and Central America.

4. Explain the various factors of the European Renaissance that prompted and promoted the exploration and settlement of the New World

5. The title of this chapter is "The Collision of Cultures." In what ways is this phrase an accurate assessment of the early relationship between the Old World and the New?

Matching Questions

A) conquered the Incan Empire
B) wrote *The Institutes of the Christian Religion* (1536)
C) was killed in the Philippines
D) began the Protestant Reformation
E) captain of the *Santa Maria*
F) led first French effort to colonize the New World
G) Spanish ruler in New Mexico
H) explored what is now the southeastern United States
I) wrote *A Brief Relation of the Destruction of the Indies*
J) attempted first English colonization of the New World

B   1. John Calvin
F   2. Jacques Cartier
E   3. Christopher Columbus
H   4. Hernando de Soto
J   5. Sir Humphrey Gilbert
I   6. Bartolomé de las Casas
D   7. Martin Luther
C   8. Ferdinand Magellan
G   9. Juan de Oñate
A   10. Francisco Pizarro

Chapter 2

ENGLAND AND ITS COLONIES

This chapter discusses the founding of the English colonies, the relationships between the various native populations and the English, and the general pattern of settlement and government of the English colonies in North America.

Chapter Outline

I. The English background to colonization
   - A. Unique features of English development
     1. Institutions that supported liberty
     2. Economic institutions that supported colonization
   - B. The development of the monarchy under the Stuarts
     1. James I advanced ideas of Divine Right
     2. Religious reforms under Charles I led to revolution
     3. The Commonwealth and Protectorate
     4. Restoration of Charles II
     5. The Glorious Revolution deposed James II

II. Patterns of English colonization
   - A. Use of the joint stock companies
   - B. Differences between English and Spanish colonization

III. Settlement of the English colonies
   - A. Virginia
     1. Founding of Jamestown
     2. Powhatan and the Virginia Indians
     3. Captain John Smith
     4. Attempts to reinforce Jamestown
     5. Tobacco
     6. Reforms of 1618–1619
     7. Indian massacre killed 350 colonists
     8. Stability as a royal colony
     9. Bacon's Rebellion
   - B. Maryland
     1. The Calverts
     2. Colonial government

   C. Plymouth
1. Differences between New England colonists and the Chesapeake Bay colonists
2. The Pilgrims
3. William Bradford's leadership
4. The Mayflower Compact
   D. Massachusetts Bay
1. The Puritans
2. The New England Company
3. John Winthrop and "a city upon a hill"
4. Trading company became provincial government
   E. Rhode Island
1. Roger Williams
2. Anne Hutchinson
   F. Connecticut
   G. New Hampshire and Maine

IV. Indians in New England
   A. White-Indian relations characterized
   B. The New England Indians
   C. Relations
1. Diseases
2. The Pequot War
3. King Philip's War

V. Effects of the English Civil War
   A. New England Confederation formed
   B. Virginia during the war
   C. Maryland Toleration Act
   D. The Restoration's effects in the colonies

VI. Restoration brought new proprietary colonies
   A. The Carolinas
1. The Lords Proprietors
2. North Carolina
3. South Carolina
4. "Fundamental Constitutions of Carolina"
5. Indian relations
   a. Trade
   b. Tuscarora War
   c. Yamasee War
   B. New York
1. Origin as New Netherland
2. English takeover
3. The Iroquois League

  C. New Jersey
  D. Pennsylvania
    1. Quakers
    2. William Penn
    3. Penn's Frames of Government
  E. Delaware
  F. Georgia
    1. James Oglethorpe
    2. Philanthropic experiment and military buffer

VII. The general pattern of English settlement

Lecture Ideas

1. Several lectures should be developed to discuss the motivations and patterns of English colonization. Not only does this set up the English story but can be used as a basis of comparison to other European colonization efforts in America. You can trace this development from forces within England all the way to the establishment of England's American colonies. A good source for this is Jack P. Greene and J. R. Pole, eds., *Colonial British America* (1984).

2. It would be useful to discuss the various Native American tribes that the English encountered in the American colonies. A discussion on the initial reactions of the various tribes as the English advanced their colonies could stimulate great discussion. You may assign groups an individual region to examine the relationship between native and English populations and have a class discussion on their findings. See James Axtell's *The Europeans and the Indian* (1981) and Edward Countryman's *Americans: A Collision of Histories* (1996).

3. A lecture is appropriate on the topic of England's success in North America. You can focus in on the adjustments England made along the way. The change in colonies, the intellectual changes by the colonists themselves, and the redefining of group and individual goals. Jack P. Greene's book *Pursuits of Happiness* (1988) is a fine source.

True/False Questions

F   1. William Laud ruled England as "Lord Protector" through most of the 1650s.

F   2. The Virginia Company of Plymouth brought the Puritans to Massachusetts Bay.

T   3. The first blacks in English America were brought to Virginia.

F   4. Nathaniel Bacon owned one of the biggest plantations in Tidewater Virginia.

T   5. The Indian wars of the mid-1670s cost proportionately more casualties than any other American war.

T   6. The "Fundamental Constitutions of Carolina" established a formal nobility and provided for religious toleration.

T   7. Much of Anne Hutchinson's problem with the Puritan leaders was because she was a woman.

T   8. Delaware was originally part of Pennsylvania.

T   9. By the mid-1670s, about a quarter of Virginia's free white adult males owned no land.

F   10. Peter Stuyvesant was the defiant governor of Rhode Island.

Multiple-Choice Questions

1. The English Civil War:
   A. led to the execution of Charles II.
   B. overturned the reforms of the Glorious Revolution.
   * C. was fought between supporters of Parliament and supporters of the monarchy.
   D. is correctly represented by all the above statements.

2. The Indian leader Powhatan was associated with the early history of which colony?
   A. Massachusetts Bay
   B. New York
   C. Plymouth
   * D. Virginia

3. Charles I:
   A. was the father of James I.
   B. was the son of James II.
   C. sympathized with the Puritans more than any other seventeenth-century English monarch.
   * D. ruled without Parliament for about a dozen years.

4. England's first permanent colony in the New World was founded:
   A. when Charles II was king.
 * B. before the English Civil War.
   C. as a royal colony.
   D. All the above are true.

5. One of the important factors aiding the survival of the early Jamestown settlers was:
   A. the large sums of money that were used to bring additional supplies to them regularly.
   B. their willingness to work hard and sacrifice for the good of the whole colony.
 * C. the assistance they received from the Indians.
   D. the lack of the diseases and hardships that afflicted other colonies.

6. England's pattern of colonization in America came primarily from English experience with:
   A. operating trading posts for Dutch merchants.
   B. establishing colonies during the Crusades against the Moors.
 * C. planting settlements in Ireland.
   D. operating tobacco plantations in India.

7. The most important cash crop in seventeenth-century Virginia was:
   A. cotton.
   B. indigo.
   C. rice.
 * D. tobacco.

8. The headright system adopted for the Virginia colony consisted of:
 * A. giving fifty acres of land to anyone who would transport himself to the colony, and fifty more for any servants he might bring.
   B. "selling" wives to single male settlers.
   C. auctioning black slaves to settlers.
   D. giving free land to all servants who came to the colony.

9. The man who became head of the Virginia Company of London in 1618 and instituted a series of reforms to save the colony was:
   A. John Rolfe.
 * B. Sir Edwin Sandys.
   C. John Smith.
   D. Peter Stuyvesant.

10. The colony of Maryland was founded:
    * A. in 1634.
    B. as part of the Chesapeake Stock Company.
    C. as a royal colony.
    D. as a refuge for French Huguenots.

11. William Berkeley was governor of:
    A. Georgia.
    B. New Jersey.
    C. North Carolina.
    * D. Virginia.

12. Bacon's Rebellion:
    * A. brought indentured servants and small farmers together against the colony's rich planters and political leaders.
    B. had the support of nearby Indian tribes.
    C. resulted from changes in the Fundamental Constitutions of Carolina that discriminated against Puritans.
    D. led to the burning of Charleston.

13. The Plymouth colony:
    A. absorbed the Massachusetts Bay colony.
    * B. was absorbed by the Massachusetts Bay colony.
    C. was founded as a royal colony.
    D. was founded as a proprietary colony.

14. After 1644, the right to vote in Massachusetts Bay was restricted to those who:
    A. owned 100 acres of land.
    B. had come in the first voyage from England.
    * C. were members of a Puritan church.
    D. had been listed as freemen in the original charter.

15. The Mayflower Compact:
    A. completely separated civil and church governments.
    B. was developed by settlers in Massachusetts Bay.
    * C. provided the original government for the Plymouth colony.
    D. called for total religious toleration.

16. Anne Hutchinson:
    A. claimed to have received direct revelations from God.
    B. challenged the legitimacy of the Puritan ministers.
    C. was banished from Massachusetts Bay.
    * D. is correctly represented by all the above statements.

17. "Separatists" established the colony of:
    A. Georgia.
    B. Maryland.
    C. Massachusetts Bay.
    * D. Plymouth.

18. The log cabin:
    A. was the essential form of housing for the early settlers in all colonies.
    B. originated in the Carolinas.
    * C. was the contribution of Scandinavian settlers in New Sweden.
    D. was first used by the Pilgrims in Plymouth colony.

19. Roger Williams's mistrust of the purity of others eventually led him to the belief that:
    A. all churches were equally valid.
    * B. there should be complete separation of church and state.
    C. the government must direct actions of the church to assure its purity.
    D. only those people who believed exactly as he did could be saved.

20. King Philip's War:
    A. was named for the French king who ordered the Indians to leave his New World colonies.
    B. led to the virtual destruction of the Pequots.
    * C. was fought in the mid-1670s.
    D. is correctly represented by all the above statements.

21. The New England Confederation:
    A. was developed to provide defense against the Dutch, French, and Indians.
    B. began during the Civil War in England.
    C. was made up of Massachusetts, Plymouth, Connecticut, and New Haven.
    * D. is correctly represented by all the above statements.

22. The Maryland Toleration Act was passed:
    A. because of Lord Baltimore's desire to extend toleration to Jews.
    B. in 1633.
    * C. to assure Puritans that they would not be molested in their religion.
    D. as a means of attracting Quakers to move to the colony from Pennsylvania.

23. The colonies established after the Restoration were all:
    A. corporate colonies.
    B. royal colonies.
 * C. proprietary colonies.
    D. in New England.

24. The Yamasee War:
 * A. was a revolt by Creek and Choctaw Indians against English control in the South.
    B. brought about the quick demise of the Iroquois League.
    C. was a rare victory for the Indians.
    D. was, in the words of John Winthrop, "a special manifestation of divine justice."

25. The colony of New York:
    A. was formed to serve as a buffer against the French in Canada.
 * B. was built upon the conquest of a Dutch settlement.
    C. was started as a royal colony by the king.
    D. had all the land divided into feudal manors consisting of 1,000 acres each.

26. Which of the following was *not* true of the Quakers?
    A. Their religion was based on individual inspiration.
    B. They refused to take oaths.
 * C. The only formal parts of the Quaker service were the pastor's sermon and the communion.
    D. They believed in the equality of the sexes and the full participation of women in religious affairs.

27. The Iroquois:
    A. was a group of five Indian tribes that united to fight the Dutch settlers who invaded their homeland.
 * B. controlled much of eastern North America during the second half of the seventeenth century.
    C. were known for their pacifism, even in the face of almost certain destruction.
    D. developed a written language and a constitutional government.

28. Of the following, which colony offered the most religious toleration?
    A. Massachusetts Bay
    B. New Hampshire
 * C. Pennsylvania
    D. Plymouth

29. Georgia was founded:
    * A. as a colonial refuge for the poor and the persecuted.
    B. in order to launch military attacks against the French in Florida.
    C. as a Quaker commonwealth, a southern counterpart to William Penn's "Holy Experiment."
    D. as a sanctuary for religious dissenters from Florida.

30. Which of the following was *not* one of the ways in which the English colonies differed from the Spanish?
    A. There was less centralized control in the English colonies than in the Spanish.
    B. The English colonies were developed with private investment funds rather than royal money.
    * C. Most of the settlers in the English colonies came from the mother country so there was less variety among the views of the settlers.
    D. The English colonies were settled in a compact geographical area.

Essay Questions

1. Do there seem to be connections between a colony's purpose and its success? That is, what type of colony seemed most apt to succeed? What type seemed most likely to fail?

2. Describe the general pattern of white-Indian relations in the English colonies.

3. Compare the settlement of Virginia and Massachusetts in regard to their founding religion, form of government, and landholding patterns.

4. Discuss the various ways in which domestic political affairs in England affected colonization in the New World.

5. According to the textbook, "The lack of plan was the genius of English colonization." What does this statement mean? How accurate is it?

Matching Questions

A) Carolina
B) Georgia
C) Maryland
D) Massachusetts Bay
E) New Jersey
F) New Netherland
G) Pennsylvania
H) Plymouth
I) Rhode Island
J) Virginia

H   1. William Bradford
C   2. Cecilius Calvert
A   3. eight "Lords Proprietors"
E   4. George Carteret
F   5. Peter Minuit
B   6. James Oglethorpe
G   7. William Penn
J   8. John Smith
I   9. Roger Williams
D   10. John Winthrop

Chapter 3

COLONIAL WAYS OF LIFE

This chapter discusses the major social and economic differences among the colonies, describes the various groups of people within colonial society, and traces the development of the Enlightenment and the Great Awakening in the American colonies.

Chapter Outline

I. The shape of early America
   A. Early American settlers
   B. British folkways brought to New World
      1. Social system
      2. British cultural legacy
   C. Seaboard ecology
      1. Indian modifications
      2. European modifications
   D. Population patterns
      1. Rapid population growth
      2. Earlier marriage age in the colonies than in England resulted in a greater frequency of pregnancies
      3. Lower death rates in the colonies resulted from scattered settlements, a younger population, and ample food
      4. The high mortality rate in the early years of the colonies made children more self-reliant
      5. Family patterns in New England compared with those in the southern colonies
      6. Impact of the frontier on values among early settlers
      7. Importance of family ties
      8. Role of women in the British colonies
      9. Women's work

II. Sectional differences among the colonies
   A. Southern colonies
      1. Advantages of the warm climate

2. Tobacco, rice, indigo, lumber, naval stores, furs, and cattle became chief exports
3. The South's favorable balance of trade with England was offset by "invisible" charges
4. Land policy came to be based on the headright system
5. Indentured servants solved some labor problems
6. Slavery developed in the southern colonies
   a. Slavery in the English colonies differed from slavery elsewhere
   b. The ethnic diversity among the slaves
   c. Perseverance of African influences
   d. Effect of color in determining groups relegated to slavery
7. The gentry
8. Religion
   a. The Church of England was the established church in the South
   b. Lack of clergy placed much control in the hands of laymen
B. The New England colonies
   1. Transformation of the English village into the New England town
      a. No headrights or quitrents
      b. System of land division used
      c. Basis used to assign land to individual families
   2. Puritan houses
   3. Exports developed in lieu of farm products
   4. Method used to offset an unfavorable balance of trade
   5. Effects of chronic shortage of hard currency
      a. Effects of use of paper money
      b. Efforts of Parliament to outlaw paper money
   6. Nature of Puritan reaction to worldly pleasures
   7. Puritan religion
      a. Form of organization in the churches
      b. Covenant theory of government
      c. Nature of church-state relationship
   8. Evidence of strain within the Puritan community in the late seventeenth century
      a. Economic strains developed
      b. Frequent challenges to authority

        c. Development of the Half-Way Covenant
        d. Witchcraft hysteria

  C. The Middle colonies
    1. Reflect elements of both the southern and New England colonies
    2. Products for export
    3. Land system used
    4. Ethnic elements represented in the population

  D. Backcountry Piedmont constituted virtually a fourth region

III. Other social and intellectual features of the colonies
  A. Isolation of colonies
  B. Urban class groupings and stratification
  C. Nature of town and city governments
  D. Means of transportation
  E. Taverns
  F. Postal service
  G. Early newspapers and editorial freedom
    1. Earliest papers
    2. Impact of the Zenger trial on freedom of the press
  H. Impact of the Enlightenment
    1. Nature of the Enlightenment
    2. Enlightenment in the British colonies
  I. Developments in education
  J. Impact of the Great Awakening
    1. Causes for the development of the movement
    2. George Whitefield and Jonathan Edwards
    3. Impact of the movement on churches and schools
    4. Long-range impact of the Great Awakening and the Enlightenment

Lecture Ideas

1. Develop a lecture on the diversity of colonial settlers. This should include a discussion on both social and economic issues, but also focus on cultural issues as well. See David H. Fischer's *Albion's Seed* (1989), Jack P. Greene's *Imperatives, Behaviors, and Identities* (1992), and Jack P. Greene's *Pursuits of Happiness* (1988).

2. A good discussion can take place by assigning groups to research and compare the three major regions of the English North American colonies. You can give a brief overview of each and then let the students present their views. Focus in on economics, religion, land use,

and so on. See Jackson Turner Main's classic, *The Social Structure of Revolutionary America* (1965).

3. A lecture on the Atlantic slave trade is a must. This lecture should include the motivation for the slave trade as well as details of the physical trade. It is important to present the cultural realities of the slave trade and a discussion of the problems from the slave traders', masters', and captives' viewpoints. See Herbert Klein's *The Atlantic Slave Trade* (1999) and Robin Law's *The Slave Coast of West Africa* (1991).

4. Lecturing on the daily life of the colonists is a good change of pace for students. A solid lecture on this can build the foundation for a good understanding of life in the colonies. You can focus in on the roles of children, men, women, the elderly, slaves, and freedmen. See David Freeman Hawke's *Everyday Life in Early America* (1988), David Eltis's *The Rise of African Slavery* (2000), and Carol Ruth Berkin and Mary Beth Norton, eds., *Women of America: A History* (1979).

5. Develop a lecture on the impact of the Enlightenment and the Great Awakening on the American colonies. Discuss the impact these movements had on both New England and the Chesapeake regions. See Frank Lambert's *Inventing the "Great Awakening"* (1999).

True/False Questions

T 1. British immigrants to America tended to retain much of their British culture.

F 2. When English settlers reached the New World, they entered a pristine environment little changed by human intervention.

T 3. People in the American colonies generally married at a younger age than those in England.

F 4. By 1700, rice and indigo were Virginia's most important export crops.

T 5. New Englanders, more than southerners, turned to the sea for their livelihood.

T 6. Puritans wore colorful clothes and enjoyed secular music.

F 7. Nearly one-third of American colonists lived in cities at the end of the seventeenth century.

F   8. A good example of the Great Awakening in American
             society was John Bartram's study of American plant life.

F   9. The Half-Way Covenant addressed the problem of New
             England's unfavorable balance of trade.

F   10. Jonathan Edwards owned the largest plantation and the
             greatest number of slaves in South Carolina.

Multiple-Choice Questions

1. Which of the following statements about the early American
    colonial population is true?
    A. The birth rate was lower than in Europe.
    B. The death rate was higher than in Europe.
    C. The number of females greatly exceeded males in the
        northern colonies.
  * D. The number of males greatly exceeded females in the
        southern colonies.

2. Women in the American colonies:
    A. generally had a lower status in society than did women in
        Europe.
  * B. often remained confined to the domestic sphere.
    C. could vote and hold office.
    D. were not likely to find eligible men to marry.

3. In 1625, the population of the English colonies in North America
    was about 2,000; by 1700, the population was about:
    A. 4,000.
    B. 9,000.
    C. 15,000.
  * D. 250,000.

4. Of the following, which was most important as an export of the
    southern colonies?
    A. corn
  * B. indigo
    C. poultry
    D. wheat

5. Indentured servants were:
    A. most common in New England.
    B. usually African Americans.

* C. usually persons who promised to work to pay for their transportation to the colonies.
    D. persons bound to a lifetime of service in the colonies.

6. Slaves who were brought to the English colonies:
    A. were mostly from eastern Africa.
* B. had a better chance to survive than those shipped to other New World destinations.
    C. were forced to learn English on the ships.
    D. generally came in at Ellis Island in New York.

7. Of all the slaves brought to the New World from Africa, how many came to the colonies of British North America?
* A. about 5 percent
    B. about 33 percent
    C. about 50 percent
    D. about 90 percent

8. It seems likely that an important factor in the enslavement of Africans was that:
    A. their common language made them an easy population to control.
    B. they were lazier and less intelligent than whites.
* C. their skin color was associated with darkness and evil by Englishmen.
    D. they clearly preferred the difficult work in rice fields and other areas for which whites were not physically well suited.

9. The southern gentry:
    A. great houses of the new colonial aristocracy became centers of sumptuous living and legendary hospitality.
    B. was often dependent on outside capital.
    C. was found mainly in Virginia and South Carolina.
* D. is correctly represented by all the above statements.

10. The established church in the southern colonies was:
    A. the Congregationalist (Puritan) church.
    B. carefully controlled by bishops and the religious hierarchy.
* C. often lax in its religious and moral standards.
    D. often in financial trouble because of the need to depend on voluntary offerings for support.

11. New England's most important staple for export was:
    A. corn.
    B. molasses.
    * C. fish.
    D. turkeys.

12. New England trade was:
    A. in most respects the same as that of the southern colonies.
    B. usually conducted along lines of the "triangle" between New England, Newfoundland, and Cuba.
    * C. based on the region's lack of suitable export crops and its potential as a commercial center.
    D. based on the great quantities of machinery and paint shipped to Europe.

13. One feature of the colonial New England economy was:
    * A. an unfavorable balance of trade; New England imported more than it exported.
    B. a favorable balance of trade; New England exported more than it imported.
    C. a steady increase in the amount of hard money (gold and silver) in circulation.
    D. the virtual nonexistence of paper money.

14. Which of the following was *not* true of Puritan beliefs?
    A. The Bible was the ultimate source of authority.
    B. Because men were depraved, sinful creatures, government was necessary to control them.
    C. The Puritans were dedicated, both in the church and in the civil government, to carry out the will of God.
    * D. Drinking was forbidden, as were sexual relations for reasons other than producing children.

15. The covenant theory from which the Puritans drew their ideas contained:
    * A. certain kernels of democracy in both church and state.
    B. the notion that the king replaced God as the head of the government of the people.
    C. the notion that men were capable of governing themselves well because they had been absolved of all sin when they entered the church.
    D. a fundamental belief in democracy.

16. The most culturally diverse of the American colonies were:
    A. in the South.
    * B. in the Middle Colonies.
    C. in New England.
    D. The colonies were roughly equal in this respect.

17. The "Middle Passage" referred to:
    A. the Anglican belief in entire sanctification.
    * B. the transportation of slaves to the New World.
    C. certain features of domestic architecture in the southern colonies.
    D. social customs in Pennsylvania.

18. The witchcraft hysteria in Salem:
    A. resulted in the execution by burning of three women.
    B. lasted nearly eight years.
    C. was led by Jonathan Edwards and the president of Harvard College.
    * D. was caused in part by the general upheaval in the political, economic, social, and religious life of the area.

19. The Middle Colonies:
    * A. included New York and Pennsylvania.
    B. lacked a suitable base for commerce.
    C. for many years had a black majority in their population.
    D. are correctly represented by all the above statements.

20. The Pennsylvania Dutch:
    A. were immigrants from Holland who settled in the backcountry of New York and Pennsylvania.
    B. migrated to Virginia and North Carolina in the late seventeenth century to escape religious persecution.
    C. were almost wiped out because of a genetic intolerance to New World viruses.
    * D. were a mixture of Mennonites, Lutherans, Moravians, Dunkers, and others.

21. After the English, the next largest white ethnic groups in the colonies were the:
    * A. Germans and Scotch-Irish.
    B. Irish and Scandinavians.
    C. French and Spanish.
    D. Dutch and Swedish.

22. The largest city in the colonies at the end of the colonial period:
    A. had a population of about 1,000,000.
    B. had a population of about 2,000.
    C. was Charleston, South Carolina.
    * D. was Philadelphia.

23. Colonial cities were marked by all the following *except*:
    A. increasingly sharp class stratification.
    * B. lack of public assistance for the poor.
    C. problems of traffic, fire, and crime.
    D. relative isolation from one another.

24. The trial of John Peter Zenger:
    A. found Zenger guilty of libel for having criticized the governor of New York.
    B. declared unconstitutional all laws that hampered freedom of the press.
    * C. encouraged editors to be more critical of public officials.
    D. denied the principle of trial by jury.

25. The Enlightenment:
    * A. led some people to the idea that God was like a master clockmaker who planned the universe and set it in motion.
    B. was rejected by most Puritan leaders.
    C. was based mainly on the writings of Martin Luther.
    D. is correctly represented by all the above statements.

26. Benjamin Franklin:
    A. epitomized the Great Awakening.
    B. wrote "Of Freedom of Will."
    C. was Hollis Professor of Mathematics and Natural Philosophy at Harvard.
    * D. was a Philadelphia printer.

27. Education in the colonies was:
    A. most advanced in the South.
    B. primarily intended for young women.
    * C. usually seen as the responsibility of family and church.
    D. hampered in New England by the Puritans' anti-intellectual tradition.

28. The Great Awakening developed in reaction to the:
  * A. Deism and skepticism associated with the Enlightenment.
    B. increasing education and sophistication of backwoods settlers.
    C. increasing role of emotionalism in religion.
    D. tendency of the Enlightenment to place great emphasis on formal religion.

29. George Whitefield:
    A. was a British customs agent.
    B. was Harvard's first Hollis Professor of Mathematics and Natural Philosophy.
  * C. was a major figure in the Great Awakening.
    D. founded the American Philosophical Society.

30. Which of the following was *not* a long-range result of the Great Awakening?
    A. the American style of evangelism and revivalism
    B. the rise of denominational colleges
    C. the encouragement of church members to exercise their individual judgment
  * D. an emphasis in American life on conformity and acceptance of established groups

Essay Questions

1. In what ways did settlement patterns, family life, population growth, and so forth differ in the New England and the southern colonies in the seventeenth century? What factors might account for these differences?

2. Describe the early development of slavery in the American colonies.

3. Describe the status of women in colonial society. What factors might account for this?

4. Which had the most far-reaching consequences on American culture: the Enlightenment or the Great Awakening? Why?

5. According to the textbook, "Both geographically and culturally the Middle Colonies stood between New England and the South." Explain this statement.

Matching Questions

A) "Sinners in the Hands of an Angry God"
B) set up "Log College" to train ministers
C) Virginia planter
D) *Principia (Mathematical Principles of Natural Philosophy)*
E) clockmaker, constructed first telescope in America
F) *Experiments and Observations on Electricity*
G) newspaper editor tried for libel
H) developed indigo as exotic staple
I) *Essay on Human Understanding*
J) crushed to death in Salem

C   1. William Byrd
J   2. Giles Corey
A   3. Jonathan Edwards
F   4. Benjamin Franklin
I   5. John Locke
H   6. Eliza Lucas
D   7. Isaac Newton
E   8. David Rittenhouse
B   9. Gilbert Tennent
G   10. John Peter Zenger

Chapter 4

THE IMPERIAL PERSPECTIVE

This chapter discusses England's changing policies in the political and economic administration of the colonies. It also discusses the structure of the colonial government, and details the relationship of England's North American colonies with the French and Native Americans.

Chapter Outline

I. English agencies of colonial policy
   A. Overall policy not coherent or efficient, generally lax
   B. Role of the king
   C. Role of the Privy Council
   D. Efforts to control colonial trade during the Protectorate
   E. Colonial consolidation by the Restoration government
      1. Theory of mercantilism
      2. Navigation Acts of the Restoration
      3. Lords of Trade created by Charles II
      4. Customs collections tightened
      5. Creation of Dominion of New England
   F. Impact of the Glorious Revolution in America
      1. Dominion of New England broken up
      2. Leisler's rebellion in New York
      3. Appointments of governors in MA, NY, and MD
      4. Influence of John Locke
      5. Recapitulation and refinement of the Navigation Acts
      6. Creation of the Board of Trade
   G. Period of salutary neglect

II. Governments in the colonies
   A. Lack of a coherent plan
   B. Role of the governor
      1. Method of election in different colonies
      2. Veto power
      3. Control over convening the assembly

        4. Selection of council members
        5. Role of the courts
        6. Other authority
  C. Role of the assemblies
        1. Conflict with governors
        2. Restrictions in various colonies on right to vote for assembly
        3. Two key powers: to approve taxes; to initiate legislation
        4. Efforts to manipulate assembly powers to gain control over governors

III. Spain and France in America
  A. Spanish decline
        1. Reasons
        2. Spanish-Indian relations
  B. French settlements
        1. Beginnings in Québec
        2. Exploration and settlement to the south: Louisiana and Mississippi
        3. French settlements compared with English settlements
        4. Early conflicts between the French and the English

IV. The colonial wars
  A. Nature of the wars
  B. King William's War (War of the League of Augsburg), 1689–1697
  C. Queen Anne's War (War of the Spanish Succession), 1701–1713
  D. King George's War (War of the Austrian Succession), 1744–1748
  E. Rivalry over the Ohio Valley in the 1740s
  F. Albany Congress, 1754
        1. Plan for union rejected
        2. Substantive results of the congress
  G. French and Indian War (Seven Years' War), 1754–1763
        1. Braddock's campaign against Fort Duquesne
        2. Use of English sea power
        3. Battle of Quebec
        4. Results of the war

Lecture Ideas

1. A lecture concerning the colonial policies in relation to economic needs is essential. In order to have the students fully appreciate this issue, trace the economic factors driving political decisions within the British Empire. Issues such as the Navigation Acts, Privy Council, and the Board of Trade should be covered. See John McCusker and Russell R. Mernard's *The Economy of British America* (1991) and Michael Kammen's *Politics of Mercantilism* (1970) as well as Jon Butler's *Becoming America* (2000).

2. Break your class up into groups and have each group research a colonial war. Have them look into cause, details, and the results of their particular war and then have presentations on each. You might list on the board the difference and similarities of each as a good comparison on this issue. See Fred Anderson's *The Crucible of War* (2000) and Howard H. Peckham's epic *The Colonial Wars* (1965).

True/False Questions

T   1. In the Dominion of New England, taxes were levied without the consent of the assembly.

F   2. The Glorious Revolution was bloodier (in terms of battle deaths) than the English Civil War.

F   3. Through the first half of the eighteenth century, the power of the colonial assemblies generally declined.

T   4. Colonial governors retained powers and prerogatives that the king no longer had.

F   5. A parliamentary act of 1696 allowed smugglers and others accused of violating the Navigation Acts to be tried by a jury of their peers.

F   6. Of the great colonial wars of the eighteenth century, King William's War was the fourth.

T   7. Benjamin Franklin headed the committee that produced the Plan of Union in 1754.

T   8. Among the enumerated articles of the Navigation Act of 1660 were rice and tobacco.

T   9. The New England colonies were hurt more than the southern colonies in the colonial wars of the first half of the eighteenth century.

F   10. Spain fought on the side of England in the Seven Years' War.

Multiple-Choice Questions

1. The ultimate source of legal authority in the colonies was:
    A. Parliament.
  * B. the king.
    C. the Lords of Trade.
    D. the people of England.

2. The Navigation Act of 1651:
    A. was the last such act not based on mercantilist principles.
  * B. required all goods imported into England or the colonies to be shipped in English vessels.
    C. was mainly an attempt to wrest the colonial trade from the French.
    D. is correctly represented by all the above statements.

3. All the following were principles of mercantilism *except*:
    A. a nation should increase its store of gold and silver.
    B. a nation should limit foreign imports and encourage the development of domestic manufacturing.
  * C. a nation should seek to specialize in the economic goods it could produce best, and depend on other countries for what it could not easily produce.
    D. colonies should be a source of raw materials and a market for finished goods from the mother country.

4. Under the Navigation Act of 1660 the enumerated articles could be:
  * A. shipped only to England or other English colonies.
    B. purchased only from England.
    C. purchased from any nation.
    D. sold to whomever the colonists wished.

5. The Navigation Act of 1663 required that:
  * A. all goods imported by the colonies come through England.
    B. the colonies carry on trade only with non-Catholic nations.

    C. all goods sold by the colonies be sold to England.

    D. the colonists pay cash for all goods purchased.

6. The most notorious of the customs officials was:
    A. Ferdinando Gorges.
    B. William Laud.
  * C. Edward Randolph.
    D. Robert Walpole.

7. The Dominion of New England:
    A. was created under King James II.
    B. included all northern colonies down through New Jersey.
    C. was ruled by a governor without an elected assembly.
  * D. is correctly represented by all the above statements.

8. The Glorious Revolution in England:
    A. resulted in the overthrow of Charles I.
    B. was a setback for English Protestants.
  * C. led to the downfall of Edmond Andros.
    D. is correctly represented by all the above statements.

9. As a result of the Glorious Revolution, Massachusetts:
    A. became a proprietary colony.
    B. became a corporate colony.
  * C. was united with Plymouth as a royal colony.
    D. established the Anglican church as the official religion.

10. John Locke's contract theory of government argued that:
  * A. men have certain rights in the state of nature, including the right to life, liberty, and property.
    B. governments were formed when strong men seized authority as kings to protect natural rights.
    C. kings have a "divine right" to rule their subjects as long as their subjects prosper.
    D. the only legitimate governments are ones that allow all adults, regardless of sex and race, to vote.

11. Reforms of the colonial system under William and Mary included all the following *except*:
    A. ordering accused violators to be tried in Admiralty Courts.
  * B. greatly lowering duties on most items imported.
    C. establishing the Board of Trade to oversee custom affairs.
    D. allowing the use of writs of assistance.

12. A writ of assistance was:
    A. an order to the public to assist police officers in arresting suspected smugglers.
    * B. a blanket search warrant that did not specify the place to be searched.
    C. the legal order that guaranteed trial by jury.
    D. a government document used to assess criminal fines on colonists suspected of smuggling.

13. During the period of salutary neglect:
    * A. the British government took less of a role in governing the American colonies.
    B. new and efficient trade regulations were introduced.
    C. William and Mary ruled England.
    D. a new trade board, the Lords of Trade and Plantations, was introduced.

14. Which of the following was *not* a power of the governor of a colony?
    A. nominating for life appointment members of his council
    B. vetoing colonial legislation
    * C. ordering the seizure of any property in the colony
    D. dissolving the assembly until new elections were held or postponing elections until he wanted them

15. The right to vote for members of the colonial assemblies was:
    A. greatly restricted because of high property qualifications.
    B. open to women in most colonies.
    * C. extended to a greater proportion of the population than anywhere else in the world.
    D. based on the same property qualifications as required to vote for Parliament in England.

16. Which of the following were the two key powers of the colonial assemblies?
    * A. the power to vote on taxes and expenditures and the power to initiate legislation
    B. the power to approve appointments of the governor and the power to override his vetoes
    C. the power to approve taxes and the power to approve the appointments of the governor
    D. the power to set times of elections and the power to grant pardons

17. The Spanish colonies in North America failed, in part, because:
    * A. the region lacked the gold and silver of Central and South America.
    B. the region had a greater native population than Central and South America.
    C. the Spanish colonizers did not pay enough attention to military matters.
    D. All the above statements are true.

18. The Iroquois Indians were most active against the:
    A. Dutch.
    B. English.
    * C. French.
    D. Spanish.

19. In general, the colonial wars were an American sideshow to larger conflicts in Europe between:
    A. England and Holland.
    B. Spain and Holland.
    C. France and Spain.
    * D. England and France.

20. In 1750:
    A. the French population in the New World outnumbered the British.
    * B. the French controlled New Orleans.
    C. the French controlled what is now Florida.
    D. All the above statements are true.

21. Which of the following was *not* an advantage that the French had in their settlements in North America?
    A. Their claims gave them access to the interior river systems.
    B. They had better relations with the Indians.
    C. Their government was more efficient and responsive to orders from the governors because there were no representative assemblies.
    * D. The population that had settled in their lands exhibited greater ethnic diversity.

22. Which of the following did the French settle first?
    A. Mobile, Alabama
    B. New Orleans
    * C. Quebec
    D. St. Augustine

23. One change brought to the American colonies after the Glorious
    Revolution was that the:
    A. concept of the Dominion of New England was extended to
       the southern colonies.
    B. colonies were inspired to lead a revolt against King
       William.
    C. new monarch showed little interest in the colonies because
       of his desire to force the French out of North America.
    * D. monarchy attempted to tighten its grip on the colonies by
       making more of them royal colonies.

24. The center of British-French conflict on the North American
    continent was the:
    * A. Ohio Valley.
    B. Great Lakes.
    C. Mississippi River.
    D. mouth of the Mississippi and New Orleans.

25. The conflict that became the French and Indian War began:
    * A. in 1754.
    B. in a conflict with the Indians in eastern Massachusetts.
    C. with the murder of Philip of Anjou.
    D. on the border between Georgia and Florida.

26. The Albany Congress:
    A. was the first official body to consider independence from
       Great Britain.
    B. signed the Peace of Utrecht, thus ending Queen Anne's
       War.
    C. unanimously accepted the Plan of Union.
    * D. met to consider precautions against the French threat.

27. The Cajuns of Louisiana were:
    A. French Protestants driven from their homeland in
       southern France.
    * B. French who escaped from the British forces when England
       took over Nova Scotia.
    C. a group of English who obtained permission from the
       French to settle in Louisiana.
    D. a group of Indians who assimilated French customs and
       language.

28. In the American colonies, the Seven Years' War was known as:
    A. Queen Anne's War.
    B. King George's War.
    * C. the French and Indian War.
    D. the War of Spanish Succession.

29. The decisive battle of the French and Indian War took place at:
    A. Charleston.
    B. Portsmouth.
    * C. Quebec.
    D. Yorktown.

30. As a result of the Peace of Paris:
    * A. Spain won control of the Louisiana Territory.
    B. France won control of Florida.
    C. Spain was pushed back to what is now Oregon and Washington.
    D. France was pushed back to what is now Oregon and Washington.

Essay Questions

1. What were the various effects of the Glorious Revolution in America?

2. Compare the relative roles played in colonial governments by the governor, the council, and the assembly. In which of these did the most power appear to reside? Explain.

3. Discuss the evolution of agencies and other means in Britain to control the colonies, and point out the weaknesses of the system that evolved before 1763.

4. Explain the nature of French colonial policy in America and show how conflict grew between the French and English.

5. Discuss Britain's mercantilist policies toward the colonies. How did the Navigation Acts implement these policies?

Matching Questions

A) British general in French and Indian War
B) surrendered Fort Necessity to French
C) hanged for treason in New York
D) argued in 1754 for colonial unity against France
E) headed Lords Commissioners for Plantations in General
F) wrote *Two Treatises on Government*
G) British war minister during French and Indian War
H) early governor of New France
I) enacted the first Navigation Act
J) governor of the Dominion of New England

J	1. Edmond Andros
A	2. Edward Braddock
H	3. Samuel de Champlain
I	4. Oliver Cromwell
D	5. Benjamin Franklin
E	6. William Laud
C	7. Jacob Leisler
F	8. John Locke
G	9. William Pitt
B	10. George Washington

Chapter 5

FROM EMPIRE TO INDEPENDENCE

This chapter opens with an assessment of the impact of the Great War for Empire, examines political actions under George III, treats the British plans to raise revenue in the colonies, then traces the counter-play between British actions and colonial reactions up to the opening of the Revolution, at which point the various causes of the revolt are assessed.

Chapter Outline

I. The heritage of war
    A. Rumblings of American nationalism
    B. Retaliation of the British government for colonial trading with the enemy
        1. Imperial forces won the war while colonists traded with the enemy
        2. Efforts to use writs of assistance to stop illegal trade
    C. Problems of managing defense in the newly captured lands to the north and east

II. Government of George III
    A. Whiggish nature of the government
    B. Privy Council supplanted by the inner cabinet
    C. Intrigue for position meant instability of ministers

III. Problem of western lands acquired in 1763
    A. Indian uprisings in the Ohio region
    B. Proclamation of 1763 to keep out British settlers
        1. Kept the British settlers out of lands beyond the Appalachians
        2. Quebec created in the western area
    C. Treaties with the Indians in 1768 gave British entry into Ohio region
    D. Land speculators sought to enter new lands

IV. Revenues needed to pay for British troops in the West
- A. Grenville program
  1. Customs agents must go to America
  2. Naval patrol of coasts
  3. New vice-admiralty court in Halifax had jurisdiction over all the colonies
  4. Sugar Act of 1764 cut molasses taxes in half
  5. Currency Act of 1764 extended prohibition of paper money to all the colonies
  6. Stamp Tax, 1765
  7. Quartering Act
- B. Colonial reaction
  1. Imbued with Whiggery
  2. Grenville program appeared to herald tyranny
  3. Cry of no taxation without representation
  4. British response of "virtual representation"

V. Stamp Act crisis
- A. Impact on the most articulate colonists
- B. Intimidation of stamp agents to encourage their resignation
- C. Adoption of non-importation agreements
- D. Stamp Act Congress, October 1765
- E. Grenville ministry replaced by Rockingham
- F. Repeal of the tax and passage of the Declaratory Act, 1766

VI. Townshend duties
- A. Musical chairs in the ministry
- B. Townshend's acts
  1. Suspended New York Assembly
  2. Revenue Act
  3. Set up Board of Customs Commissioners
  4. Creation of additional vice-admiralty courts
  5. Use made of duties collected
- C. Reactions to Townshend Acts
  1. John Dickinson's opposition to any parliamentary taxation to levy revenue
  2. Sam Adams and the Sons of Liberty
  3. James Otis's Circular Letter
  4. Customs racketeering
  5. Rise of Lord North in the Parliament
  6. Boston Massacre
  7. Parliament repealed all Townshend duties except tax on tea, April 1770
  8. Two years of relative peace

VII. Backcountry dissent
- A. Creation of state of Vermont
- B. "Paxton Boys" of Pennsylvania took revenge on Indians
- C. South Carolina regulators demanded protection against thieves and Indians
- D. North Carolina people protested abuses and extortion of easterners

VIII. Other protest acts
- A. *Gaspee* (a patrol vessel) burned, 1772
- B. Committees of correspondence formed
- C. Lord North's Tea Act of 1773
  1. Terms of the act
  2. Colonials refused to accept the tea
  3. Boston Tea Party

IX. British responded with Coercive Acts
- A. Closed port of Boston
- B. Allowed trials of government officials to be transferred to England
- C. New quartering act for soldiers
- D. Massachusetts Council and law-enforcement officers made appointive
- E. No town meetings
- F. Quebec Act also fueled movement for colonial unity

X. Colonial response
- A. Support for Boston
- B. First Continental Congress, September 1774
  1. All colonies present except Georgia
  2. Rejected plan for union
  3. Endorsed Suffolk Resolves
  4. Adopted Declaration of American Rights
  5. Adopted Continental Association
  6. Called another congress for May 1775

XI. British response
- A. Declared Massachusetts in rebellion
- B. Loyal authorities losing control
- C. Gage moved to confiscate supplies in Concord
- D. Battle of Lexington

XII. Other acts of protest
- A. Second Continental Congress
- B. Seizures in New York
- C. Congress adopted Continental Army

      D. Battle of Bunker Hill
      E. Olive Branch Petition and Declaration for Taking Up Arms
      F. Congress gradually assumed functions of general government
      G. Thomas Paine's *Common Sense*, January 1776
      H. Declaration of Independence, July 1776

XIII. Assessment of the causes of the Revolution

XIV. Independence Day

Lecture Ideas

1. A general lecture on the causes of the American Revolution can be a great tool for future discussion. A good lecture should go into all aspects of the War, including the nature of those leading it and dispelling myths about the unity against the British. See Ray Raphael's *A People's History of the American Revolution* (2001) and the classic by John Shy, *People Numerous and Armed* (1976).

2. Assign a specific event that lead to the American Revolution, for example, The French and Indian War, The Stamp Act, and so on, and have groups of students investigate the impact each had on the Revolution. Each group should present their topic in class and see if the class can determine any common element of each. Then have them reflect on how different events and peoples came together to fight against the British. See Robert Middlekauf's *The Glorious Cause* (1982) and Michael Kammen's *Empire and Interest* (1970).

3. A good lecture on the American radicals and radicalism of the Revolution in general should give you an opportunity to discuss revolutionary war literature. One of the most important radicals is Thomas Paine. A lecture could focus in on him and his book *Common Sense*. Other leaders that should be discussed are Thomas Dickinson, Thomas Jefferson, and Samuel Adams. See Gordon S. Wood's *The Radicalism of the American Revolution* (1992), Bernard Bailyn's *The Ideological Origins of the American Revolution* (1967), Eric Foner's *Thomas Paine and Revolutionary America* (1976), and Jack P. Greene and J. R. Pole, eds., *The Blackwell Encyclopedia of the American Revolution* (1991).

4. A lecture on the writing and meaning of the Declaration of Independence is essential. You might give a supplemental reading assignment concerning the Declaration, then read it out loud and follow with a discussion. A good assigned reading is Gary Wills's *Inventing America* (1994). Also see Pauline Maier's *American Scripture* (1997).

True/False Questions

T   1. The *Gaspee* incident involved the burning of a grounded British patrol boat.

T   2. The Quartering Act required the colonies to provide provisions and barracks for British soldiers.

F   3. The Stamp Act placed the first tax on the new colonial postal system.

F   4. George Grenville opposed the idea of virtual representation.

T   5. John Adams defended the British soldiers accused of murder in the Boston Massacre.

T   6. The Townshend duties brought in more revenue than the Stamp Act.

T   7. The Coercive Acts were called the "Intolerable Acts" in the colonies.

F   8. George Washington led the colonial militias at Lexington and Concord.

F   9. John and Sam Adams, the "Patriot brothers of Philadelphia," urged their fellow colonists to reject the arguments of *Common Sense*.

T   10. Thomas Jefferson was the chief author (or "draftsman") of the Declaration of Independence.

Multiple-Choice Questions

1. Which one of the following is *not* a true statement concerning the years during the Great War for Empire?
   A. Colonists continued to trade with the enemy.
   B. Colonists showed a growing sense of nationalism.
   * C. Since southern colonists were forced to bear the brunt of the war, they became more confident of their military superiority.
   D. Colonial sensibilities were offended by brutal British military discipline.

2. Under George III:
   * A. British ministries changed frequently.
   B. political patronage was outlawed.
   C. colonial policies finally became stable and consistent.
   D. Whigs lost almost all their influence in British politics.

3. The Proclamation Line of 1763:
   A. was along the crest of the Appalachian Mountains.
   B. was designed in part to keep settlers out of the Indians' land.
   C. did not remain intact for long.
   * D. is correctly represented by all the above statements.

4. In 1763:
   A. American colonists were taxed much more heavily than people in England.
   * B. the British customs service in America was grossly inefficient.
   C. Americans continued to smuggle goods into the colonies rather than pay taxes on them.
   D. All the above statements are true.

5. The Sugar Act:
   A. was designed strictly to protect the English sugar industry.
   B. doubled the existing tax.
   * C. halved the existing tax.
   D. was designed to regulate trade rather than to raise revenue.

6. The Currency Act of 1764:
   * A. prohibited the colonies from making their currency legal tender.
   B. created terrible inflation in the colonies.
   C. was designed to ease the shortage of hard money in the colonies.
   D. said that lenders had to accept paper money in payment of debts.

7. The writings of the "Real Whigs":
   A. supported the policies of Grenville.
   * B. were inspired by John Locke.
   C. supported the Quartering Act.
   D. were inspired by Benjamin Franklin.

8. When Americans objected to the Stamp Act with the cry of "no taxation without representation," the British reply was:
   A. that Americans would be permitted to vote on the measure in each of the colonial assemblies.
   * B. that, by means of virtual representation, the interests of Americans had been considered in Parliament.
   C. an agreement that the funds collected from the taxes would be used to improve roads in the colonies.
   D. that because this was an internal tax, no approval from the Americans was needed.

9. The Stamp Act Congress:
   A. consisted of delegates from all the colonies.
   * B. acknowledged that Parliament could legislate to regulate colonial trade but had no right to levy taxes.
   C. established the Sons of Liberty to protest the Stamp Act.
   D. is correctly represented by all the above statements.

10. Of the colonists' methods to protest the Stamp Act, probably the most effective was:
    * A. boycotting British goods through non-importation agreements.
    B. threatening the safety of British officials in the American colonies.
    C. selling the stamps to the French to use on mail to England.
    D. sending an endless stream of petitions to the king.

11. With the Declaratory Act, Parliament:
    A. announced that it would no longer attempt internal taxation in the colonies.
    B. announced its findings that the colonists bore "full and total responsibility" for the Boston Massacre.
    * C. asserted its power to make laws for the colonies.
    D. repealed the Quartering Act.

12. The Townshend Acts did *not* include which of the following?
    * A. refusal to permit any of the colonial governors to make new appointments without the approval of Parliament
    B. suspension of the New York Assembly until it agreed to provide quarters for the British troops stationed in the colony
    C. taxes on various colonial imports
    D. establishment of a Board of Customs Commissioners to prevent smuggling

13. One of the special objections of the colonists to the Revenue Act of 1767 was that the:
    A. taxes were internal rather than external.
    B. taxes did not raise enough revenue to pay the debts of the war.
    * C. revenue raised could be used to pay governors and other colonial officials and thus release those officials from dependence on the colonial assemblies.
    D. colonial assemblies themselves were required to oversee the collection of the taxes.

14. In the long run, the most important item taxed by the Townshend Acts was:
    A. lumber.
    B. rum.
    * C. tea.
    D. tobacco.

15. *Letters of a Pennsylvania Farmer*:
    A. argued that Parliament could pass internal, but not external, taxes.
    * B. argued that Parliament had no right to levy taxes for revenue.
    C. were a protest against the Tea Act of 1773.
    D. were a major factor in the repeal of the Stamp Act.

16. "Customs racketeering" referred to:
    A. efforts by the colonial merchants to avoid the payment of taxes by declaring their ships to be empty.
    B. hiring groups of youngsters to make noise while the customs officials were visiting ships, in order to distract them from finding illegal goods.
    * C. techniques of customs officials who ignored strict enforcement of rules for a time, then insisted on strict enforcement in order to catch merchants and shippers off guard.
    D. the organization of groups of merchants who sought to get around the laws by acting together.

17. Which of the following sequences of British ministers is in correct chronological order regarding the periods of their major influence on colonial trade policy?
    A. Townshend, North, Grenville
    B. North, Grenville, Rockingham
    C. Townshend, Grenville, Rockingham
    * D. Grenville, Townshend, North

18. The Boston Massacre:
    A. developed in protest to the Boston Tea Party.
    B. involved the slaughter of slaves in Boston by British troops.
    * C. grew out of crowd reaction and heckling of British soldiers in Boston.
    D. was the unprovoked slaughter of dozens of Boston patriots by British troops.

19. The so-called Regulator movement involved:
    A. attempts to push the colonies into an early war of independence against the British.
    B. efforts to control Parliamentary taxation.
    * C. demands by people in the backcountry for more effective and responsive government.
    D. the refusal of people in the backcountry to pay taxes to support the government of England.

20. Colonists opposed the Tea Act of 1773 because it:
    A. almost doubled the price of tea.
    * B. gave agents of the East India Tea Company a virtual monopoly on the tea trade.
    C. was internal rather than external taxation.
    D. forbade them from re-exporting surplus stocks of tea.

21. The Continental Congress met in:
    A. Baltimore.
    B. Boston.
    C. New York.
    * D. Philadelphia.

22. Which one of the following was *not* a result of the Coercive Acts?
    A. The port of Boston was closed to commerce.
    B. The governor was permitted to transfer Massachusetts officials to England.
    C. Massachusetts's council and law-enforcement officers were made appointive rather than elective.
    * D. Town meetings were called by the governor to raise taxes to pay for the tea tossed into Boston Harbor.

23. The Declaration of American Rights:
    A. declared the Townshend Acts null and void.
    B. was passed in Parliament by a small margin.
    C. was defeated in Parliament by a small margin.
    * D. denied Parliament's authority with respect to internal colonial affairs.

24. The First Continental Congress adopted the position that:
    - A. colonists could veto laws (but not taxes) passed by Parliament.
    - * B. each colony was a separate realm, subject only to the crown, not to Parliament.
    - C. the colonies were subject to laws of Parliament only in regard to taxes.
    - D. the colonies were independent of the empire, Parliament, and the king.

25. Shots were fired at Lexington and Concord because:
    - A. the colonial militias tried to march on Boston by going through those towns.
    - * B. British officials sent patrols out from Boston to take the colonial supply depot located at Concord.
    - C. British officials sent patrols to arrest all colonists who would not swear allegiance to the king.
    - D. British soldiers threatened to burn the Anglican churches in those towns.

26. At the meeting of the Second Continental Congress:
    - * A. the Massachusetts militia that surrounded Boston was adopted as the Continental Army.
    - B. General Washington was authorized to begin a tour of the colonies to recruit an American army.
    - C. delegates refused to fund efforts for colonial defense.
    - D. all American ships were ordered to become part of an American navy under the command of John Paul Jones.

27. At the Battle of Bunker Hill:
    - * A. the British lost about half of their troops.
    - B. the colonists held their position on Breed's Hill.
    - C. British General William Howe was killed.
    - D. the "Green Mountain Boys" defeated a larger British army.

28. What new element did *Common Sense* bring into the debate with Britain?
    - A. It emphasized that neither internal nor external taxes could be imposed on the colonies.
    - B. It suggested that Parliament was not fit to rule the colonies.
    - * C. It was an attack on the king rather than Parliament.
    - D. It argued that the colonies were already free of British rule.

29. The Continental Congress passed the resolution "that these United Colonies are, and of right ought to be, free and independent states" on:
    * A. July 2, 1776.
      B. July 4, 1776.
      C. July 4, 1778.
      D. November 28, 1778.

30. The Declaration of Independence based its argument for freedom of the colonies primarily on:
      A. the ideas of the Great Awakening.
    * B. the contract theory of government developed by John Locke.
      C. Benjamin Franklin's theory of the dominion status of the colonies.
      D. the concept of judicial review, which allowed the courts of England to declare America free.

Essay Questions

1. Which was more important in the coming of the Revolution: the development of a set of intellectual assumptions in the American colonies regarding liberty, equality, and so forth, or changes in British imperial policy?

2. In what ways did the French and Indian War pave the way for the Revolution?

3. How might a British colonial official defend British actions toward the American colonies in the dozen years before the American Revolution?

4. At what point (if any) did the Revolution become inevitable? Why?

5. Summarize the argument for independence presented in the Declaration of Independence. How did this compare with earlier colonial arguments concerning the relationship between England and the colonies?

Matching Questions

A) Massachusetts governor
B) named commander-in-chief of Continental Army
C) proposed Stamp Act
D) led Green Mountain Boys
E) wrote *Letters of a Pennsylvania Farmer*
F) British commander at Bunker Hill
G) introduced independence resolution
H) was killed at Boston Massacre
I) organized Sons of Liberty
J) wrote *Common Sense*

I   1. Samuel Adams
D   2. Ethan Allen
H   3. Crispus Attucks
E   4. John Dickinson
F   5. Thomas Gage
C   6. George Grenville
A   7. Thomas Hutchinson
G   8. Richard Henry Lee
J   9. Thomas Paine
B   10. George Washington

Chapter 6

THE AMERICAN REVOLUTION

This chapter treats the principal battles of the Revolution by chronology and region, investigates loyalist and patriot strengths, surveys problems of the Continental Army and the financing of the war, examines the degree to which a revolution occurred at home, covers the technical moves for independence at state and national levels, and discusses in some detail the impact of the Revolution on social status, slavery, women, landholding, and religion. It closes with a discussion of nationalism in the new nation, as expressed in painting, literature, education, and other cultural forms.

Chapter Outline

I. 1776: Washington's narrow escape
   A. Howe assembled largest British army ever
   B. Battle of Long Island
   C. Thomas Paine's *The American Crisis*
   D. Washington's attack on Trenton, Christmas 1776
   E. Washington's second minor success at Princeton
   F. Washington wintered in Morristown, N.J.

II. American society at war
   A. Division of support in the colonies
      1. Three groups: Patriots, Tories, and an indifferent middle group
      2. Tories' cause was hurt by licentiousness of British troops
      3. Patriot groups materialized when troops were needed, then vanished
   B. Analysis of the colonial war effort
      1. The militia
      2. The Continental Army
      3. Supplies obtained directly from farmers
      4. Financing of the war
         a. Heavy reliance on issuing paper currency

III. Setbacks for the British
  A. Problems of the British war effort
  B. Three-pronged attack in New York led to turning point of the war
    1. Howe took Philadelphia
    2. Washington retired to Valley Forge for the winter
    3. Burgoyne moved south in New York
    4. Battle of Saratoga
  C. Saratoga escalated war to worldwide proportions
    1. French entered war to help Americans
    2. Spain entered as ally of France
    3. Dutch brought in by British attack on them

IV. Both sides regroup
  A. War in the East in 1778
    1. Clinton replaced Howe
    2. Washington's winter of despair gave way to a spring of renewal
    3. Stalemate
  B. Western successes of colonials
    1. George Rogers Clark in Illinois
    2. Iroquois power broken
    3. Daniel Boone in Kentucky
    4. Later effects of battles with frontier Indians

V. Southern campaign
  A. Reasons for the move south
  B. Reasons for lack of British success in the South
  C. Savannah and Charleston captured by the British
  D. Cornwallis routed Gates's forces at Camden, S.C.
  E. Tarleton and Ferguson defeated at Kings Mountain by overmountain men
  F. Greene placed in command of colonials in the South
  G. Morgan's victory at Cowpens
  H. Greene won pyrrhic victory over Cornwallis at Guilford Court House
  I. Cornwallis defeated at Yorktown
    1. Nature of the Yorktown campaign
    2. Results and their significance

VI. Peace negotiations
  A. Negotiators
  B. Nature of the problems with France and with Spain
  C. American initiatives with Britain
  D. Terms of the Peace of Paris, September 3, 1783

VII. The Revolution at home
   A. Nature of the revolutionary concepts developed in America
      1. Lack of a feudal tradition
      2. Nature of republican governmental ideas
   B. Changes in state governments
      1. Concept of written constitutions
      2. Concept of constitutional convention
      3. Other principles in new state governments
   C. Articles of Confederation
      1. Difficulties in obtaining ratification
      2. Powers of central government under the Articles

VIII. Impact of the Revolution on equality in the colonies
   A. Impact of independence on lower socioeconomic groups
   B. Impact of the Revolution on land tenure
   C. Impact of the Revolution on slavery
   D. Impact of the Revolution on women
   E. Impact of the Revolution on religion

IX. Sense of nationalism inspired by the Revolution
   A. Variety of heroes and legends from the war
   B. First generation of native artists
   C. Impact of nationalism on education
      1. Development of state universities
      2. Development of general systems of education
      3. Work of Noah Webster
   D. General impact of nationalism

Lecture Ideas

1. For a lecture on the strategies of the Revolutionary War and motivation for fighting by the Americans, see Ray Raphael's *A People's History of the American Revolution* (2001), Russell F. Weigley's *The American Way of War* (1973), and Stephen Conway's *British Isles and the War of American Independence* (2000).

2. A good class project could center on the issues of minority groups in the Revolution. Divide the class into groups and have each group analyze a different minority, for example, women, blacks, Native Americans, and so forth. See Mary Beth Norton's *Liberty's Daughters* (1980), Charles E. Claghorn's *Women Patriots of the American Revolution* (1991), Barbara Graymont's *The Iroquois in the American Revolution* (1971), Sylvia R. Frey's *Water From the Rock* (1991), and Benjamin Quarles's classic *The Negro in the American Revolution* (1961).

3. A lecture on the Loyalists—who they were and why they remained loyal to England—can be based on the pertinent chapters in Wallace Brown's *The Good Americans* (1961). Mary Beth Norton's "The Loyalist Critique of the Revolution," in the Library of Congress's *The Development of a Revolutionary Mentality* (1972), argues that the Loyalists, like the revolutionaries, were motivated by Whig thought.

4. A very clear lecture on the peace process and the Peace of Paris of 1783 will help students better understand the end of the war and the next phase of America's history. See Richard B. Morris's *The Peacemakers* (1965).

5. For a lecture on the social effects of the Revolution, begin with J. Franklin Jameson's *The American Revolution Considered as a Social Movement* (1926). Frederick B. Tolles revises some of Jameson's findings in "The American Revolution Considered as a Social Movement: A Re-evaluation" (*American Historical Review*, Oct. 1954). More important, see James Henretta's *The Evolution of American Society, 1700–1815* (1973) to see how the Revolution changed American society.

6. A comparison of the American Revolution with other national revolutions could be enlightening for students. See R. R. Palmer's "The Revolution," in C. Vann Woodward, ed., *The Comparative Approach to American History* (1968). John R. Kayser's "Life, Liberty, and the Pursuit of Happiness: America's Modest Revolution" (*USA Today Magazine [Society for the Advancement of Education]*, July 1990), compares the French and American Revolutions. (Kayser's article is reprinted in Robert James Maddox, ed., *Annual Editions: American History*, 11th Edition [1991].)

True/False Questions

F   1. The first conflicts of the American Revolution took place in South Carolina.

T   2. Many Loyalists emigrated from the American colonies during and after the American Revolution.

T   3. Inflation was a big problem for Americans during the Revolution.

T   4. In 1778, Parliament adopted a program that granted all the American demands made prior to independence.

F   5. Benedict Arnold, originally a British officer, switched to the American side halfway through the war.

T   6. Before the Revolution was over, the British were fighting the Spanish, the French, and the Dutch, as well as the Americans.

T   7. After 1778, most of the fighting in the Revolution was done in the South.

T   8. The Articles of Confederation left many powers to the states.

T   9. Except in Virginia, the Anglican church was disestablished before the Revolutionary War was over.

T   10. The delay in ratifying the Articles of Confederation was caused mainly by the insistence that western lands be surrendered to the national government.

Multiple-Choice Questions

1. *The American Crisis*:
   A. dealt primarily with the justification for American independence.
   B. developed a military grand strategy for defeat of the British.
 * C. bolstered the declining morale of the American troops.
   D. encouraged Americans to compromise their principles and return control to their mother country.

2. Which city did the British capture early in the American Revolution and hold for the remainder of the war?
   A. Atlanta
   B. Boston
 * C. New York
   D. Philadelphia

3. Loyalists in the colonies:
 * A. often lived in urban and coastal areas.
   B. were also called "Whigs."
   C. were probably twice as numerous as the so-called "Tories."
   D. are correctly represented by all the above statements.

4. The state militia units:
    A. generally refused to ambush the British or to engage in hand-to-hand combat.
    *   B. often seemed to appear at crucial moments and then evaporate.
    C. provided the most seasoned troops of the war because of their past experience fighting the Indians.
    D. were highly successful as organized units even though they refused to wear uniforms.

5. Which of the following provided most of the money raised by the Continental Congress for the Revolution?
    A. loans from foreign countries
    B. requisitions from the states
    *   C. new issues of paper money
    D. direct taxes on the American people

6. The final result of the British attack on New York State was:
    *   A. an American victory at Saratoga.
    B. the capture of the British army in New York City.
    C. the successful splitting of New England from the rest of the states.
    D. the defeat of Burgoyne at Fort Ticonderoga.

7. The victory at Saratoga was important for the Americans because it:
    A. made the British resolve to fight with greater determination.
    *   B. brought the French into the war against Britain.
    C. opened the way for the Americans to enter the Great Lakes.
    D. convinced the Indians to join the American side against the British.

8. A problem with the Spanish entry into the Revolution against Britain was that Spain:
    *   A. entered as an ally of France rather than of the United States.
    B. demanded that the United States surrender Georgia as the price for its help.
    C. agreed to fight the British but only on the open seas.
    D. said it would attack only the British colonies in South America.

9. During the American Revolution, most Indian tribes on the frontier:
   A. refused to get involved in the fighting.
   B. opposed the Americans.
   C. assisted the Americans in their fight for freedom.
 * D. strengthened their hold on the trans-Appalachian West.

10. Washington's army spent the winter of 1777–1778 in:
    A. Morristown.
    B. New York City.
    C. Saratoga.
 * D. Valley Forge.

11. The great exploit of George Rogers Clark was the:
    A. conquest of the Canadian side of the Great Lakes.
 * B. conquest of the western frontier.
    C. termination of Pontiac's Rebellion in the Ohio Valley.
    D. destruction of the Cherokees on the Carolina frontier.

12. "Hessians" were:
 * A. German mercenaries who fought for the British.
    B. German mercenaries who fought for the Americans.
    C. French blockade runners who helped supply the Americans.
    D. Spanish blockade runners who helped supply the Americans.

13. A major reason for the British shift to campaigns in the southern colonies late in the war was the:
 * A. expectation of significant Tory help in the South.
    B. need to protect the South from conquest by the Spanish.
    C. southern colonies produced fewer valuable staple crops.
    D. extremely harsh winter of 1780–1781, which made major troop movements north of Virginia impossible.

14. The British campaign in the South:
 * A. was more brutal than in the North.
    B. was led by Daniel Morgan and Patrick Ferguson.
    C. began immediately after the fall of Philadelphia in September 1777.
    D. led to the fall of Atlanta and Columbia.

15. An important American victory—"the turning point of the war in the South"—was at:
    A. Savannah.
    B. Camden.
    * C. Kings Mountain.
    D. Charleston.

16. The American commander for the southern theater known as the "fighting Quaker" was:
    A. William Howe.
    B. Henry Clinton.
    C. Charles Cornwallis.
    * D. Nathanael Greene.

17. The victory over the British at Yorktown was made possible by:
    A. a sudden storm that kept several thousand British troops from landing before the battle.
    B. Burgoyne's capitulation at Guilford Courthouse the week before.
    C. the Spanish forces waiting in the Chesapeake.
    * D. the French navy.

18. An important factor in the conclusion of the peace negotiations was the:
    * A. American decision to negotiate separately with the British.
    B. decision to abandon claims to western lands.
    C. support that the French gave to the Americans in the peace negotiations.
    D. French decision to give Florida to England in return for Canada.

19. The peace negotiations took place in:
    A. Ghent.
    B. London.
    * C. Paris.
    D. Philadelphia.

20. Which of the following was *not* one of the provisions of the treaty ending the American Revolution?
    A. Florida was given to Spain.
    B. Congress would not prevent British merchants from collecting debts owed them by Americans.

      C. the Mississippi River was recognized as the western boundary of the United States.

* D. Congress would restore all property confiscated from Loyalists during the war.

21. The Articles of Confederation were ratified by the states:

*   A. in 1781.
    B. in 1785.
    C. despite the opposition of John Dickinson.
    D. because most people wanted a strong central government.

22. The first state constitutions:

    A. avoided separation of governmental powers as a way to prevent abuse.
*   B. tended to limit the powers of governors.
    C. tended to limit the powers of the legislatures.
    D. did not address issues of individual rights.

23. Which of the following was *not* a power of the national government under the Articles of Confederation?

    A. full authority over foreign affairs
*   B. the right to levy taxes on trade and commerce
    C. control of government in the western territories
    D. authority to coin money, run a postal service, and direct Indian affairs

24. Under the Articles of Confederation:

    A. an amendment required the approval of all the states.
    B. most important actions required approval of nine of the thirteen states.
    C. there was no executive or judicial branch.
*   D. All the above were true.

25. During the Revolutionary period:

    A. voting was limited to a small group, because only property owners could vote.
    B. old habits of deference became stronger.
*   C. the social base of the new state legislatures was much broader than that of the old assemblies.
    D. interest in local political matters decreased.

26. Among the social effects of the Revolution were all the following *except*:
    - A. voting qualifications were lowered.
    - B. Pennsylvania approved universal manhood suffrage.
    - * C. lands confiscated from Loyalists were returned.
    - D. legislative representation for the backcountry was increased.

27. Which of the following statements about the effects of the Revolution on slavery is *not* true?
    - A. The British army freed thousands of slaves.
    - B. Slaves who fought for the colonies were given their freedom.
    - C. Northern states began to outlaw slavery.
    - * D. Southern states made manumission more difficult.

28. As a result of the Revolution and the ideas it inspired, women:
    - A. secured the right to vote in most new state constitutions.
    - B. gained equal access to higher education.
    - * C. showed a new willingness to challenge old concepts.
    - D. no longer lost control of their property when they married.

29. The Virginia Statute of Religious Freedom was written by:
    - A. John Adams.
    - B. Alexander Hamilton.
    - * C. Thomas Jefferson.
    - D. Thomas Paine.

30. John Trumbull:
    - A. wrote "The World Turned Upside Down."
    - B. compiled the new nation's first dictionary.
    - C. was the influential first president of the University of North Carolina.
    - * D. was an American artist whose paintings depicted many patriotic themes.

Essay Questions

1. Describe the problems in America of finance, supplies, and troops during the Revolution. How did Americans attempt to solve these problems? How successful were they?

2. In what ways were the campaigns in the North different from those in the South?

3. Discuss the validity of the following assertion: "Without the cooperation of the French, American victory in the Revolution would not have been possible."

4. Discuss the social effects of the Revolution. In what areas was the revolutionary promise or spirit most fulfilled? In what areas was it least fulfilled?

5. Describe the basic military strategy (or strategies) of the two sides during the Revolution. How might the British have been more successful?

Matching Questions

A) mentioned concern for slavery in his *Notes on Virginia*
B) *The American Crisis*
C) "I have not yet begun to fight"
D) Revolutionary patriotic painter
E) brutal British leader in the South
F) major American peace negotiator
G) lost at Saratoga
H) won at Saratoga
I) fought often with Indians in Kentucky
J) contributed to distinctive American spelling

I	1. Daniel Boone
G	2. John Burgoyne
F	3. Benjamin Franklin
H	4. Horatio Gates
A	5. Thomas Jefferson
C	6. John Paul Jones
B	7. Thomas Paine
D	8. Charles Willson Peale
E	9. Banastre Tarleton
J	10. Noah Webster

Chapter 7

SHAPING A FEDERAL UNION

This chapter covers the accomplishments and limitations of the Confederation government, the movement for a new constitution, the key developments in the convention, a brief analysis of the historiographical controversy over the writing of the Constitution, and the movement for the ratification of the Constitution. The chapter closes as plans are laid for inauguration of the new government.

Chapter Outline

I. Government of the Confederation period
  A. Called the "critical period"
  B. Nature of congressional administration during the war
  C. Financial problems of the government
    1. Robert Morris, secretary of finance
    2. Use of public debt to secure support for the nation
    3. Scheme for a national bank failed to receive unanimous approval
    4. Newburgh Conspiracy
    5. Meeting of Pennsylvania militiamen
    6. Growth of domestic debt from $11 million to $28 million
  D. Development of a land policy
    1. Direct congressional authority prevailed
    2. Geographic areas covered by the policy
    3. Early land ordinances set precedents for future treatment of territories
    4. The Northwest Ordinance
    5. Indian treaties made to gain claim to western lands
  E. Effects of the war on the economy
    1. Fighting seldom affected farming except to bring price increases
    2. Merchants suffered more
    3. Trade treaties opened new markets
    4. Commerce and exports in "critical period" compared to colonial era

F. Diplomatic problems
  1. Problems with Britain
     a. British retained forts along the Canadian border
     b. Americans refused to pay prewar debts to British
     c. Treatment of Loyalists
  2. Problems with Spain
     a. Southern boundary
     b. Right of United States to navigate to mouth of Mississippi River
G. Efforts of states to exclude imperial trade
H. Effects of shortage of cash
  1. Demands for legal paper currency
  2. Depreciation of paper currency varied
  3. Rhode Island legal tender paper money declared unconstitutional
I. Shays's Rebellion
  1. Farmers demanded paper money to pay off taxes
  2. Militia scattered "Shays's Army"
  3. Legislature lowered taxes for the next year
J. Demands grow for stronger central authority

II. Adopting the Constitution
A. Preliminary steps to the convention
  1. Mount Vernon meeting of 1785
  2. Annapolis meeting of 1786
  3. Call for the constitutional convention
B. Nature of the convention
  1. Nature of the delegates
  2. James Madison
  3. Political philosophy represented at the convention
C. Major issues of dispute in drafting the Constitution
  1. Basis for representation of the states
     a. Virginia plan
     b. New Jersey plan
     c. Great Compromise
  2. Disputes between North and South over counting of slaves
D. Principles incorporated into the Constitution
  1. Separation of powers
  2. Nature of the office of president
  3. Nature of the judicial branch
  4. Examples of countervailing forces in the government
  5. Ratification provisions

III. The fight for ratification
 A. Nationalists vs. Antifederalists
 B. Charles Beard's argument for economic motivation of the delegates
 C. Arguments of *The Federalist* for ratification
 D. Views of Federalists and Antifederalists
 E. The pattern of ratification
  1. Several smaller states acted first
  2. New Hampshire was ninth state
  3. Efforts to convince Virginia and New York
  4. North Carolina joined in 1789
  5. Rhode Island held out until 1790
 F. Plans for transition to a new government

Lecture Ideas

1. Shays's Rebellion is a good introduction to the problems facing the new nation. See Robert A. Gross, ed., *In Debt to Shays* (1993) and David P. Szatmary's *Shays' Rebellion* (1980).

2. Break the class up into groups and assign each one a different Founding Father. Have them research all aspects of their lives and then lead a class discussion comparing each. There are many biographies on the major figures of this era; some excellent recent works include Joseph Ellis's *American Sphinx* (1997) and *Founding Fathers* (2000). Also see David McCullough's *John Adams* (2001).

3. A lecture on the Constitution might explain what the country would have been like without it. See Timothy Foote's "Imagining a Consti-tutionless Past" (*Smithsonian*, June 1988). For a lecture on how the Constitution has fared over the last two centuries, see *A Workable Government? The Constitution after 200 Years*, edited by Burke Marshall (1987).

True/False Questions

T   1. Near the end of the Newburgh Conspiracy incident, George Washington said: "I have grown not only gray but blind in the service of my country."

T   2. Adam Smith's *The Wealth of Nations* argued for free trade.

T   3. Merchants suffered more than farmers by the separation from Great Britain.

T   4. The "New Jersey Plan" proposed to keep a unicameral legislature with equal representation for each state.

F   5. The Constitution mentioned the word "slave" (or "slavery") eighteen times.

T   6. The Articles of Confederation required unanimous approval for amendment.

F   7. Under the Constitution, each slave would count as one person for purposes of representation, but as only half a person for taxation.

F   8. The Constitution immediately outlawed the foreign slave trade.

F   9. Federalists favored a decentralized federal system of government.

T   10. The essays that made up *The Federalist* were originally published in New York newspapers during the fight for ratification.

Multiple-Choice Questions

1. The years of the Confederation government were later called the:
   A. Age of Excess.
   * B. Critical Period.
   C. Gilded Age.
   D. Reconstruction Era.

2. In the Newburgh Conspiracy:
   * A. George Washington sympathized with the end but not the means of the conspirators.
   B. unpaid Pennsylvania troops tried to kidnap Alexander Hamilton.
   C. Robert Morris and Alexander Hamilton tried to divert congressional appropriations for their own use.
   D. two army officers and one enlisted man were murdered.

3. Which one of the following gave the Confederation government the most trouble?
   * A. finances
   B. Indian affairs
   C. land policy
   D. postal service

4. The United States departed from the colonial policies of Great Britain by:
   * A. promising equal statehood to all unsettled western territory.
   B. prohibiting national control of trade with other nations.
   C. promising citizenship for all western Indians.
   D. prohibiting the movement of slaves between states, except for sale.

5. The terms of the Land Ordinance of 1785 favored:
   A. settlers from the existing states who wanted to settle in new lands.
   * B. speculators who could afford to purchase large blocks of land.
   C. small farmers who did not require much land.
   D. Revolutionary War veterans, who were given first choice of all lands.

6. Which one of the following early leaders was not present at the Constitutional Convention because of his diplomatic responsibilities in Europe?
   * A. Thomas Jefferson
   B. Luther Martin
   C. George Mason
   D. George Washington

7. Which of the following was not part of the Northwest Ordinance?
   A. Slavery was prohibited in the territory above the Ohio River.
   B. Statehood was allowed when a territory had a population of 60,000 people.
   C. Religious freedom was guaranteed in a "bill of rights."
   * D. New states formed from the Northwest Territory had to allow Indians "perpetual representation" in the state governments.

8. In the lands south of the Ohio River:
   A. settlement proceeded more slowly than in the Northwest.
   B. there was little or no resistance from the Indians as white settlers encroached on their land.
   * C. Georgia, North Carolina, and Virginia temporarily kept their titles to the western lands.
   D. policy was set in the Land Ordinance of 1787.

9. After the Revolutionary War, American trade was officially prohibited with:
   * A. the British West Indies.
   B. China.
   C. England.
   D. all the above.

10. Diplomatic disagreements continued with Britain after the peace treaty of 1783 over all of the following issues *except*:
   A. Britain's refusal to vacate forts along the northern boundary.
   * B. British efforts to keep troops stationed in New York and Massachusetts.
   C. Americans' refusal to pay debts owed to the British.
   D. the confiscation of Loyalist property in America.

11. The nation with which the United States had a major diplomatic dispute over navigation of the Mississippi River was:
   A. Canada.
   B. France.
   C. Great Britain.
   * D. Spain.

12. Shays's Rebellion:
   A. was caused by too much paper money in circulation (inflation).
   B. showed the problems of a central government that was too strong.
   * C. resulted in some relief the following year by the state legislature.
   D. is correctly represented by all the above statements.

13. Who said, "The tree of liberty must be refreshed from time to time with the blood of patriots and tyrants"?
   A. Abigail Adams
   B. John Jay
   * C. Thomas Jefferson
   D. George Washington

14. The movement for the Constitution grew out of:
   A. a resolution from the Confederation Congress to develop a stronger government.
   B. a need to solve problems between the government and the Indians in the West.
   * C. meetings called to discuss commercial issues and interstate cooperation on rivers.
   D. a movement to open trade with British territory.

15. The Constitutional Convention met in:
    A. New York.
    B. Washington, D.C.
    C. 1782.
    * D. 1787.

16. The differences in political philosophy among the delegates to the Constitutional Convention:
    A. were great because few had done extensive reading in law, history, or philosophy.
    * B. were narrow; they agreed on many fundamentals.
    C. resulted in a two-year delay before agreement could be reached.
    D. were most evident in the debates over the judiciary.

17. The so-called "Great Compromise" at the Constitutional Convention addressed the issue of:
    A. slavery.
    * B. representation.
    C. foreign trade.
    D. taxation.

18. The "Virginia Plan" proposed a:
    A. unicameral legislature.
    * B. Congress divided into two houses.
    C. unified government with executive, legislative, and judicial functions contained in one branch.
    D. weak central government, with the states retaining most of their powers.

19. One of the chief differences between the Virginia and New Jersey plans was whether:
    A. the national or state governments would control western lands.
    B. the national government would have the authority to levy taxes directly on the people.
    * C. representation in Congress would be apportioned by state or by population.
    D. Congress would be given the power to regulate commerce between the states.

20. A key issue of disagreement between the northern and southern states at the Constitutional Convention was:
    A. where the new capital city would be located.
    * B. whether to count slaves in the population for determining representation in Congress.

C. whether slavery should be abolished by the Constitution.
D. whether slaves should be considered citizens of the United States.

21. The Constitution:
  * A. had checks and balances similar to those found in many of the first state constitutions.
  B. specified that women could hold political office but could not vote.
  C. authorized judicial review and ex post facto laws.
  D. allowed the direct popular election of the chief executive.

22. According to the Constitution, the president has the authority to do all the following except:
  A. veto acts of Congress.
  * B. declare war.
  C. recommend legislation to Congress.
  D. act as commander-in-chief of the armed forces.

23. According to the Constitution, Congress has the authority to do all the following *except*:
  A. levy taxes.
  B. regulate trade.
  C. raise an army.
  * D. appoint diplomats and federal judges.

24. According to the Constitution, which part of the new government would be elected directly by the people?
  A. the president
  * B. the House of Representatives
  C. the Senate
  D. the federal courts

25. The Constitution was to be considered ratified as soon as it had been approved by:
  A. the Constitutional Convention.
  B. the Continental Congress.
  C. all thirteen states.
  * D. nine of the states.

26. According to Charles A. Beard, the delegates at the Constitutional Convention were motivated mainly by:
  * A. economic self-interest.
  B. the desire to expand slavery.
  C. their wishes for an aristocracy in America.
  D. their desire to restore power to the states.

27. *The Federalist* argued that:
    * A. the size and diversity of the large new country would make it impossible for any one faction to control the government.
    B. the Constitution was necessary to prevent one faction from taking control of the nation.
    C. a republican form of government could not work in a nation as large as the United States, and therefore the Constitution was necessary.
    D. the Constitution would promote control of the government by one faction, which would be good for the nation.

28. Which of the following was an Antifederalist?
    A. Alexander Hamilton
    B. John Jay
    * C. Richard Henry Lee
    D. James Madison

29. Antifederalist leaders:
    A. often were better organized and prepared than their Federalist opponents.
    B. tended to be younger than their Federalist counterparts.
    C. had been the chief proponents of a stronger central government at the Constitutional Convention.
    * D. wanted a Bill of Rights to protect individuals from the new government.

30. The last of the thirteen original states to ratify the Constitution was:
    A. Delaware.
    B. New York.
    * C. Rhode Island.
    D. Virginia.

Essay Questions

1. Describe the weaknesses of the Articles of Confederation. Why had the Articles been written that way?

2. Describe the system of checks and balances in the Constitution.

3. Discuss the effects of the Revolutionary War on the agriculture, trade, diplomacy, and finances of the new nation.

4. Discuss the conflict between Federalists and Antifederalists in the writing and ratification of the Constitution.

5. What major compromises were made at the Constitutional Convention, and what issues did they settle? What issues remained unsettled?

Matching Questions

A) oldest member of the Constitutional Convention
B) proposed "Great Compromise" at Constitutional Convention
C) drafted land ordinance of 1784
D) Confederation superintendent of finance
E) briefly represented New York at the Constitutional Convention
F) claimed to "smell a rat" at Constitutional Convention
G) Western intrigues with Spain
H) *An Economic Interpretation of the Constitution*
I) destitute and disgruntled Massachusetts farmer
J) "Father of the Constitution"

H   1. Charles A. Beard
A   2. Benjamin Franklin
E   3. Alexander Hamilton
F   4. Patrick Henry
C   5. Thomas Jefferson
J   6. James Madison
D   7. Robert Morris
I   8. Daniel Shays
B   9. Roger Sherman
G   10. James Wilkinson

Chapter 8

THE FEDERALIST ERA

This chapter covers the major developments of the first two presidential administrations of the new government. Significant attention is given to Hamilton's proposals for the economic development of the new nation and to the clash of philosophies between Hamilton and Jefferson. Diplomatic problems with Britain, with France, and with Spain are treated in some detail. Land policy through 1804 is summarized, and there is a summary of Washington's farewell address. The focus of the treatment of the Adams administration is on the conflict with France and its domestic ramifications in the Alien and Sedition Acts. The elections of 1796 and 1800 are both explained. The chapter closes with the outgoing Federalist administration packing the judiciary.

Chapter Outline

  I. Organizing the new government
      A. America in 1789
      B. The convening of Congress
      C. The first president
      D. Structure of the government
         1. Cabinet posts and appointments
         2. Court system
      E. Bill of Rights added to the Constitution
         1. Proposals
         2. Ratification
      F. Revenue for the government
         1. Import duties
         2. Tonnage duties
         3. Protection of American trade

 II. Hamilton's vision of America
      A. Hamilton's background
      B. Establishing the public credit
         1. Provisions of the Report on Public Credit
            a. Funding federal debt at face value
            b. Federal assumption of state debts

        2. Other credit reports
           a. Proposal for an excise tax on liquor
           b. Proposal for a national bank and mint
           c. Report on Manufactures
        3. Reactions to Hamilton's credit proposals
           a. Concern about rewarding speculators
           b. Sectional differences
        4. Compromise solution
           a. Location of the capital in the South
           b. States with small debts to receive grants
    C. Hamilton's plan for a national bank
        1. Advantages of a bank
           a. Uniform currency
           b. Source of capital for business
           c. Perform housekeeping needs for the federal treasury
        2. Controversy over the constitutionality of the bank
           a. Position of Madison and Jefferson
           b. Hamilton's response
           c. Washington's approval of the bill
    D. Hamilton's Report on Manufactures
        1. Advantages of governmental development of manufacturing
        2. Techniques to promote manufacturing
        3. Reactions to the proposals

III. Development of political parties
    A. Madison's and Jefferson's general reactions
    B. Jefferson's and Hamilton's views compared
    C. Development of party support

IV. Crises foreign and domestic
    A. Foreign affairs
        1. Impact of the French Revolution
        2. Washington's neutrality proclamation
        3. Actions of Citizen Genêt
        4. Aggressive French action
    B. Jay's Treaty
        1. Jay's instructions
        2. Terms accepted by Jay
        3. Public reactions to the treaty
        4. Congressional reaction

    C. Frontier problems
        1. Battle of Fallen Timbers
        2. Treaty of Greenville
    D. Whiskey Rebellion
        1. Basis for the rebellion
        2. Army sent to disperse the rebellion
        3. Effects of the incident
    E. Pinckney's Treaty
        1. Spanish intrigues in the West
        2. Reasons for Spanish willingness to negotiate
        3. Terms of the treaty
    F. Development of land policy
        1. Conflict over basic principles of land policy
        2. Relationship of land policy to the political parties
        3. Congressional changes in land policy from 1796 to 1804
    G. The Wilderness Trail
        1. Daniel Boone
        2. Pioneer life
    H. Washington's farewell
        1. Summary of his achievements as president
        2. General principles of the Farewell Address

V. The Adams administration
    A. Election of 1796
        1. Candidates
        2. Hamilton's scheme
        3. Outcome of the election
    B. Adams the man
    C. Troubles with France
        1. The XYZ Affair
        2. Creation of a navy
        3. Organization of a new army
        4. The Convention of 1800
    D. The Alien and Sedition Acts
        1. Terms of the acts
        2. Arrests and prosecutions under the acts
        3. Kentucky and Virginia Resolutions

VI. Election of 1800
    A. Candidates
    B. Outcome of the election
    C. Packing the judiciary

Lecture Ideas

1. A general overview lecture on the new nation will be very helpful to your students' understanding of this period. See Merrill Jensen's *The New Nation* (1950), Seymour M. Lipset's *The First New Nation* (1963), and James R. Sharp's *American Politics in the New Republic* (1993).

2. The ultimate political discussion for your class is on the tension between Hamilton and Jefferson. Divide the class into the Jeffersonian's and the Hamiltonian's. Let each side make their case and then segue into a discussion on the origins of political parties in America. Noble E. Cunningham Jr.'s *Jefferson vs. Hamilton* (2000), Richard Hofstadter's *The Idea of a Party System* (1968), and Richard Buel, Jr.'s *Securing the Revolution* (1974).

3. George Washington's administration deserves serious consideration for a lecture in light of the fact that all other administrations will be judge against it. See Mark J. Rozell et. al, *George Washington and the Origins of the American Presidency* (2000) and Richard Brookhiser's *Founding Father: Rediscovering George Washington* (1996).

4. For a lecture on one of the major domestic policies of Washington's administration, see Gerald Carson's "A Tax on Whiskey? Never!" (*American Heritage*, Aug. 1963). Buel's *Securing the Revolution*, mentioned above, could serve for a brief overview of foreign policy during the Federalist years (and later).

True/False Questions

F   1. George Washington won thirty-eight of sixty-nine electoral votes to become the first president.

F   2. Congress initially set the number of Supreme Court justices at nine.

F   3. In foreign policy, Federalists tended to favor the French.

F   4. On the issue of the assumption of state debts, James Madison agreed with Alexander Hamilton.

F   5. Washington's first presidential veto was on Hamilton's bill for a national bank.

T   6. Thomas Jefferson's supporters were called "Republicans."

T   7. According to Alexander Hamilton, the United States needed a national bank to provide a stable currency and to assure capital for development.

F   8. Almost without exception, Americans praised Jay's Treaty.

T   9. The slogan "Millions for defense but not one cent for tribute" is associated with the XYZ Affair.

T   10. Thomas Jefferson was elected the third president of the United States.

Multiple-Choice Questions

1. Which of the following statements about the United States in 1790 is *not* true?
   * A. The South had the most ethnically diverse population.
   B. England and Spain continued to stir up the Indians against American authority.
   C. The United States was still largely a rural society.
   D. Most white Americans continued to view Native Americans as "merciless Indian savages."

2. America's first vice-president was:
   * A. John Adams.
   B. Aaron Burr.
   C. Alexander Hamilton.
   D. Thomas Pinckney.

3. A major achievement of John Adams's administration was avoidance of war with:
   A. England.
   * B. France.
   C. Mexico.
   D. Spain.

4. Washington's secretary of state was:
   A. John Hancock.
   * B. Thomas Jefferson.
   C. James Madison.
   D. Edmund Randolph.

5. The Bill of Rights:
    A. was strongly opposed by James Madison.
    B. became effective in 1786.
  * C. for the most part concerned the fundamental rights of individuals.
    D. was opposed by most Antifederalists.

6. The Tenth Amendment to the Constitution:
  * A. said that powers not specifically given to the national government remained with the states or the people.
    B. guaranteed certain civil rights for African Americans.
    C. guaranteed free speech and the right of assembly.
    D. prohibited the national government from interfering in the religious beliefs or practices of any citizen.

7. Alexander Hamilton's philosophy:
    A. came from an aristocratic background.
  * B. provided the seeds for the first national political parties.
    C. generally favored a weak central government.
    D. said, "Those who labor in the earth are the chosen people of God."

8. The objections to paying off the national debt at full value included:
  * A. the unfairness of allowing speculators to make money on bonds they had bought at reduced prices.
    B. the damage it would do to the honor and reputation of the national government.
    C. the great percentage of the debt that was held by people in the South.
    D. all the above.

9. The question of assumption of the state debt:
    A. received little debate in Congress.
    B. was divided along sectional lines, eastern seaboard against western backcountry.
    C. was the subject of Hamilton's Report on Manufactures.
  * D. was resolved in a compromise involving the location of the national capital.

10. Madison and Jefferson objected to the national bank primarily because:
  * A. they believed in a strict interpretation of the Constitution.
    B. they felt it was not powerful enough to meet the nation's financial needs.
    C. it would cost the government too much money.
    D. it would be located in New York rather than Virginia.

11. Hamilton's plan to encourage manufacturing included:
    A. protective tariffs.
    B. government paid bounties and premiums to encourage industry.
    C. encouragement of internal improvements in transportation.
  * D. all the above.

12. The preferred crop of pioneers on the Wilderness Trail was:
  * A. corn.
    B. cotton.
    C. tobacco.
    D. wheat.

13. Daniel Boone is usually associated with the development of:
    A. California.
  * B. Kentucky.
    C. Missouri.
    D. Texas.

14. Thomas Jefferson:
    A. supported the vision of an urban, industrial America.
    B. "feared anarchy and loved order."
  * C. was, among other things, an architect who read seven languages.
    D. paid little attention to the needs of small farmers.

15. An early development of the Republican party was the alliance of the South with an anti-aristocratic group among:
    A. the conservative Puritans of Massachusetts.
  * B. New York politicians.
    C. Pennsylvania Quakers.
    D. the commercial interests of Rhode Island and Connecticut.

16. When Britain and France went to war in 1793, the United States:
    A. support Britain because of its conservative government.
    B. support France because of the Franco-American alliance.
  * C. expressed neutrality, warning Americans not to aid either side.
    D. allied with other nations to oppose both Britain and France.

17. Edmond Genêt:
    A. came to the United States to escape the revolutionary excesses of the French Revolution.

     *   B. encouraged Americans to attack foreign territory on the frontier.

         C. quickly won the sympathy of Alexander Hamilton and the Federalists.

         D. is correctly described by all the above statements.

18. As a result of Jay's Treaty:
    * A. the British agreed to evacuate their northwest posts by 1796.
    B. the border with Canada was adjusted in favor of America.
    C. all American trade with the British West Indies was legalized.
    D. duties on most items imported from England were cut in half.

19. The Treaty of Greenville was an agreement between the United States and:
    A. England.
    B. France.
    C. Spain.
    * D. Indians on the northwest frontier.

20. The Whiskey Rebellion ended when:
    A. Congress removed the tax on whiskey.
    B. Federalists agreed to financial aid for the disgruntled farmers.
    * C. Washington sent an army larger than any he had ever commanded in the Revolution to put down the revolt.
    D. a compromise was reached in which the leaders were executed and the tax was gradually lowered.

21. As the result of a treaty with Spain in the 1790s:
    * A. the United States won the right to navigate the Mississippi River and deposit goods at New Orleans.
    B. Florida passed into the hands of the United States.
    C. Louisiana passed into the hands of the United States.
    D. the United States and Spain joined forces against hostile Indians in the Old Southwest.

22. On the issue of land policy:
    A. Federalists and Republicans agreed.
    B. Republicans won out in the Land Act of 1796.
    C. Federalists pushed for the sale of small parcels of land to settlers, rather than large parcels to speculators.
    * D. Jefferson said that frontiersmen would settle the land regardless of what Congress decided.

23. In his Farewell Address, Washington:
    A. decried the growing spirit of sectionalism.
    B. decried the spirit of political parties.
    C. urged Americans not to become involved in permanent arrangements with foreign nations.
  * D. All the above statements are true.

24. In the election of 1796:
    A. John Adams defeated George Washington.
  * B. Alexander Hamilton's scheming against John Adams allowed Thomas Jefferson to win the vice-presidency.
    C. the nation experimented for the first time with the direct election of the president.
    D. George Washington announced his support for Thomas Jefferson.

25. The XYZ Affair:
  * A. led Congress to raise an army and prepare for war against France.
    B. involved American diplomats in England.
    C. resulted in a declaration of war by the United States against Spain.
    D. ended when American officials agreed to pay a bribe rather than risk war.

26. In the Convention of 1800:
    A. the United States and Spain agreed on a boundary in the Northwest.
    B. the United States and France agreed on the Canadian boundary.
    C. the United States and England agreed on the Canadian boundary.
  * D. France agreed to suspend its alliance with the United States.

27. The Sedition Act:
    A. was aimed primarily at the British.
    B. was a partisan attempt to stifle the Federalists.
  * C. resulted in ten convictions.
    D. was ruled unconstitutional by the Supreme Court in 1795.

28. The Virginia and Kentucky Resolutions argued that:
  * A. states could decide if laws were unconstitutional.
    B. taxes imposed by Congress were unconstitutional.

    C. immigrants should be expelled from the country if they were not loyal to the American cause.

    D. the "freedom of speech" clause in the Bill of Rights did not apply to purely political rhetoric.

29. Jefferson's election in 1800:
    A. continued the Federalist domination of the United States government.
  *   B. had to be settled by the House of Representatives.
    C. was assured when Aaron Burr agreed to withdraw as a candidate for president.
    D. was assured when George Washington announced his support of Jefferson just three weeks before the election.

30. The Judiciary Act of 1801:
    A. created three new positions on the Supreme Court.
    B. was the first act passed by the Republicans.
    C. allowed federal judges to be impeached under the Sedition Act.
  *   D. was the legacy of the Federalists as they left office.

Essay Questions

1. Compare the arguments of Jefferson and Hamilton on the constitutionality of the Bank of the United States.

2. Describe the conflict between the United States and France in the late 1790s. How did the conflict end? What was the effect of the conflict on domestic policy?

3. What were the major points of the Federalists' foreign policy? What factors influenced that policy?

4. What was George Washington's greatest achievement as president? What was his worst failure? Overall, was his administration a success for the nation? Was it a success for the Federalists?

5. Trace the development of political parties during Washington's administration and describe their basic philosophies.

Matching Questions

A)   led Americans at the Battle of Fallen Timbers
B)   issued neutrality proclamation in 1793
C)   with future third president, wrote Kentucky and Virginia Resolutions
D)   first secretary of the treasury
E)   negotiated treaty with Spain
F)   designed the Virginia Capitol and the University of Virginia
G)   edited the *National Gazette*
H)   Federalist presidential candidate in 1800
I)   convicted under the Sedition Act
J)   first chief justice of the United States

H	1. John Adams
G	2. Philip Freneau
D	3. Alexander Hamilton
J	4. John Jay
F	5. Thomas Jefferson
I	6. Matthew Lyon
C	7. James Madison
E	8. Thomas Pinckney
B	9. George Washington
A	10. Anthony Wayne

Chapter 9

THE EARLY REPUBLIC

This chapter focuses on the political events of the years 1801–1815, including the War of 1812. Beginning with a description of the new city of Washington, the chapter covers in some detail Jefferson's two terms in office, the *Marbury* v. *Madison* decision, the Louisiana Purchase, and the Burr Conspiracy. The history and historiography of the War of 1812 is traced. The major battles of the war are covered. The chapter concludes with the peace that ended the war and a brief reflection on the immediate aftermath of the war.

Chapter Outline

I. The new capital city

II. Jefferson in office
   - A. The "Revolution of 1800"
       1. An orderly transfer of power
       2. Jefferson's role as party leader
   - B. Jefferson and the judiciary
       1. Repeal of the Judiciary Act of 1801
       2. Importance of the *Marbury* v. *Madison* ruling
       3. Impeachment of justices
   - C. Conflicts with Federalist policies
       1. Acceptance of the national bank
       2. Repeal of excise taxes
       3. Sources of good revenue
       4. Land policies
       5. Treatment of army and navy
       6. Foreign slave trade outlawed
   - D. Conflict with the Barbary pirates
       1. Causes for conflict
       2. United States actions
   - E. The Louisiana Purchase
       1. Interest in the territory
       2. Negotiating the purchase
       3. Republican reaction to constitutional issues

    F. Exploring the continent
      1. Lewis and Clark
      2. Zebulon Pike
    G. Political schemes of the Federalist camp
      1. Thomas Pickering and the Essex Junto considered secession
      2. Burr's duel ended his political career

III. Divisions within the Republican party
    A. Election of Jefferson and Clinton in 1804
    B. Emergence of John Randolph and the Tertium Quids
      1. John Randolph
      2. Randolph's final break with Jefferson
    C. The Burr conspiracy
      1. Burr's background and character
      2. Burr's excursion
      3. Disposition of the charge of treason
        a. Jefferson's use of "executive privilege"
        b. Rigid definition of treason adopted
      4. Burr's later life

IV. War in Europe
    A. Napoleon's victories
    B. Harassment of shipping by Britain and France
      1. Mutual blockades
      2. Impressment of sailors
    C. The Jefferson Embargo
      1. Nature of the act
      2. Impact of the embargo
    D. Madison and Clinton elected in 1808
    E. The drift toward war
      1. Non-Intercourse Act
      2. Macon's Bill No. 2
      3. Intrigues with Britain and France over the trade restrictions
    F. Madison's request for war

V. The War of 1812
    A. Causes of the war
      1. Demand for neutral rights
      2. Geographical distribution of war sentiment
        a. Farming regions and shippers
        b. Concern for the Indians
        c. Desire for new land in Florida and Canada

      3. Indian uprisings
      4. National honor
  B. Preparations for war
      1. Banking problems affecting financing of the war
      2. Problems with building an army
      3. State of the navy
  C. War in the North
      1. Three-pronged strategy failed
      2. Detroit and Fort Dearborn forces surrendered
      3. Niagara contingent refused to fight in Canada
      4. Champlain group would not march to Canada
      5. Perry's exploits on Lake Erie
      6. Harrison won victory at Battle of the Thames
  D. War in the South
      1. Creek aggressions
      2. Jackson's raid
  E. Macdonough's victory on Lake Champlain
  F. Invasions at Washington and Baltimore
  G. Battle of New Orleans
  H. Treaty of Ghent
      1. Issues to be resolved
      2. Terms of the treaty
   I. The Hartford Convention
      1. Composition
      2. Actions taken
      3. Consequences of the gathering
   J. Aftermath of the war
      1. Inspired patriotism and nationalism
      2. Action against the pirates of the Barbary Coast
      3. Reversal of roles by Republicans and Federalists

Lecture Ideas

1. A good overview lecture of the Jefferson administration will help students understand this chapter. See Peter Onuf's *Jefferson's Empire* (1999), Merrill D. Peterson's *Thomas Jefferson and the New Nation* (1970), and Joseph J. Ellis's *American Sphinx: The Character of Thomas Jefferson* (1997).

2. The Lewis and Clark explorations could be used to illustrate a number of points, such as the Louisiana Purchase and westward expansion. A good source for a lecture on Lewis and Clark is David F. Hawke's *Those Tremendous Mountains* (1980). Walter LaFeber offers a different perspective on Jefferson's expansionism in "The Louisiana Purchase:

A Dangerous Precedent," in Stephen B. Oates, ed., *Portrait of America* (6th ed., 1995) and James Ronda's *Lewis and Clark Among the Indians* (1984).

3. The War of 1812 fascinates students once they realize its causes and outcomes. Divide the class into two groups and have them look at the war from both the United States and British perspectives. See J. C. A. Stagg's *Mr. Madison's War* (1983), Donald R. Hickey's *The War of 1812: A Forgotten Conflict* (1989), and Steven Watts's *The Republic Reborn: War and the Making of Liberal America, 1790–1820* (1987).

True/False Questions

T   1. The "Revolution of 1800" refers to the election of Thomas Jefferson.

T   2. Thomas Jefferson signed an act outlawing the foreign slave trade as of 1808.

F   3. Once in office, Jefferson set out to dismantle Hamilton's Federalist economic program.

T   4. President Jefferson ignored a subpoena requiring him to appear in court with certain documents in his possession.

T   5. *Marbury* v. *Madison* was sparked by one of President Adams's "midnight appointments."

F   6. From 1763 to 1803, the Louisiana Territory belonged to France.

F   7. Most "War Hawks" were New England Federalists.

F   8. Tecumseh was a Shawnee leader who supported the United States in the War of 1812.

T   9. James Madison followed Thomas Jefferson as president.

F   10. William Henry Harrison was the American hero at the Battle of New Orleans.

Multiple-Choice Questions

1. The first president to be inaugurated in Washington, D.C., was:
   A. George Washington.
   B. John Adams.
   * C. Thomas Jefferson.
   D. James Madison.

2. Who said, "We are all Republicans—we are all Federalists"?
   A. Alexander Hamilton
   * B. Thomas Jefferson
   C. Francis Scott Key
   D. James Madison

3. Thomas Jefferson's inaugural address reflected:
   A. his strong partisan desire to oppose the Federalists now that he was in office.
   B. his desire to adopt Federalist principles now that he was in office.
   C. an affirmation of educational elitism and commitment to continued governmental formality.
   * D. a tone of simplicity and conciliation.

4. Thomas Jefferson's secretary of state was:
   A. Aaron Burr.
   B. Alexander Hamilton.
   * C. James Madison.
   D. John Marshall.

5. In order to bring about the "wise and frugal government" he promised in his inaugural address, Jefferson:
   * A. cut back on military spending.
   B. ended Hamilton's funding and assumption schemes.
   C. raised the excise tax on whiskey.
   D. decreased the sale of western lands for revenue.

6. In the case of *Marbury* v. *Madison*:
   A. Jefferson was forbidden to change appointments made to the Supreme Court.
   * B. a law of Congress was declared unconstitutional.
   C. the Supreme Court acknowledged that it had no power over the president.
   D. the Federalists won the assurance that they would keep their appointments in the judicial branch of government.

7. Jefferson's problems with the Barbary States:
    A. began when American smugglers killed the captain of an Algerian frigate.
    B. were over issues involving fishing rights in the North Atlantic.
    C. led to an uneasy temporary alliance with the French.
  * D. were temporarily settled when the United States agreed to pay ransom for a kidnapped ship's crew.

8. The Louisiana Purchase:
    A. was favored by New England Federalists.
    B. cost the United States $3 million.
  * C. more than doubled the size of the United States.
    D. for the first time gave Americans a strip of land from the Atlantic Ocean to the Pacific.

9. The Louisiana Purchase was a problem for Jefferson because:
    A. the cost was too high for the United States to pay.
    B. acquisition of new Indian lands was contrary to his principles and beliefs.
    C. the territory was ideal for slavery, which he opposed.
  * D. he believed that the Constitution did not give authority to acquire new land.

10. Alexander Hamilton was killed in a duel with:
    A. John Quincy Adams.
  * B. Aaron Burr.
    C. Timothy Pickering.
    D. Charles C. Pinckney.

11. The Essex Junto was:
    A. a group of New Englanders who supported the Louisiana Purchase.
    B. the name given to Republican supporters of Aaron Burr.
  * C. an extremist group of Federalists in New England who developed the idea of secession from the Union.
    D. the primary supporter of Jefferson's Embargo.

12. The overwhelming election success of Jefferson and the Republicans in 1804 led to:
  * A. splits in the Republican party.
    B. an almost equal party division in the new Congress.
    C. riots by disgruntled Federalists in South Carolina.
    D. the rejuvenation of the Federalist party.

13. The "Old Republicans":
    A. believed in a strong central government.
    B. supported the Louisiana Purchase.
    C. opposed Jefferson because he refused to compromise his republican principles, no matter what the circumstances.
  * D. were led by John Randolph.

14. Who was tried for treason for his vague intrigues concerning Louisiana?
  * A. Aaron Burr
    B. Andrew Jackson
    C. Edwin Pakenham
    D. Timothy Pickering

15. In the *Essex* case:
  * A. a British court ruled that enemy goods were subject to seizure even if shipped through neutral ports.
    B. a French gunboat that ran aground in North Carolina was burned.
    C. the American navy seized and improperly searched a British ship.
    D. certain provisions of Pinckney's Treaty were violated.

16. American shipping after 1805 was hampered by:
    A. the British policy of impressment.
    B. the British Orders in Council that created a blockade of continental Europe.
    C. the French blockade of the British Isles.
  * D. all the above.

17. Jefferson's response to British and French interference with American shipping was:
    A. an effort to woo France into an alliance.
    B. an effort to woo England into an alliance.
  * C. what he called a policy of "peaceable coercion."
    D. to ignore the matter and continue trading with both.

18. The Embargo Act of 1807:
    A. was passed over Jefferson's veto.
    B. was not a success because too many items were exempted.
  * C. did not hurt the French very much.
    D. had the support of most New England Federalists.

19. Macon's Bill No. 2:
    A. opened trade with all countries except France and England.
    * B. opened trade with both France and England.
    C. authorized the president to reopen trade with England or France whenever these countries dropped their trade restrictions against America.
    D. failed to pass Congress.

20. The greatest support for the declaration of war in 1812 came from:
    A. the New England area.
    B. the areas in which commerce and international trade were a primary occupation.
    C. the manufacturing centers.
    * D. the agricultural regions of the South and West.

21. Which of the following was *not* one of the important causes of the War of 1812?
    A. British restriction of American neutral rights at sea
    * B. British efforts to invade and regain control of the Ohio Valley area
    C. an American desire to obtain more land from Britain
    D. an American fear of British aid to Indians who attacked frontier settlements

22. One of the greatest hindrances to American success in the War of 1812 was:
    A. the lack of western enthusiasm for the war.
    B. the lack of nearby British territory that could be attacked.
    * C. the lack of military preparation for war.
    D. continued French attacks on American shipping.

23. In the Battle of Tippecanoe:
    A. British forces defeated a larger American army.
    B. American forces defeated a larger British army.
    C. American frontiersmen battled Spanish settlers in Florida.
    * D. the hope of an Indian confederation to protect their hunting grounds was ended.

24. During the War of 1812, the most effective victories for the United States occurred:
    A. at sea, with attacks on the British navy in the Azores.
    B. on land, with the invasion of Canada.

      C. along the eastern seaboard, where British efforts to invade were repeatedly repelled.

*   D. on the Great Lakes, where the small American navy repeatedly raised morale with victories over British ships.

25. The greatest humiliation to the United States in the War of 1812 occurred when the British:
    A. sank the *Leopard* just outside territorial waters off Virginia.
*   B. invaded and burned Washington, D.C.
    C. captured Fort McHenry and Baltimore.
    D. attacked New Orleans two weeks after the war ended.

26. The provisions of the treaty ending the War of 1812 included:
*   A. the restoration of the same boundaries as before the war started.
    B. British evacuation of their forts in the Northwest Territory.
    C. an end to British violations of American neutral rights.
    D. British access to the Mississippi River and removal of American warships from the Great Lakes.

27. The treaty ending the War of 1812 was negotiated in:
*   A. Ghent.
    B. London.
    C. Paris.
    D. Vienna.

28. At the Hartford Convention, delegates from the New England states:
    A. voted to secede from the Union.
*   B. proposed a series of constitutional amendments to limit Republican influence in government.
    C. denounced New England merchants who had traded with the British during the war.
    D. voted to join the Republican party.

29. In the aftermath of the War of 1812:
*   A. Americans took decisive action against the Barbary pirates in the Mediterranean.
    B. the Barbary pirates defeated the small United States Navy and forced President Madison into an expensive settlement.
    C. the U.S. government paid tribute to the Barbary pirates to avoid an additional war with them.
    D. America and the Barbary States reached a peaceful settlement concerning shipping rights off the Barbary coast.

30. Following the War of 1812:
    A. Federalists and Republicans returned to their prewar positions.
    B. Federalists argued for a broad construction of the Constitution.
 * C. Republicans argued for a national bank and a peacetime army.
    D. both parties opposed spending money on internal improvements.

Essay Questions

1. Assess the degree to which Jefferson's election as president can accurately be called the "Revolution of 1800."

2. "Strict construction of the Constitution is more a matter of politics than principle." Discuss this statement in light of the conflicts described in this chapter.

3. Political dissension seemed to be an important factor in the era of Jefferson. This can be seen in the appearance of, among other things, the Tertium Quids, the Burr Conspiracy, the Essex Junto, and the Hartford Convention. How can you account for these examples, and what generalizations can you draw from them?

4. Why did the United States go to war with England in 1812? Which groups of people supported and opposed the war? Why?

5. "The War of 1812 was an unnecessary conflict that solved nothing and brought no benefit to either side." Discuss the validity of this assertion.

Matching Questions

A) appointed justice of the peace in the District of Columbia
B) elected president in 1804
C) negotiated Louisiana Purchase
D) naval hero against the Barbary pirates
E) impeached Federalist justice
F) saw British attack of Fort McHenry from Baltimore Harbor
G) became vice-president in 1801
H) Chief Justice
I) American naval hero in the War of 1812
J) explored Louisiana Purchase and Far West

G 1. Aaron Burr
E 2. Samuel Chase
D 3. Stephen Decatur
B 4. Thomas Jefferson
F 5. Francis Scott Key
J 6. Meriwether Lewis
C 7. Robert R. Livingston
A 8. William Marbury
I 9. John Marshal
H 10. Oliver H. Perry

Chapter 10

NATIONALISM AND SECTIONALISM

This chapter focuses on the effects of nationalism following the War of 1812 on the economy, on government centralization, on diplomacy, on Supreme Court decisions, and on politics, as well as the expressions of sectionalism in the era. It follows the shifting political party patterns while narrating key developments of the administrations of Monroe and Adams. The chapter concludes with the election of Andrew Jackson in 1828.

Chapter Outline

I. Economic nationalism
   A. Impact of the War of 1812 on nationalism
      1. Impact on the economy
      2. Call for a stronger national government
   B. National bank
      1. Effects of the expiration of the national bank in 1811
      2. Proposal for a new national bank
      3. The bank's supporters and opponents
   C. Protective tariff
      1. Changing sectional attitudes
      2. Proposal for Tariff of 1816
   D. Internal improvements
      1. Call for constitutional amendment
      2. State actions for internal improvements
      3. Calhoun's bill and its fate
      4. Status of internal improvements

II. An era of political harmony
   A. James Monroe characterized
   B. Monroe's cabinet
   C. Election of 1820 and demise of the first party system

III. Diplomatic developments
   A. Rush-Bagot Agreement of 1817 to limit naval forces on the Great Lakes

    B. Convention of 1818
       1. Northern boundary of Louisiana Purchase
       2. Joint occupation of Oregon
       3. Fishing rights off Newfoundland
    C. Trade with the West Indies
    D. Acquisition of Florida
       1. Spain's powerlessness in Florida
       2. Jackson sent on campaign against the Seminoles
       3. Reactions to Jackson's campaign
       4. Adams negotiates a treaty with Spain to acquire Florida

IV. Portents of diminishing political harmony
    A. Panic of 1819
       1. Speculative binge
       2. Easy credit
       3. State banks lent beyond their means
       4. Bank of the United States added to speculative mania
       5. Wildcat banks forced to maintain specie reserves
    B. The Missouri Compromise
       1. Balance of slave and free states
       2. Tallmadge resolution relating to Missouri slavery
       3. Arguments for and against slavery
       4. Compromise to admit Missouri
          a. Maine and Missouri balanced each other
          b. Slavery excluded in the northern Louisiana Purchase
       5. Clay's "Second Missouri Compromise"

V. Judicial nationalism
    A. Court membership
    B. Cases asserting judicial review
       1. *Marbury* v. *Madison* (1803)
       2. *Fletcher* v. *Peck* (1810)
       3. *Martin* v. *Hunter's Lessee* (1816) and *Cohens* v. *Virginia* (1821)
    C. Protection of contract rights in *Dartmouth College* v. *Woodward* (1819)
    D. Curbing state powers in *McCulloch* v. *Maryland* (1819)
    E. National supremacy in commerce in *Gibbons* v. *Ogden* (1824)

   VI. Nationalist diplomacy
       A. Negotiating Russia out of Oregon
       B. The Monroe Doctrine
           1. Impact of Napoleonic wars on Latin America
           2. British efforts to protect Latin America
           3. The Monroe Doctrine asserted
           4. Reactions to the doctrine

  VII. One-party politics
       A. The candidates in 1824
       B. The system for nomination
       C. The candidates and issues
       D. Outcome of the race
       E. Charges of "Corrupt Bargain"

 VIII. Presidency of John Quincy Adams
       A. Adams's character and plans
       B. Adams's mistakes
           1. Demeaning voters
           2. Conjuring notions of a royal family
           3. Political activities that hurt him
           4. Tariff of 1828
               a. Provisions
               b. Calhoun's proposal to defeat a tariff increase
               c. Calhoun's protest

   IX. Election of 1828
       A. Opposition to Jackson
       B. His appeal to different groups
       C. Extensions of suffrage in the states
       D. Other domestic trends
       E. Outcome of the election

Lecture Ideas

1. A lecture on the development of America's early national economy
   will expose the students to many of the challenges facing the early
   republic. This discussion should include the issue of a national bank,
   federal tariffs, and internal improvements. See John L. Larson's
   *Internal Improvements: National Public Works and the Promise of Popular
   Government in the Early United States* (2001) and George Taylor's *The
   Transportation Revolution, 1815–1860* (1951).

2. A lecture on James Monroe's presidency will facilitate a class discussion on the accomplishments under his administration. Have students look at domestic and foreign affairs under Monroe's presidency. See George Danderfield's *The Awakening of American Nationalism, 1815–1828* (1965), Ernest R. May's *The Making of the Monroe Doctrine* (1994), Harry Ammon's *James Monroe: The Quest for National Identity* (1971), and Glover Moore's *The Missouri Compromise, 1819–1821* (1953).

3. What happened to the Federalists when their party disappeared? According to Clifford S. Griffin's *Their Brothers' Keepers* (1960), Federalists set up various private benevolent societies (the "benevolent empire") to bring about their vision of America, when they could no longer effect change from government positions. If you introduce this idea now, you can return to it later (Chapter 12).

4. For a lecture on the important topic of the Supreme Court's nationalist decisions, see Alfred H. Kelly, Winfred A. Harbison, and Herman Belz's *The American Constitution: Its Origins and Development* (7th ed., 1991). Interesting details on the major cases mentioned in the text can be found in *Quarrels That Have Shaped the Constitution*, edited by John A. Garraty (1964). For a short discussion of John Marshall, see Brian McGinty's "The Great Chief Justice" (*American History Illustrated*, Sept. 1988).

True/False Questions

T   1. The United States experienced a period of economic prosperity in the years after the War of 1812.

F   2. The Second Bank of the United States was chartered in 1826.

F   3. Support for the Tariff of 1816 came primarily from the South.

F   4. James Monroe was the first president from New York.

T   5. Langdon Cheves was president of the Second Bank of the United States.

F   6. As a territory, Missouri had not allowed slavery.

T   7. The Monroe Doctrine was part of President Monroe's annual message to Congress.

T   8. The Missouri Compromise was almost undone when Missouri put into its constitution a provision excluding free Negroes and mulattoes.

T   9. Four presidential candidates received electoral votes in 1824.

F   10. During the 1820s, the tariff level generally declined.

Multiple-Choice Questions

1. Ironically, Thomas Jefferson's embargo in 1807:
   * A. led to a significant increase in American manufacturing.
   B. ended Republican control of the government.
   C. encouraged farmers to grow less foodstuffs and more cotton.
   D. helped perpetuate slavery.

2. In his first annual message to Congress after the War of 1812, President Madison recommended all the following *except*:
   A. a permanent army and a strong navy.
   B. protection for American industries.
   C. a system of roads and canals.
   * D. an end to the Bank of the United States.

3. Which of the following opposed a national bank in 1816?
   A. John C. Calhoun
   * B. Daniel Webster
   C. Henry Clay
   D. James Madison

4. The Tariff of 1816:
   * A. was the first intended more for protection than revenue.
   B. hurt American manufacturing.
   C. passed only by a narrow margin.
   D. came at a time when sources of cheap British imports were drying up.

5. John C. Calhoun accepted the Tariff of 1816 because he:
   A. saw it as a way to lessen the importance of slavery to southern planters.
   B. saw it as a means to protect slavery in the South.

    *   C. expected the South would become a manufacturing center.

          D. sympathized with New England shippers and southern farmers.

6. In the first half of the nineteenth century, internal improvements:
   A. finally became the responsibility of the national government.
   * B. were supported mainly by people in the West.
   C. were supported mainly by people in New England and the South.
   D. were supported mainly by people who held to a strict interpretation of the Constitution.

7. Whose presidential administration was characterized as the "Era of Good Feelings"?
   A. John Q. Adams
   B. Andrew Jackson
   C. James Madison
   * D. James Monroe

8. "This momentous question like a firebell in the night awakened and filled me with terror." Thomas Jefferson said this about the:
   * A. debate over the Missouri Compromise.
   B. Panic of 1819.
   C. case of *Marbury* v. *Madison*.
   D. Second Bank of the United States.

9. Which of the following phrases best characterizes James Monroe as president?
   A. the president who "out-Federalized Federalism"
   * B. a strong adherent to Republican principles who could not accept the onrush of the new nationalism
   C. a broad constructionist who supported strong legislation to promote American industries and internal improvements
   D. a president whose political innocence was surpassed only by the ineptitude of his cabinet

10. The Rush-Bagot Agreement:
    A. settled the boundary dispute with Florida.
    B. was a formal treaty dealing with trade with the British West Indies.
    * C. ended naval competition on the Great Lakes by limiting naval forces there.
    D. dealt with fishing rights off Newfoundland.

11. The Convention of 1818 did all the following *except*:
    A. settle the northern limit of the Louisiana Purchase.
    B. open Oregon to joint occupation by the United States and Great Britain.
  * C. return control of the Southwest to Spain.
    D. acknowledge the right of Americans to fish off Newfoundland and Labrador.

12. In 1825, Florida belonged to:
    A. France.
    B. Great Britain.
    C. Spain.
  * D. the United States.

13. The Panic of 1819:
    A. was started by the sudden collapse of the Second Bank of the United States.
    B. encouraged greater loans from banks all over the United States.
  * C. was brought on by a severe drop in cotton prices.
    D. demonstrated the financial soundness of government land sale policies.

14. The controversy over admitting Missouri as a state arose because:
    A. there were more slave states than free states.
    B. there were more free states than slave states.
    C. in the Convention of 1818 the United States had, in part, agreed to exclude slavery from the western territories.
  * D. a New York congressman wanted to end slavery in Missouri after it became a state.

15. The Missouri Compromise:
    A. was debated almost wholly on moral grounds.
    B. brought Vermont into the Union as a free state.
    C. allowed for the freedom of all slaves in Missouri at the age of twenty-five.
  * D. prohibited slavery in the rest of the Louisiana Territory north of Missouri's southern border.

16. *South Carolina Exposition and Protest* was published in response to the:
    A. election of 1824.
  * B. Tariff of 1828.
    C. Missouri Compromise.
    D. the Second Bank of the United States.

17. The lack of a national bank during the War of 1812:
    * A. led to a muddling of the nation's finances.
    B. restricted the lending ability of state-chartered banks.
    C. increased the value of state banknotes.
    D. helped regulate the amount of currency in circulation.

18. Monroe's reelection as president in 1820 was:
    A. a resounding triumph over Rufus King, the Federalist candidate.
    B. a narrow victory over Henry Clay, the Federalist candidate.
    C. a victory for Virginia Federalists.
    * D. without real opposition.

19. In the case of *McCulloch* v. *Maryland,* the Supreme Court:
    A. began to retreat from the nationalism of the Marshall years.
    B. upheld the right of immigrants to vote.
    C. upheld the right of state banks to issue currency.
    * D. denied the right of states to tax the Bank of the United States.

20. The Supreme Court ruled that congressional power to regulate commerce "is complete in itself" and "may be exercised to its utmost extent" in:
    A. *Fletcher* v. *Peck.*
    * B. *Gibbons* v. *Ogden.*
    C. *Dartmouth College* v. *Woodward.*
    D. *Cohens* v. *Virginia.*

21. The decisions of the Supreme Court in the early nineteenth century were generally:
    * A. strongly in favor of national authority over the states.
    B. protective of the rights of state governments.
    C. based on a literal and strict interpretation of the Constitution.
    D. hostile to the development of business.

22. In 1824 the United States signed a treaty with Russia concerning:
    A. claims in Alaska.
    * B. claims in Oregon.
    C. trading rights in the Atlantic.
    D. trading rights in the Pacific.

23. Which one of the following were *not* part of the Monroe Doctrine?
    A. The American continents were closed to further European colonization.
    B. Any attempt to extend the European political system in the Americas would be considered dangerous to the peace and safety of the United States.
    * C. The United States would work for the independence of any remaining European colonies in this hemisphere.
    D. The United States would stay out of the internal affairs of European nations.

24. Andrew Jackson:
    * A. was elected to the United States Senate from Tennessee in 1823.
    B. served as President Monroe's secretary of state.
    C. supported a national bank and a protective tariff.
    D. is correctly represented by all the above statements.

25. All of the following were presidential candidates in 1824 *except*:
    A. John Q. Adams.
    * B. John C. Calhoun.
    C. Henry Clay.
    D. Andrew Jackson.

26. The presidential election of 1824:
    A. witnessed a brief revival of the Federalist party.
    * B. was lost by the candidate with the most popular and electoral votes.
    C. was decided in the Senate since no candidate received a plurality of the popular vote.
    D. was one of the first to turn more on issues of substance rather than on personalities or sectional allegiance.

27. John Quincy Adams:
    * A. said the national government should promote internal improvements, set up a national university, finance scientific explorations, and create a Department of the Interior.
    B. was accused of collaborating with Andrew Jackson in a "corrupt bargain" in the election of 1824.
    C. was the grandson of President John Adams.
    D. was known as "Old Hickory."

28. The Tariff of 1828:
    A. included very high duties on raw materials.
    B. was intended to increase support for Andrew Jackson.
    C. led to a reversal of position by John C. Calhoun.
    * D. is correctly described by all the above statements.

29. Prior to the election of 1828:
    A. the Federalist party had been revived to support John Quincy Adams.
    B. the Supreme Court had ruled that the electoral college system of choosing a president was "unjust and arbitrary" and against the constitutional guarantee of "one man, one vote."
    * C. white male suffrage had been gaining ground.
    D. all the above had occurred.

30. In the presidential election of 1828:
    A. John C. Calhoun won the South but lost in New England.
    B. John C. Calhoun won New England but lost in the South.
    C. most of Andrew Jackson's support was in New England.
    * D. Adams won all of New England except for one of Maine's nine electoral votes.

Essay Questions

1. Contrast the expressions of nationalism and sectionalism in the period from 1815 to 1828 and explain which force was dominant in that period.

2. In what ways might the foreign policy of this period be called nationalistic?

3. How might one account for the rise of Andrew Jackson to victory in the election of 1828?

4. In what ways did the Supreme Court act as a force for nationalism in this period?

5. What factors led to the decline of the first party system?

Matching Questions

A) nationalist chief justice
B) the "Great Compromiser"
C) came in second in popular votes in 1824 presidential election
D) president at the end of the War of 1812
E) wrote *South Carolina Exposition and Protest*
F) introduced amendment to ban slavery from Missouri
G) led war against the Seminoles
H) presidential candidate in 1824 from Georgia
I) elected president in 1816
J) Massachusetts senator who favored a protective tariff in 1828

C   1. John Q. Adams
E   2. John C. Calhoun
B   3. Henry Clay
H   4. William Crawford
G   5. Andrew Jackson
D   6. James Madison
A   7. John Marshall
I   8. James Monroe
F   9. James Tallmadge, Jr.
J   10. Daniel Webster

Chapter 11

THE JACKSONIAN IMPULSE

This chapter focuses on the controversies of Jackson's presidency and the emergence of a new party system. It narrates and explains the nullification controversy, the bank war, and Indian policy. The economic issues of the Van Buren administration and the emergence of a second party are treated. There is a final historiographical assessment of the Jacksonian period.

Chapter Outline

I. The Jacksonian presidency
   A. Inauguration
   B. Nature of appointments
   C. Political rivalry between Van Buren and Calhoun
   D. Jackson's democratic concept of rotation in office
   E. The Peggy Eaton affair

II. Policies of conflict with Calhoun
   A. Internal improvements
       1. Jackson's veto of the Maysville Road Bill, 1830
       2. Attitude toward other internal improvements
   B. The nullification issue
       1. South Carolina's concern about the tariff
       2. Calhoun's theory of nullification
       3. The Webster-Hayne Debate
           a. Original issue of the debate
           b. Views of Hayne and Webster
       4. Jackson's toast at the Jefferson Day Dinner
   C. The final break with Calhoun
       1. Crawford's letter relating to Calhoun's disciplining of Jackson
       2. Cabinet shake-up
       3. Van Buren's appointment to England killed by Calhoun
       4. Calhoun takes lead of nullifcationists

III. The nullification crisis
   A. The tariff problem
   B. South Carolina's actions of nullification
   C. Jackson's response
      1. Nullification Proclamation
      2. Troop reinforcements
      3. Force Bill
      4. Lowering the tariff
   D. Resolution of the crisis

IV. Jackson's Indian policy
   A. Jackson's attitude
   B. Indian Removal Act and treaties
   C. Indians in the Old Southwest
   D. Black Hawk War
   E. Seminole War
   F. Cherokees' Trail of Tears
      1. Georgia's legal actions against the Indians
      2. Supreme Court rulings
      3. Jackson's reaction
      4. Cherokee removal

V. The bank controversy
   A. The bank's opponents
   B. Jackson's views
   C. Biddle's effort to recharter
   D. Jackson's grounds for veto
   E. The election of 1832
      1. Innovations of the Anti-Masonic party
      2. National conventions of the National Republicans
         and the Democrats
      3. Results of the election
   F. Jackson's removal of deposits
      1. Basis for his actions
      2. Changes in the Secretary of the Treasury
      3. Removals to pet banks
   G. Economic reaction to the removal
      1. Contraction of credit in Biddle's bank
      2. Speculative binge
      3. Increase in land sales
      4. State indebtedness
   H. Bursting the bubble
      1. Distribution Act
      2. Specie Circular

3. International complications
   a. Specie from England, France, and Mexico
   b. Decrease in British investments
4. Banks begin to collapse
I. Political impact of the controversy

VI. Van Buren and the new party system
   A. Emergence of the Whigs
      1. Sources of support
      2. Whig philosophy
   B. Democratic nominees
   C. Whig coalitions
   D. Results of the election

VII. Van Buren's administration
   A. Van Buren characterized
   B. The Panic of 1837
      1. Causes and effects
      2. Government reaction
   C. Proposal for an independent treasury
      1. Basis for the concept
      2. Passage in 1840
   D. Other issues of the times
      1. Slavery in the District of Columbia
      2. The northern boundary

VIII. The election of 1840
   A. Democratic nominees
   B. Whig nominees
   C. Nature of the campaign
   D. Results of the election

IX. Assessing the Jacksonian years
   A. Voter participation increased
   B. Historical interpretations
   C. A closing assessment

Lecture Ideas

1. A general overview of the nature and character of Andrew Jackson
   will develop the theme for the rest of this chapter. See Robert V.
   Remini's *Andrew Jackson: The Course of American Empire* (1977, three
   volumes) and *Andrew Jackson and the Source of American Freedom*
   (1981), Donald B. Cole's *The Presidency of Andrew Jackson* (1993), and
   Arthur M. Schlesinger Jr.'s, *Andrew Jackson: The Age of Jackson* (1945).

2. Give each group in your class a specific issue related to the Jackson administration, for example, the Nullification Crisis, the bank, Native American relations, and have them research and present the issue to the class. See Robert V. Remini's *The Legacy of Andrew Jackson* (1988), William W. Freehling's *Prelude to Civil War* (1966), John M. McFaul's *The Politics of Jacksonian Finance* (1972), Richard Latner's *The Presidency of Andrew Jackson: White House Politics, 1829–1837* (1979), and Ronald N. Satz's *American Indian Policy in the Jacksonian Era* (1975).

3. Lecture on the split between the Democratic and Whig parties and the realignment of the political party system in America during the Jacksonian Era. See Richard Hofstadter's *The Idea of a Party System* (1969), Michael F. Holt's *The Rise and Fall of the American Whig Party* (1999), and Glenn C. Altschuler and Stuart M. Blumin's *Rude Republic: Americans and Their Politics in the Nineteenth Century* (2000).

True/False Questions

F   1. Martin Van Buren opposed the establishment of an Independent Treasury.

T   2. The Tariff of 1828 was also known as the "Tariff of Abominations."

T   3. John C. Calhoun was born in South Carolina.

F   4. President Jackson's response to the nullification crisis was to ask Congress to raise the tariff.

T   5. The Cherokee Indians were forced westward on the route that came to be known as the Trail of Tears.

T   6. Osceola led the Seminole resistance to their removal from their lands.

F   7. The Distribution Act provided for each veteran of the War of 1812 to receive 360 acres of land in the West.

F   8. Most Whigs were states' rights advocates.

F   9. Martin Van Buren was a native of North Carolina and had served two terms as that state's governor.

F   10. Henry Clay was Andrew Jackson's second vice-president.

Multiple-Choice Questions

1. In his first inaugural address, Andrew Jackson announced that he favored:
   - A. retirement of the national debt.
   - B. a proper regard for states' rights.
   - C. rotation in federal offices.
   - * D. all the above.

2. The spoils system:
   - A. reached its peak during President Jackson's first year in office.
   - B. was more of a problem in the national government than in state governments.
   - * C. was a way of rewarding political supporters.
   - D. was another name for "pork barrel" legislation.

3. Jackson's first vice-president was:
   - * A. John C. Calhoun.
   - B. Henry Clay.
   - C. John Randolph.
   - D. Martin Van Buren.

4. As a result of the Eaton affair, President Jackson:
   - A. drew closer to John C. Calhoun.
   - * B. drew closer to Martin Van Buren.
   - C. began to distrust Martin Van Buren.
   - D. began to distrust John Eaton.

5. Jackson's veto of the Maysville Road Bill demonstrated his:
   - * A. belief that the federal government should not fund purely local projects.
   - B. belief that the federal government should assist states with internal improvements projects.
   - C. tremendous respect for Henry Clay.
   - D. initial support for John C. Calhoun's policies.

6. *South Carolina Exposition and Protest*:
     A. argued that southern states had the right to take drastic actions to prevent slave insurrections.
     B. condemned the use of military force to protect escaped slaves.
     C. was written in response to the Indian Removal Act.
   * D. was written in response to the Tariff of 1828.

7. The "Force Bill" of 1833 was:
     A. opposed by President Jackson.
   * B. issued in response to the South Carolina Ordinance.
     C. supported by John C. Calhoun.
     D. overturned by the Supreme Court.

8. The theory of nullification:
     A. allowed Congress to nullify laws passed by the state legislatures.
     B. was first raised in the congressional debates over the sale of public lands.
     C. is usually associated with the name of Daniel Webster.
   * D. is usually associated with the name of John C. Calhoun.

9. In the Webster-Hayne Debate, Robert Y. Hayne argued that:
     A. within its jurisdiction the Supreme Court's authority was "full and complete."
   * B. the Union was created by a compact of the states.
     C. Congress had no right to pass tariffs to raise revenue.
     D. the northern and southern states had to unite against the West on issues involving public lands.

10. In the Webster-Hayne Debate, Daniel Webster argued that:
     A. each section of the country had to stand up and fight, if necessary, for its rights.
     B. states had the right to nullify national laws.
     C. the Union was made up of sovereign states.
   * D. a state could neither nullify a federal law nor secede from the Union.

11. The rift between Jackson and Calhoun:
     A. ended in the attempted impeachment of Calhoun.
   * B. led to the removal of Calhoun's supporters from the cabinet.
     C. caused Calhoun to support Martin Van Buren as minister to Great Britain.
     D. ended Jackson's hopes for a second term as president.

12. How many states joined South Carolina in repudiating the tariff acts of 1828 and 1832?
    * A. none
    B. two southern states and one northern state
    C. three northern states and one southern state
    D. five states, all in the South

13. The Indian Removal Act of 1830:
    A. allowed Indians who wished to become American citizens to remain on their homeland.
    B. became law after Congress overrode Jackson's veto.
    * C. proposed moving Indian tribes to areas west of the Mississippi River.
    D. contained loopholes designed to exclude peaceful Indians from removal.

14. President Jackson's attitude toward the Supreme Court's decision in *Worcester* v. *Georgia* was:
    A. elation.
    B. sadness.
    C. acquiescence.
    * D. defiance.

15. Nicholas Biddle:
    A. led the opposition to Van Buren's appointment as ambassador to Great Britain.
    * B. headed the Bank of the United States.
    C. opposed the Bank of the United States because it seemed to favor business and the wealthy.
    D. opposed the Bank of the United States because it allowed state and local banks to expand their issue of notes.

16. In the case of *Cherokee Nation* v. *Georgia*, the Supreme Court:
    A. ordered the Cherokees to vacate their lands east of the Mississippi River.
    B. ordered the state of Georgia to enforce Indian voting rights.
    C. prohibited the intermarriage of Indians and whites.
    * D. announced that the Cherokees had "an unquestionable right" to their lands.

17. President Jackson vetoed the bill to recharter the Bank of the United States:
    A. but the veto was overturned by the Senate.
    B. on the advice of Henry Clay and Daniel Webster.
    * C. four years before the Bank's charter expired.
    D. although he felt the bank served many useful functions.

18. "Pet banks" were:
    * A. state banks that received federal government deposits.
    B. allowed to issue notes that were not covered by specie reserves.
    C. those established by Jackson's executive order in 1829.
    D. chartered in 1832 for the express purpose of handling foreign investments.

19. The Anti-Masonic party:
    * A. was the first national third party.
    B. was also known as the "Know-Nothing" party.
    C. finished a close second in the presidential race of 1832.
    D. is correctly represented by all the above statements.

20. As a result of Jackson's bank policies:
    A. sales of public land instantly declined.
    * B. banks printed new bank notes with abandon.
    C. worried investors pulled out of risky projects.
    D. All the above statements are true.

21. The Specie Circular of 1836:
    A. distributed the federal surplus to the states.
    B. ordered banks to issue notes only up to the amount that could be covered by their specie reserves.
    * C. said that only gold and silver would be accepted as payment for public lands.
    D. was an attempt to increase private investments.

22. The one thing that united all members of the new Whig party was opposition to:
    A. the Bank of the United States.
    * B. Andrew Jackson.
    C. internal improvements.
    D. high protective tariffs.

23. In the presidential election of 1836:
    A. Daniel Webster was the Republican candidate.
    B. Henry Clay was the Democratic candidate.
    C. no candidate received a majority of the electoral vote.
    * D. the Whig party put up three candidates.

24. All the following factors contributed to the Panic of 1837 *except* the:
    A. withdrawal of European investments.
    B. failure of the 1836 wheat crop.
    * C. tariff of 1835, which had lowered duties to dangerous levels.
    D. depression in England.

25. Discontent during Van Buren's administration:
    * A. was brought on in part by a depressed economy.
    B. cost him the Democratic presidential nomination in 1840.
    C. started when the Bank of the United States went bankrupt in 1837.
    D. is correctly represented by all the above statements.

26. In 1840 the Whigs:
    * A. feared splitting their party and hence had no platform.
    B. nominated Winfield Scott for president.
    C. campaigned for a program similar to the "American System."
    D. tried to play down their candidate's war record.

27. In the election of 1840:
    A. Martin Van Buren won by the smallest electoral margin of any nineteenth-century presidential election.
    * B. voter turnout was high.
    C. Martin Van Buren became the first president in the second party system to win re-election.
    D. both parties alienated many voters by their stands on controversial issues.

28. According to the "progressive" historians, Jackson:
    * A. led a vast democratic movement against the abuses of the "Monster" bank.
    B. promoted democratic reforms only for political expediency.
    C. caused a decline in voter turnout during the 1830s by his lack of concern for issues touching the daily lives of the common man.
    D. supported the national bank and federal aid to internal improvements because he stood to benefit financially from them.

29. In political philosophy, Andrew Jackson was closest to:
    A. Henry Clay.
    B. Alexander Hamilton.
    * C. Thomas Jefferson.
    D. Daniel Webster.

30. The irony of Jackson's political philosophy is that:
    A. the special privileges he urged for business led to wide-scale abuse.
    B. his opposition to an independent treasury was based on his belief in centralizing the functions of government.
    * C. his laissez-faire rationale for republican simplicity became the justification for the unregulated growth of centers of economic power.
    D. his concern for the common man came at a time of extremely low voter participation.

Essay Questions

1. Discuss the presidential elections of 1832, 1836, and 1840, describing the candidates and the major issues.

2. What was Jackson's most important accomplishment as president? What was his greatest failure?

3. Why was the banking controversy so important in the 1830s? What actions did Jackson take toward the Bank? Why?

4. Describe and explain the tariff/nullification controversy.

5. Describe the new party system that emerged in the 1830s.

Matching Questions

A) offered as toast at Jefferson Day Dinner: "Our Union—It must be preserved!"
B) husband of woman snubbed by wives of cabinet members
C) called the "Little Magician"
D) tried for early recharter of the Bank of the United States
E) resigned vice-presidency, 1832
F) proposed "American System"
G) won the presidency with his "Log Cabin and Hard Cider" campaign
H) Massachusetts senator, said "Liberty and Union, now and forever, one and inseparable."
I) presidential candidate for Anti-Masonic party, 1832
J) 1840 Whig vice-presidential candidate

D   1. Nicholas Biddle
E   2. John C. Calhoun
F   3. Henry Clay
B   4. John Eaton
G   5. William Henry Harrison
A   6. Andrew Jackson
J   7. John Tyler
C   8. Martin Van Buren
H   9. Daniel Webster
I   10. William Wirt

Chapter 12

THE DYNAMICS OF GROWTH

This chapter traces economic and social developments from about 1800 to 1860, including developments in agriculture, transportation, technology, industrial production, corporate organization, urbanization, immigration, labor unions, land policy, the distribution of wealth, and urban culture.

Chapter Outline

I. Agriculture
    A. The importance of cotton to the economy
        1. Invention of the cotton gin
        2. Revolutionary impact of the gin
            a. Impact on slavery
            b. Encouragement of westward migration
            c. Cotton became an important export
    B. The westward movement
        1. Statistical evidence
        2. Changes in land laws
            a. Land law of 1820
            b. Preemption Act of 1830
            c. Graduation Act of 1854
        3. Development of improved iron plows
        4. Cyrus McCormick's mechanical reaper

II. Improvements in transportation
    A. Opening new roads
        1. Turnpikes
        2. National Road
    B. River transportation
        1. Steamboats
        2. Flatboats
        3. Growth of canals
    C. Development of railroads
        1. Early roads

      2. Travel on the early railroads
      3. Water travel compared to rail
    D. Ocean transport
      1. Transatlantic packet service
      2. Clipper ships
    E. Financing internal improvements
      1. Turnpikes funded by private investment
      2. States sponsor canals
      3. Railroads first came from private investment
      4. Federal railroad assistance
    F. Communications revolution
      1. Impact of new modes of transportation
      2. Delivery of mail

III. Industrialization
    A. The growth of industry
      1. Persistence of the handicraft system
      2. Britain's lead in industrial production
      3. Early industrial mills in the United States
      4. Impact of War of 1812 on early textile manufacturing
    B. Advances in technology
      1. Emphasis on practical application of science in the
        United States
      2. Examples of the impact of inventions
    C. Emergence of the factory
      1. Slow development of power-driven machinery
      2. Emergence of the factory system
        a. Lowell idea
          (1) Use of young women
          (2) Failure of Lowell idea
        b. Family system

IV. Popular culture
    A. Urban recreation
      1. Sports
      2. Alcohol consumption
      3. Performing arts
        a. Theatre
        b. Minstrel shows

V. Urbanization
    A. Leading cities of the antebellum period
    B. Interaction of manufacturing with urbanization

VI. Immigration
    A. Continuing need for labor
    B. Ebb and flow of immigration
    C. Characteristics of ethnic groups
        1. Irish
            a. Reasons for immigration
            b. Irish immigrant life
            c. Led to growth of Catholic Church
        2. Germans
        3. British
        4. Scandinavians
        5. Chinese
    D. Nativist reaction to immigrants
        1. Reasons for antagonism toward immigrants
        2. Examples of nativist activity
        3. Nativist organizations
            a. Early associations
            b. Know-Nothing party formed in 1854

VII. Labor organization
    A. Daily life of the skilled urban working class
    B. Importance of *Commonwealth* v. *Hunt* decision, 1842
    C. Efforts to create national trade unions
    D. Urban labor politics
        1. Working Men's parties
        2. Factionalization of labor unions
        3. Locofocos in New York
        4. Impact of labor parties
    E. Producers' and consumers' cooperatives
    F. Continuing activities of unions

VIII. The rise of professions
    A. Growing sophistication of American life
        1. Henry Day
        2. Reading revolution
    B. Rise of education
        1. Law
        2. Medicine
        3. Engineering
    C. Changing role of women

IX. Jacksonian inequality
    A. Examples of self-made men
    B. Distribution of wealth

Lecture Ideas

1. A good introductory lecture on the agricultural, industrial, and transportation revolutions will serve the students well in understanding this era. See Thomas C. Cochran's *Frontiers of Change: Early Industrialization in America* (1981), George R. Taylor's *The Transportation Revolution, 1815–1860* (1951), Wilbur Cash's *The Mind of the South* (1941), and Paul W. Gates's *The Farmer's Age of Agriculture, 1815–1860* (1966).

2. For a lecture on the economic aspects of early nineteenth-century society, a handy source is Edward Pessen's *Jacksonian America* (rev. ed., 1978), which emphasizes the "Jacksonian inequality" of the period. The first "overview" chapter of Herbert Gutman's *Work, Culture, and Society in Industrializing America* (1976) describes the life of the early factory workers. For a lecture describing the everyday lives of Americans in this period, see Jack Larkin's *The Reshaping of Everyday Life, 1790–1840* (1988).

3. For two lecture ideas on the Erie Canal, see Julius Rubin's "Canal or Railroad?" (*Transactions of the American Philosophical Society*, Nov. 1961), which describes how three cities—Baltimore, Boston, and Philadelphia—reacted to New York's Erie Canal; and Paul Johnson's *A Shopkeeper's Millennium* (1978), which describes the growth and changes that the Erie Canal brought to Rochester and how the Second Great Awakening (Chapter 13) can be seen in part as a response to that growth.

4. Have each student trace his or her family roots to determine where their descendants came from. You can then give an introductory lecture on the issue of immigration prior to the Civil War in America, integrating your students' background into the lecture if possible. See John Bodnar's *The Transplanted: A History of Immigrants in America* (1985) and Maldwyn A. Jones's *American Immigration* (1960).

5. Ray Allen Billington's "The Know-Nothing Uproar" (*American Heritage*, Feb. 1959) would be a good source for a lecture on nativism and the American party.

True/False Questions

F   1. As late as 1860, three-fourths of the American people lived within twenty-five miles of the Atlantic Ocean.

F   2. Before 1845, steamships were used more for transportation on the ocean than on internal waterways.

T   3. Church attendance and temperance were enforced among early workers at Lowell.

F   4. The United States had caught up with England's textile production by 1815.

T   5. One advantage of New England for manufacturing was that the fall line and the power it provided were near the coast where water transportation was available.

F   6. Irish immigrants to the United States tended to join the Republican party.

T   7. Chinese immigrants to the United States often did the heavy work of construction.

T   8. Most of the growth of the Catholic church in America in the mid-nineteenth century can be attributed to immigration from Ireland.

F   9. The greatest proportionate influx of immigrants in the history of the United States came in the 1820s.

T   10. The American party was based on nativism.

Multiple-Choice Questions

1. The cotton gin was invented:
   A. by John Deere.
   B. by John Oliver.
   * C. in the 1790s.
   D. in the 1830s.

2. The widespread use of the cotton gin:
   A. made millions of dollars for the inventor.
   B. made cotton easier to pick.
   C. kept cotton out of the "Old Southwest."
   * D. made cotton a major export commodity.

3. Thomas Rice:
   * A. sang about "Jim Crow."
   B. was the controversial leader of the Equal Rights party.
   C. invented the first successful steam locomotive.
   D. wrote *Iron Rails to Baltimore*.

4. The Preemption Acts of 1830 and 1841:
   A. gradually raised the price of unsold public lands.
   * B. allowed squatters to stake out claims ahead of the land surveys.
   C. limited the amount of cotton exported per year.
   D. set guidelines for the construction of new roads.

5. Before 1820, most of the nation's important roads:
   A. were in the South.
   * B. were north of South Carolina.
   C. ran beside canals.
   D. ran alongside navigable rivers.

6. Steamboats:
   A. were commercially profitable by the 1790s.
   B. generally had at least twelve-foot drafts.
   * C. brought cheaper and faster two-way traffic to the Mississippi Valley.
   D. are correctly represented by all the above statements.

7. The Erie Canal was located in:
   A. New Jersey.
   * B. New York.
   C. Ohio.
   D. Pennsylvania.

8. The decade that witnessed the most growth in American railroads (in terms of mileage constructed) was the:
   A. 1820s.
   B. 1830s.
   C. 1840s.
   * D. 1850s.

9. The advantages of water travel over railroads in 1860 included:
   * A. comfort.
   B. cost.
   C. speed.
   D. all the above.

10. Clipper ships:
    A. were slower than steamships.
    B. had more cargo space than steamships.
    * C. became popular in the 1840s because of the California gold rush and the market for Chinese tea.
    D. quickly became the standard method of ocean transport and remained so until Word War I.

11. Internal improvements in the first half of the nineteenth century were financed by:
    A. state governments.
    B. the federal government.
    C. private enterprise.
    * D. all the above.

12. Jacob Bigelow:
    A. invented a power loom for weaving carpets.
    * B. was a Harvard botanist who lectured on the importance of technology.
    C. invented the "spinning mule," a device that could do the work of 200 hand spinners.
    D. established the New England Protective Union.

13. Jefferson's embargo in 1807 and the War of 1812:
    A. almost destroyed American manufacturing.
    B. had little effect on the growth of textile manufacturing in America.
    * C. encouraged rapid growth in American manufacturing.
    D. restricted exports and thereby hurt the growth of American manufacturing.

14. The factory system, in which all the manufacturing processes were brought under one plant:
    A. did not develop in America until after the Civil War.
    * B. was promoted by the Boston Associates.
    C. was more widespread in the South than in New England.
    D. produced most American textiles by 1820.

15. The first American factories produced:
    * A. cotton textiles.
    B. leather goods.
    C. tobacco products.
    D. glass products.

16. Early factory workers at Lowell were:
    * A. mostly young women.
    B. usually widows or older unmarried women.
    C. among the first factory workers to have a standard forty-hour week.
    D. usually immigrants who could speak little English.

17. The first American city to have a population of more than one million was:
    A. Baltimore.

    B. Boston.
*   C. New York.
    D. Philadelphia.

18. In the first half of the nineteenth century, most European immigrants entered the United States at:
    A. Boston.
    B. Charleston.
*   C. New York.
    D. Savannah.

19. Most nineteenth-century Irish immigrants:
*   A. came to America to escape economic depression and famine.
    B. were Protestants.
    C. were skilled artisans.
    D. moved to the South.

20. Americans were hostile to mid-nineteenth-century immigrants largely because of differences in:
    A. family traditions.
    B. languages.
    C. political philosophies.
*   D. religious practices.

21. The German migration to the United States:
    A. included few educated professionals or skilled workers.
    B. peaked in 1831.
    C. was in most respects similar to that of the Irish.
*   D. often ended in St. Louis, San Antonio, or Milwaukee.

22. The largest group of immigrants living in America in 1860 was:
    A. British.
    B. Chinese.
*   C. Irish.
    D. Scandinavian.

23. The Know-Nothing party:
*   A. was established in 1854.
    B. was weakest in New England.
    C. was based on prejudice against the Negro.
    D. is correctly represented by all the above statements.

24. The Equal Rights party was also known as:
*   A. the Locofocos.
    B. Tammany Hall.
    C. the National Trades' Union.
    D. the Industrial Workers of the World.

25. "Locofocos" were:
   * A. members of the Equal Rights party.
     B. railroad workers who went on strike in 1844 for higher wages.
     C. special detectives hired to break up the early unions.
     D. Irish factory workers.

26. In the case of *Commonwealth* v. *Hunt*, the Massachusetts Supreme Court ruled that:
     A. immigration quotas established in the late 1830s were constitutional.
     B. immigration quotas established in the late 1830s were unconstitutional.
     C. forming a trade union was illegal.
   * D. forming a trade union was not illegal.

27. The various working men's parties failed for all the following reasons *except*:
     A. they often splintered into factions.
     B. labor politicians were inexperienced.
     C. they were vulnerable to charges of radicalism.
   * D. the major parties refused to adopt any of their causes.

28. The shoemakers' strike at Lynn and Natick, Massachusetts:
     A. was one of the few of this period that the workers won.
     B. spread to include perhaps 25 towns and 20,000 workers.
     C. concerned mainly demands for higher wages.
   * D. is correctly represented by all the above statements.

29. The trade unions of the 1840s and 1850s:
     A. were mostly affiliate unions of the National Labor Council.
     B. were composed mainly of unskilled workers.
   * C. tended to be local and weak.
     D. were mainly concerned with immigration reform.

30. Apprentices were provided all of the following *except*:
     A. room.
     B. board.
     C. training.
   * D. tools.

Essay Questions

1. What factors account for the tremendous growth in cotton cultivation from 1790 to 1860?

2. Compare the growth of roads, river transportation, and railroads through 1860. What were the advantages and disadvantages of each means of transport?

3. Explain the unique character of American technological development in the first half of the nineteenth century.

4. Why is the "age of the common man" or "the age of Jacksonian Democracy" an ironic name for this period?

5. Describe the general immigration trends of the period. What forms did the nativist response to this immigration take?

Matching Questions

A) invented the telegraph
B) invented the sewing machine
C) with Boston Associates, formed the Boston Manufacturing Company
D) wrote "Oh! Susanna"
E) America's wealthiest man in 1840s
F) invented the practical grain reaper
G) preached anti-Catholic sermons
H) invented process for condensed milk
I) improved steamboat
J) used his memory to bring industrial technology from England to the United States.

E   1. John Jacob Astor
G   2. Lyman Beecher
H   3. Gail Borden
D   4. Stephen Foster
I   5. Robert Fulton
B   6. Elias Howe
C   7. Francis Cabot Lowell
A   8. Samuel F. B. Morse
F   9. Cyrus McCormick
J   10. Samuel Slater

Chapter 13

AN AMERICAN RENAISSANCE:
RELIGION, ROMANTICISM, AND REFORM

This chapter explores intellectual currents prior to the Civil War. It reviews the important literary accomplishments of the first half of the nineteenth century, the developments in religion and education, and surveys major reform movements including temperance, prison reform, aid to the insane, women's rights, and utopian communities. Antislavery is discussed in Chapter 15 on slavery and the Old South.

Chapter Outline

I. The impact of the Enlightenment on nineteenth-century America
   A. The concept of mission in the American character
   B. The development of deism
       1. Roots in rationalism and Calvinism
       2. Nature of the beliefs
   C. The development of Unitarianism
       1. Nature of the beliefs
       2. Role of William Ellery Channing
       3. Creation of American Unitarian Association
   D. The development of Universalism
       1. Role of John Murray
       2. Nature of the beliefs
       3. Comparison with Unitarianism

II. The Second Great Awakening
   A. Origins of the revival movement
   B. The frontier phase of revivalism
       1. Development of the camp meeting
       2. Frontier reception of the revivals
       3. Role of Presbyterian and Congregational denominations
       4. Role of the Baptists
       5. The Methodists' impact
       6. Spread of revivals on the frontier

  C. Revivals in western New York State
   1. Role of Charles Grandison Finney
   2. Nature of Oberlin College
  D. Development of new religious groups
   1. Tendency for schisms
   2. Creation of the Disciples of Christ church
   3. Rise of the Mormon church
    a. Role of Joseph Smith, Jr.
    b. Characteristics of the church
    c. Persecution of Mormons
    d. The move to Utah
  E. The revival movement and democracy

III. Romanticism in America
  A. Nature of the Romantic revolt
  B. Transcendentalism as a Romantic expression
   1. Nature of Transcendentalism
   2. Margaret Fuller
   3. Ralph Waldo Emerson
   4. Henry David Thoreau
   5. The impact of Transcendentalism

IV. The flowering of American literature
  A. Nathaniel Hawthorne
  B. Emily Dickinson
  C. Washington Irving
  D. James Fenimore Cooper
  E. Edgar Allan Poe
  F. William Gilmore Simms
  G. Herman Melville
  H. Walt Whitman
  I. Feminist fiction
  J. The popular press
   1. Impact of advances in printing technology
   2. Sensational New York daily papers
   3. *New York Tribune* (1841)
   4. Growth of magazines

V. Education
  A. Level of literacy
  B. Early public schools

    C. Rising demand for public schools in the 1830s
       1. Basis of demand
       2. Role of Horace Mann
       3. Leadership of North Carolina in the South
    D. Hindrances to success
    E. Secondary-level schools
    F. Developments in higher education
       1. Post-Revolutionary surge in college formation
       2. Conflicts over offering broader levels of education
       3. Slow growth of technical education
       4. Development of law schools
    G. Education for women

VI. Movements for reform
    A. Roots of reform
    B. Temperance
       1. Heavy consumption of alcohol in the United States
       2. Arguments for temperance
       3. Early efforts at reform
       4. The American Temperance Union
    C. Prison reform
       1. Growth of public institutions to treat social ills
       2. Prevention and rehabilitation versus punishment for crime
       3. Auburn prison system
       4. Elimination of prison for debtors
    D. Reform in treatment of the insane
       1. Early state institutions for the insane
       2. Work of Dorothea Lynde Dix
    E. Crusade for women's rights
       1. Catharine Beecher and the "cult of domesticity"
       2. Advantages of domestic role for women
       3. Jobs for women
       4. Status of women in the antebellum period
       5. Seneca Falls Conference (1848)
       6. Hindrances to success
       7. Evidence of success of the movement
       8. Women in education and other professions
    F. Utopian communities
       1. Proliferation of utopian communities
       2. Nature of the Shaker communities
       3. Development and contributions of the Oneida Community
       4. The importance of Brook Farm
       5. The impact of the utopian communities

Lecture Ideas

1. Give each group in your class a particular reform group other than abolition (that will come in a later chapter) to research. It could consist of education, temperance, women's rights, and others. Give a short overview of the spirit of reform and then let each group contribute on their specific topic. See Steven Mintz's *Moralists and Modernizers: America's Pre-Civil War Reformers* (1995) and Ronald G. Walters's *American Reformers, 1815–1860* (1978).

2. For a good overview of the Second Great Awakening—its origins, revival phase, and its impact on religion in America—see Nathan O. Hatch's *The Democratization of American Christianity* (1989), and Paul K. Conkin's *American Originals* (1997).

3. For a lecture on Catharine Beecher and her view of women's role in society, see the essay by Kathryn Kish Sklar in *Portraits of American Women*, edited by G. J. Barker-Benfield and Catherine Clinton (1991).

True/False Questions

F   1. Of the major denominations, Baptists and Methodists were among the least affected by the frontier phase of the Second Great Awakening.

F   2. Peter Cartwright was president of Oberlin College.

T   3. Mormons often believed in popular magic and conjuring.

T   4. Margaret Fuller edited *The Dial*, a Transcendentalist journal.

F   5. Edgar Allan Poe based several of his novels (such as *Typee* and *Omoo*) on his experiences aboard an Australian whaler.

F   6. Public school teachers at first were mostly older unmarried women.

T   7. The word "teetotaler" originated with a temperance society's use of the letter T to signify Total Abstinence.

F   8. Lucretia Mott wrote *A Treatise on Domestic Economy*.

F   9. A major reform of the 1830s was the establishment of debtors' prisons.

F   10. Despite the temperance movement, per capita consumption of alcohol almost doubled between 1830 and 1860.

Multiple-Choice Questions

1. Which of the following religious movements arising in the
   nineteenth century attracted mainly workers and poor people?
   A. Calvinism
   B. Deism
   C. Unitarianism
   * D. Universalism

2. God "had planned the universe, built it, set it in motion, and
   then left it to its own fate." Which of the following emphasized
   this image of God?
   A. Calvinism
   * B. Deism
   C. Universalism
   D. Unitarianism

3. Unitarianism stressed:
   * A. reason and conscience.
   B. creeds and confessions.
   C. belief in the Holy Trinity.
   D. ritualistic practices.

4. Francis Asbury:
   A. founded the American Unitarian Association.
   * B. was the original Methodist "circuit rider."
   C. was a theology professor at Yale who criticized the
     emotionalism of the Second Great Awakening.
   D. taught Universalism as a professor of religion at Harvard.

5. The "Burned-Over District" was:
   A. the southern frontier.
   B. the coastal areas of the Carolinas.
   * C. western New York.
   D. the Appalachian region.

6. The first American college to admit both blacks and women was:
   A. Duke.
   * B. Oberlin.
   C. Vassar.
   D. William and Mary.

7. Which Protestant denomination "stressed the equality of all before God" and had no authority higher than the congregation?
    * A. Baptist
    B. Lutheran
    C. Methodist
    D. Presbyterian

8. Brigham Young:
    A. was found guilty of murdering Joseph Smith, Jr.
    B. was shot and killed in 1844 by an anti-Mormon lynch mob.
    * C. led the Mormons to their settlement near the Great Salt Lake in Utah.
    D. wrote the golden tablets that became the basis for the Mormon faith.

9. In the first half of the 1840s, the Mormons lived in:
    A. Charleston, South Carolina.
    B. Charlotte, North Carolina.
    C. Green Bay, Wisconsin.
    * D. Nauvoo, Illinois.

10. Romanticism in America:
    A. was a reaction to the Transcendental excesses of the Enlightenment.
    * B. stressed individualism and emotions over conformity and reason.
    C. opposed the Quaker doctrine of the inner light.
    D. was supported by Benjamin Franklin and Thomas Paine.

11. Transcendentalism:
    * A. stressed intuition over experience.
    B. was strongest in the South.
    C. expressed a strong belief in science and reason.
    D. grew directly out of the Enlightenment.

12. The author of "Civil Disobedience":
    A. was Ralph Waldo Emerson.
    B. was Margaret Fuller.
    * C. emphasized the Transcendentalist theme that men must follow their consciences.
    D. argued that violent resistance to an unjust law was justified.

13. Nathaniel Hawthorne:
    * A. used the themes of guilt and evil in many of his stories.
    B. became a writer on a bet with his wife.
    C. wrote "Rip Van Winkle" and "The Legend of Sleepy Hollow," both of which relied extensively on German folk tales.
    D. began the American literary renaissance with his poem "Thanatopsis."

14. Emily Dickinson:
    A. was the first American poet to gain an international reputation.
    B. edited several important Transcendentalist publications.
    * C. published just two poems before she died.
    D. invented the detective story.

15. Thoreau described which of the following as: "the greatest democrat the world has seen":
    A. Alexander Campbell.
    B. Herman Melville.
    C. William Gilmore Simms.
    * D. Walt Whitman.

16. Who wrote *Moby Dick*?
    A. James Fenimore Cooper
    B. Nathaniel Hawthorne
    C. Washington Irving
    * D. Herman Melville

17. Which one of the following is best identified as a southern writer?
    A. Emily Dickinson
    B. Nathaniel Hawthorne
    * C. William Gilmore Simms
    D. Henry David Thoreau

18. Walt Whitman:
    A. was a strong defender of slavery.
    B. wrote several essays attacking "the excesses of Emerson."
    * C. shocked many people with the sexual frankness of his works.
    D. first gained fame with the publication of his *Twice-Told Tales*.

19. Feminine fiction between 1830 and 1850:
    * A. stressed domestic topics.
    B. emphasized women's rights.
    C. opposed the writings of Catharine Beecher.
    D. was greatly condemned by men.

20. Horace Greeley:
    * A. was editor of the *New York Tribune*.
    B. promoted sensationalism in journalism.
    C. wrote the phrase, "If the law is of such a nature that it requires you to be an agent of injustice to another, then, I say, break the law."
    D. was the liberal president of the University of Virginia.

21. The literacy rate for Americans in 1840 was:
    A. lower than anywhere else in the Western world.
    B. high because every state had modern public school systems.
    C. ironically, higher for blacks than for whites.
    * D. about 80 percent of the total population.

22. Most of the institutions of higher education founded in the 1830s:
    A. were tax supported.
    * B. were attached to a religious denomination.
    C. stressed technical education.
    D. were coeducational.

23. The Declaration of Sentiments of the Seneca Falls Convention said that:
    A. institutions for the blind and deaf should be improved.
    B. excessive drinking destroyed many families.
    C. slavery should be immediately abolished.
    * D. "all men and women are created equal."

24. The American Temperance Union lost many members in 1836 when it:
    A. allowed women to join.
    * B. called for abstinence from all alcoholic beverages.
    C. allowed members to drink beer and wine.
    D. began to push immigration reform as "the only sure way to rid America of demon rum."

25. The Auburn Penitentiary:
    A. kept sane and insane prisoners in the same cells.
    B. was designed by Calvin H. Wiley.
    * C. was widely copied as a model for prison reform.
    D. is correctly represented by all the above statements.

26. Dorothea Lynde Dix directed her reform efforts at:
    * A. insane asylums.
    B. public education.
    C. women's rights.
    D. slavery.

27. The woman who argued that "woman's sphere" was the home was:
    * A. Catharine Beecher.
      B. Harriet Hunt.
      C. Lucretia Mott.
      D. Lucy Stone.

28. The women's rights movement of the 1850s had the support of all the following *except*:
      A. Ralph Waldo Emerson.
      B. Walt Whitman.
    * C. Herman Melville.
      D. William Lloyd Garrison.

29. Members of the Shaker community:
      A. believed that Jesus Christ had returned to earth in the 1820s.
      B. practiced free love and polygamy.
      C. were not permitted to leave after their "initiation."
    * D. followed "Mother Ann" Stanley.

30. George Ripley:
      A. wrote *The Blithedale Romance*.
    * B. founded Brook Farm.
      C. founded the United Society of Believers in Christ's Second Appearing.
      D. invented the steel animal trap produced at the Onedia community.

Essay Questions

1. Describe the various religious movements of the era—the "rational religions," the Second Great Awakening, the Mormons, etc.—characterizing the origin and adherents of each.

2. According to the text, the Romantic movement was a "great victory of heart over head." Explain this statement.

3. Describe the various trends in the rise of education (public, private, and higher) during this period.

4. Describe the various facets and accomplishments of the women's movement of the first half of the nineteenth century.

5. Using specific examples, discuss the objectives, membership, practices, and success of the nineteenth-century utopian communities.

Matching Questions

A)   set up Seneca Falls Convention
B)   wrote *Walden, or Life in the Woods*
C)   invented rotary press that printed 20,000 sheets an hour
D)   founded Mormonism
E)   dietary reformer
F)   wrote about Natty Bumppo ("Hawkeye") in *The Leather-Stocking Tales*
G)   promoted statewide school systems
H)   wrote *Leaves of Grass*
I)   wrote *The Scarlet Letter*
J)   leading Unitarian minister

J   1. William Ellery Channing
F   2. James Fenimore Cooper
E   3. Sylvester Graham
I   4. Nathaniel Hawthorne
C   5. Richard Hoe
G   6. Horace Mann
D   7. Joseph Smith
A   8. Elizabeth Cady Stanton
B   9. Henry David Thoreau
H   10. Walt Whitman

Chapter 14

MANIFEST DESTINY

This chapter covers the period 1841–1848, focusing on Tyler's domestic problems, the Webster-Ashburton Treaty, the settlement of the Far West, Polk's election, the acquisition of Texas and Oregon, and the Mexican War and its results.

Chapter Outline

I. The Tyler years
    A. Harrison's brief term
    B. Tyler's position on issues
    C. Domestic affairs
        1. Failure of Clay's program
        2. Tyler left without a party
    D. Foreign affairs
        1. Problems with Britain needing solution
            a. Suppression of African slave trade
        2. Compromises of the Webster-Ashburton Treaty
            a. Canada-U.S. borders settled
            b. Joint patrols of Africa

II. Westward expansion
    A. The idea of "manifest destiny"
        1. John L. O'Sullivan
    B. The western Indians
        1. Plains Indians
        2. Pressures from white expansion
    C. The Spanish West
        1. American attitudes toward area
        2. Spanish colonization not successful in Texas
    D. The Mexican Revolution
        1. Movements for independence
        2. Opened area for American expansion
    E. Movement to Santa Fe
    F. Fur trappers in the Rockies

      G. Move to Oregon country
         1. Joint occupation with Britain
         2. Mass migration of Americans by 1843
      H. Eyeing California
         1. Early California history
         2. Ship trading with the area
         3. Sutter's colony
       I. Life on the overland trail
         1. Statistics
         2. Indians rarely attacked
         3. Difficulties
         4. Gender roles
         5. The Donner party
      J. Frémont's mapping activities
      K. Efforts to acquire California

III. Annexing Texas
      A. American settlements
         1. Role of Stephen F. Austin
         2. Mexican edict against immigration
      B. Independence for Texas
         1. American demands
         2. Santa Anna's actions
         3. Independence declared
      C. War for Texas independence
         1. Battle of the Alamo
         2. Role of Sam Houston
         3. Santa Anna's trade
      D. The Republic of Texas
         1. President Sam Houston
         2. Efforts for annexation
            a. Jackson's delayed recognition
            b. Calhoun's treaty rejected

IV. The election of 1844
      A. Desire to keep the Texas issue out of the campaign
      B. Whig refusal to refer to Texas questions
      C. Democrats nominate a dark horse—James K. Polk
      D. Polk's victory

V. Polk's presidency
      A. Polk's background
      B. Polk's program
      C. Annexation of Texas by Tyler

    D. Oregon demands
      1. British hesitancy about war
      2. Compromise treaty

VI. Mexican War
    A. Negotiations with Mexico
    B. Provocation of an attack
    C. The request for war
    D. Opposition to the war
      1. In various parts of the country
      2. In New England
    E. Preparation for war
      1. Troops compared
      2. Comparisons of other factors
      3. Selection of a commander
    F. Taylor's conquest of northern Mexico
    G. Annexation of California
      1. Frémont's efforts
      2. Republic of California
      3. Stockton's claim of governorship
      4. Kearny's move to California
    H. Taylor's battles
      1. Victory at Monterrey
      2. Polk's assumptions and suspicions
      3. Santa Anna's return to power
      4. Battle of Buena Vista
      5. Taylor granted leave and returns home
    I. Scott's move to Mexico City
      1. Amphibious attack on Vera Cruz
      2. Troop reinforcements
      3. Attack on Mexico City
    J. Treaty of Guadalupe Hidalgo
      1. Terms of the treaty
      2. Ratification
    K. The war's legacy
      1. Gains and losses
      2. Innovations

Lecture Ideas

1. A good overview of Manifest Destiny is a must. See Frederick Merk and Lois Bannister Merk's *Manifest Destiny and Mission in American History* (1963), Anders Stephanson's *Manifest Destiny* (1995), and Albert K. Weinberg's *Manifest Destiny: A Study of Nationalist Expansionism in American History* (1957).

2. Create a lecture on westward migrations and the conditions that settlers faced. See Ray A. Billington's *The Far Western Frontier, 1830–1860* (1956) and Frederick Merk's *History of the Westward Movement* (1978).

3. Divide the class into two groups and research the origins, details, and results of the Mexican War. One group takes the Mexican perspective and the other group takes the American.See Robert W. Johannsen's *To the Halls of Montezumas: The Mexican War in the American Imagination* (1985) and John S. D. Eisenhower's *So Far From God: The U.S. War with Mexico, 1846–1848* (1989).

4. A good lecture could center on James K. Polk. A presentation of is administration's achievements could lead to the conclusion that he was one of America's most successful presidents. See Sam W. Haynes's *James K. Polk: Centinentalist, 1843–1846* (1966) and Paul H. Bergeron's *The Presidency of John K. Polk* (1987).

True/False Questions

F   1. John Taylor favored Henry Clay's American System.

T   2. Indians seldom attacked wagon trains.

T   3. The term "Bear Flaggers" refers to supporters of the Republic of California.

T   4. There were more than 200 different Indian tribes west of the Mississippi River in 1840.

T   5. Christopher "Kit" Carson was one of the most famous and knowledgeable of the mountain men.

F   6. Henry Clay was the Democratic presidential candidate in 1844.

F   7. The United States annexed California during Tyler's presidency.

T   8. The Great Plains was virtually devoid of a human presence until the Spaniards introduced the horse and the gun.

F   9. President Andrew Jackson wanted to purchase California primarily because of the gold discoveries there.

F   10. Zachary Taylor's decisive victory at the Battle of Buena Vista (February 1847) led to an immediate Mexican surrender.

Multiple-Choice Questions

1. Which leader is described as "a president without a party"?
   A. William Henry Harrison
   B. Sam Houston
   C. James K. Polk
   * D. John Tyler

2. William Henry Harrison:
   A. was the last president elected from the Jacksonian Democratic party.
   B. developed a close association with Henry Clay during his presidency.
   * C. was elected more on his military record than for his stand on the issues.
   D. was the first president to be assassinated.

3. The *Creole* incident:
   A. strained relations between the United States and France.
   * B. involved the British freeing American slaves after they mutinied and escaped.
   C. involved the seizure and destruction of an American steamboat at Niagara Falls.
   D. was solved almost singlehandedly by Henry Clay.

4. As a result of the Webster-Ashburton Treaty:
   A. the United States acquired Louisiana from Great Britain.
   B. the British government agreed to pay reparations for the destruction of the *Creole*.
   * C. the boundary dispute in Maine was settled.
   D. the United States gave up all claims to the territory west of the Mississippi River.

5. Of the following, the Spanish were most successful at colonizing what is now:
   A. Arizona.
   * B. New Mexico.
   C. Texas.
   D. Oregon.

6. Large-scale American emigration to the Oregon country:
   * A. began in earnest in the early 1840s.
   B. started as a result of rumors of gold discoveries.

C. was greatly hampered by hostile Indians.

D. was usually along a southern route, through Texas, New Mexico, and California.

7. *Rancheros*:
   * A. usually used Indians as slaves.
   B. were the small farms that the Mexican government allowed American settlers to own in California.
   C. was a spicy cheese and potato dish favored by Santa Anna's soldiers.
   D. was the derogatory name American settlers used to refer to native Mexicans in Texas.

8. John A. Sutter:
   A. was the captain of the *Creole*.
   B. intrigued with the British for control of Oregon.
   * C. established the trading post that became Sacramento.
   D. negotiated the Webster-Ashburton Treaty for the United States.

9. Most of the women who traveled the Overland Trail:
   A. were single.
   B. died during the trip.
   C. were slaves.
   * D. found that the constant toil soon exhausted their enthusiasm for the trip.

10. Mexico obtained its independence from:
    A. France in 1807.
    B. Spain in 1807.
    * C. Spain in 1821.
    D. the United Sates in 1821.

11. Most of the American settlers in Texas went there because of:
    A. furs.
    B. gold and other mineral deposits.
    * C. cheap cotton lands.
    D. trading opportunities with the Indians and the Mexicans.

12. The Mexican ban on American immigration to Texas:
    * A. was ineffective.
    B. halted the flood of immigrants to the area.
    C. went into effect in 1820.
    D. was necessary because Americans in Texas already numbered almost half the Mexican population there.

13. The Battle of the Alamo:
    A. was the first victory for Texans in their war for
       independence from Mexico.
    * B. inspired the rest of Texas to fanatical resistance.
    C. claimed the life of Sam Houston.
    D. is correctly represented by all the above statements.

14. Mexican General Santa Anna was captured:
    A. by the U.S. Army in 1833.
    B. and executed by rebel Texans at the Alamo.
    * C. but won his freedom by agreeing to independence for Texas.
    D. at the Battle of Monterrey.

15. All the following contributed to the failure of the United States
    to annex Texas before 1845 *except*:
    A. sectional divisions in the Senate.
    B. fear of war with Mexico.
    C. addition of a new slave state.
    * D. the reluctance of Texans.

16. The phrase "fifty-four forty or fight!" referred to:
    A. California.
    B. Florida.
    * C. Oregon.
    D. Texas.

17. The so-called "spot resolutions" were introduced in Congress:
    A. immediately before the Battle of the Alamo.
    B. immediately after the Battle of the Alamo.
    * C. to oppose the Mexican War.
    D. to support the annexation of California.

18. The Republic of Texas:
    A. at first shied away from annexation by the United States.
    B. drafted a constitution emancipating its slaves.
    C. was recognized by President Andrew Jackson early in his
       administration.
    * D. developed trade relations with England and France.

19. According to Henry Clay, annexation of Texas:
    * A. was "dangerous to the integrity of the Union."
    B. should wait until the people in Texas asked the American
       government to take control of the area.

       C. was "the manifest destiny of the American republic."

       D. should have the support of all members of the new Republican party.

20. George Donner:
    A. was John Tyler's vice-president.
    B. was a Spanish priest known for his sympathy for the Indians.
    C. was the expansionist-minded editor of the *Sacramento Bee*.
  * D. led a party of settlers on the Oregon Trail.

21. James K. Polk:
    A. won the presidential nomination of the Whig party in 1844 for his expansionist stance.
    B. got his start in politics as a Federalist in Massachusetts.
    C. argued that annexation of Oregon was "not called for by any general expression of public opinion."
  * D. won the 1844 Democratic presidential nomination as a "dark horse" candidate.

22. In the presidential election of 1844:
    A. Martin Van Buren ran against James K. Polk.
  * B. the popular vote was very close.
    C. both parties supported expansionism in their platforms.
    D. both parties opposed expansionism in their platforms.

23. As president, Polk supported all the following *except*:
    A. the reestablishment of the Independent Treasury.
    B. a reduction in the tariff.
  * C. the immediate abolition of slavery.
    D. the acquisition of California.

24. On the question of Oregon:
    A. Polk privately favored compromise with the British.
    B. England did not think the issue worth going to war.
    C. most of the border was drawn at the Forty-ninth Parallel.
  * D. All the above statements are true.

25. Which one of the following supported the Mexican War?
    A. Abraham Lincoln
    B. John Quincy Adams
    C. residents of New England
  * D. residents of the Mississippi Valley

26. At the beginning of the Mexican War:
    A. American forces were prepared, since war with Britain had been threatening for over a year.
    * B. American forces were outnumbered by Mexican forces by more than four to one.
    C. Polk had no plan of action.
    D. Polk named Thomas Hart Benton as his first commander in Texas.

27. The Republic of California:
    A. was recognized by Great Britain in 1827.
    B. lasted nearly twice as long as the Republic of Texas.
    C. sided with Mexico in the Mexican War.
    * D. had a confused and unruly government.

28. The American capture of Mexico City was led by:
    A. John C. Frémont.
    B. Stephen Kearny.
    * C. Winfield Scott.
    D. Zachary Taylor.

29. All the following statements about the Treaty of Guadalupe Hidalgo are true *except*:
    A. Mexico gave up all claims to Texas.
    B. Mexico ceded California to the United States.
    C. The United States agreed to pay Mexico $15 million.
    * D. The treaty was never ratified by the U.S. Senate.

30. Which of the following statements about the Mexican War is *not* true?
    A. It was America's first successful offensive war.
    B. The annexations following the war completed what is now the continental United States.
    * C. Over 1,700 Americans died in battle, and over 11,000 died of disease.
    D. The fighting lasted less than two years.

Essay Questions

1. Why was Henry Clay and not the incumbent, John Tyler, nominated by the Whig party in 1844?

2. Explain the phrase "manifest destiny." What factors were most important in drawing Americans to the West, both mentally and physically?

3. In which territory—Texas, California, or Oregon—was America's claim best? In which was it worst?

4. Discuss the American movement to annex Texas between 1820 and 1845.

5. Why were many Americans opposed to the Mexican War?

Matching Questions

A) introduced "spot resolutions" in Congress
B) led American forces at Vera Cruz
C) was elected vice-president in 1840
D) was killed at the Alamo
E) California "governor"
F) secretary of state who negotiated treaty concerning the boundaries for Maine and the Great Lakes region
G) "the Pathfinder"
H) died after one month in office
I) president of the Republic of Texas
J) "Young Hickory"

G 1. John Charles Frémont
H 2. William Henry Harrison
I 3. Sam Houston
A 4. Abraham Lincoln
J 5. James K. Polk
B 6. Winfield Scott
E 7. Robert F. Stockton
D 8. William B. Travis
C 9. John Tyler
F 10. Daniel Webster

Chapter 15

THE OLD SOUTH

This chapter discusses the Old South, slavery, and the development of the antislavery movement up to the early 1840s. Included are an effort to sort myth from reality in the life of the Old South, statistics on the economic development of the South, a description of white society and black slavery in the South, the condition of free blacks in both the South and the North, the growth of antislavery sentiment and action, and the major defenses of slavery.

Chapter Outline

    I. Myth and reality in the Old South

        A. Southern mythology

        B. The southern condition

            1. Causal effects of the environment and of human decisions and actions

            2. Factors that contribute a sense of sectional distinction

                a. The weather

                b. A biracial population

                c. Highly native population

                d. Architecture, work ethic, penchant for the military, country-gentleman ideal

                e. Preponderance of farming

        C. Myth of the cotton kingdom

            1. Actual variety of staple crops

                a. Cotton

                b. Tobacco in upper South

                 c. Indigo in colonial era

                d. Rice in tidewater area

                e. Sugar along the lower Mississippi River

                f. Hemp and flax

            2. Voracious demand for cotton

            3. The reality of high proportions of other agricultural products

                a. Grains, potatoes, and general crops

                b. Livestock

            4. Exhaustion of the soil

    D. Proposals for diversification
        1. Edmund Ruffin and agricultural reform
        2. Levels of manufacturing and trade
        3. A "colonial" economy
    E. Demands for economic development
        1. Examples of existing southern industry
            a. Tredegar Iron Works in Richmond, Virginia
            b. Daniel Pratt's various industries in Alabama
    F. Causes for southern lag in economic development
        1. Traditional claims
            a. Claims that blacks were unsuited to factory
               work
            b. Contention that aristocratic prestige precluded
               trade ventures
        2. Profitability of slaves

II. White society in the South
    A. The planter
        1. Relative ownership of slaves
        2. Style of life
        3. The plantation mistress
    B. The middle class
        1. Largest group of whites
        2. Land ownership
        3. General style of life
    C. Poor whites
        1. General characteristics
    D. Honor and violence in the Old South

III. Black society in the South
    A. Free blacks
        1. Methods of obtaining freedom
        2. Occupations for free blacks
    B. Slaves
        1. Statistics of population and value
        2. Domestic slave trade replaces foreign slave trade
        3. Plantation slave life
            a. Classes among plantation slaves
            b. Provision of the necessities of life
            c. Work schedules
            d. Punishment
        4. The nature of slavery as an institution
    C. Forging the slave community
    D. The experience of slave women

E. Slave religion and folklore
   1. Syncretic nature of the religion
   2. Use of religion as an instrument of white control and black refuge
   3. The uses of folklore
F. The slave family
   1. Legal status
   2. Importance of the nuclear family
   3. Sexual exploitation of slaves

IV. The culture of the southern frontier
   A. The "Old Southwest"
      1. Largely unsettled until 1820s
      2. A "land of promise"
   B. The decision to migrate
      1. For men, East had decreasing economic opportunity
      2. Women more hesitant to move
      3. Worse conditions for slaves
   C. Journey and settlement
      1. Steady stream of settlers
      2. For many, an opportunity to prosper
      3. Difficulties
   D. A masculine culture
      1. Violence and alcoholism
      2. Celia, a slave girl
         a. White owner attacked her repeatedly
         b. She killed him and was executed

V. Antislavery movements
   A. Early opposition to slavery
      1. Establishment of the American Colonization Society
         a. Appeals to different groups of whites
         b. Acquisition of and settlement in Liberia
   B. The movement toward abolition
      1. William Lloyd Garrison's call for immediate emancipation
      2. The Liberator
   C. Creation of the American Anti-Slavery Society
      1. Predecessor societies
      2. Aims of the organization
      3. Propaganda efforts
   D. The antislavery movement split
      1. Garrison and the radical wing refuse compromise
      2. Others only want to purge American society of slavery

3. Showdown comes in 1840 over women's rights in the society
4. Garrisonians win the right of women to participate
5. New Yorkers break away

E. Black antislavery advocates
1. Conflicts over the right of blacks to participate in antislavery activities
2. Former slaves who became public speakers

F. Discrimination against blacks in the North

VI. Reactions to antislavery agitation
   A. The "gag rule" in Congress
   B. Development of the Liberty party (1840)
   C. Defenses of slavery
      1. Biblical arguments
      2. Inferiority of blacks
      3. Practical considerations
      4. George Fitzhugh's comparison to northern wage slavery

Lecture Ideas

1. A lecture on society in the Antebellum South will help students better understand the decisions made by southern leaders as the country headed toward civil war. See John B. Boles's *The South Through Time: A History of an America Region* (1995), Bruce Collins's *White Society in the Antebellum South* (1985), and Eugene D. Genovese's *Roll Jordan Roll: The World the Slaves Made* (1974).

2. A lecture on slavery could take several directions. For a sampling of the rich literature on the subject, see the bibliography in the textbook. Kenneth M. Stampp's *The Peculiar Institution* (1956) remains one of the best overviews of slavery. Chapters 1 and 6 of Stanley M. Elkins's *Slavery* (3rd ed., 1976) describe how historians have viewed slavery over the years. Many of the recent studies have used various types of first-person accounts of slavery; for example, Paul D. Escott, in *Slavery Remembered* (1979), used slave narratives to come up with a composite picture of slavery. A good selection of first-person slave narratives can be found in *Slave Testimony*, edited by John Blassingame (1977). The introduction to Blassingame's book, a briefer version of which was published as "Using the Testimony of Ex-slaves: Approaches and Problems" (*Journal of Southern History*, Aug. 1975), is a good discussion of how historians can use such examples of oral history.

3. A Good follow-up lecture to the one on slavery will be to develop one on slave rebellions. See Douglas R. Egerton's *Gabriel's Rebellion: The Virginia Slave Conspiracies of 1800 and 1802* (1993), Stephen B. Oates's *The Fires of Jubilee: Nat Turner's Fierce Rebellion* (1975), and Eugene D. Genovese's *From Rebellion to Revolution: Afro-American Slave Revolts in the Making of the Modern World* (1979).

4. A lecture on abolitionism is a must. Divide your class into two groups and research and report on the two movements of white abolitionism and black abolitionism. See Ronald G. Walters's *The Antislavery Appeal: American Abolitionists After 1830* (1976), William S. McFeely's *Frederick Douglas* (1990), and Wendy Hamand Venet's *Neither Ballots nor Bullets: Women Abolitionists and the Civil War* (1991).

5. For an interesting discussion of the Underground Railroad, see Charles L. Blockson's "Escape from Slavery: The Underground Railroad" (*National Geographic*, July 1984).

True/False Questions

T   1. The South's staple crops tended to exhaust the soil and lead to erosion.

T   2. White abolitionists tended to favor the formation of separate black antislavery organizations.

T   3. Economically, the South was a sort of colonial dependency of the North.

T   4. David Walker was a black abolitionist.

F   5. Agricultural diversity in the Old South was practically nonexistent.

F   6. Men on the southern frontier tended to drink less alcohol than men in the eastern states.

T   7. The American Colonization Society established the African nation of Liberia as a new home for free American blacks.

F   8. The "Lane rebels" were northern seminary students who supported slavery.

F   9. The northern states had little racial discrimination and segregation before the Civil War.

T   10. After about 1830, southern intellectuals presented slavery
            as a positive good rather than as a necessary evil.

Multiple-Choice Questions

1. All the following might be used to explain the South's
   distinctiveness *except*:
   A. its climate.
   B. its preponderance of farming.
   C. its biracial population.
   * D. the large number of immigrants who came to the South
      after 1760.

2. Southerners became especially conscious that they were a
   minority within the United States around:
   A. 1750.
   B. 1780.
   C. 1800.
   * D. 1820.

3. The plantation mistress:
   A. usually led a life of idle leisure.
   B. often criticized the prevailing social order and racist
      climate.
   * C. generally confronted a double standard in terms of moral
      and sexual behavior.
   D. is correctly represented by all the above statements.

4. Cotton production increased between 1815 and 1860:
   A. despite a diminished demand from French and British
      markets.
   B. because of the sustained high prices for cotton.
   * C. partly because of the cultivation of new lands in the
      Southwest.
   D. from 1 million to almost 2 million bales per year.

5. Corn as a crop in the Old South:
   * A. was used mainly for immediate consumption.
   B. generally went into the market.
   C. was found almost exclusively in the upper South.
   D. was found almost exclusively in the Deep South.

6. The Tredegar Iron Works:
    *   A. was the most important single manufacturing enterprise in the Old South.
        B. employed over half of the population of Cartersville, Georgia.
        C. refused to use black workers.
        D. is correctly represented by all the above statements.

7. Manufacturing in the Old South lagged behind that in the North because:
        A. black labor was incompatible with industry.
        B. white leaders in the South were more concerned with prestige than with profits.
        C. the South lacked important natural resources.
    *   D. cotton was a more profitable investment.

8. The South's "lazy diseases" were:
    *   A. often caused by dietary deficiencies.
        B. usually the result of genetic inbreeding.
        C. usually fatal.
        D. eliminated by the time of the Civil War.

9. What portion of the South's white families owned slaves?
        A. one-tenth
    *   B. one fourth
        C. one-half
        D. two-thirds

10. "Free persons of color":
        A. were not allowed to own slaves.
        B. enjoyed legal (if not social) equality with whites.
        C. were usually very wealthy.
    *   D. were often mulattos.

11. Approximately how many slaves lived in the South in 1860?
        A. 30,000
        B. 100,000
        C. 1 million
    *   D. 4 million

12. The end of the foreign slave trade:
        A. made slaves more valuable.
        B. gave rise to a flourishing domestic trade.
        C. had the unexpected effect of tempering some of slavery's harsher features.
    *   D. is correctly represented by all the above statements.

13. Nat Turner's slave insurrection:
    A. resulted in the death of seven whites and at least five blacks.
    B. was betrayed by Jehu Jones, a free black man.
  * C. was the largest in the country.
    D. never passed the planning stage.

14. The most numerous white southerners were the:
    A. planters.
  * B. yeoman farmers.
    C. "poor whites."
    D. manufacturers.

15. "Gullah" refers to the:
  * A. slave culture of coastal Georgia and South Carolina.
    B. labor system used on most large plantations.
    C. slave "cabins" on large plantations.
    D. slave overseer.

16. Slave religion:
    A. was often used by whites to teach humility and obedience.
    B. was often used by slaves to release their emotions and soothe their troubles with the promise of a better life to come.
    C. was a mixture of African and Christian elements.
  * D. is correctly represented by all the above statements.

17. Slave folklore:
    A. contained little humor.
    B. included many stories about superhuman heroes.
    C. was simple and easily understood by whites.
  * D. included many "trickster tales."

18. Slave families:
    A. were not allowed by most slave owners.
    B. were generally headed by mothers.
    C. were "legalized" in the 1840s by state laws allowing marriages between slaves.
  * D. provided a means for socializing children into slave culture.

19. Celia was:
    A. the penname of Harriet Jacobs.
  * B. a slave girl executed for killing her abusive master.
    C. a free black woman who opened the first school for slave children in New Orleans.
    D. the most effective black abolitionist speaker.

20. The "Old Southwest":
    A. included Texas, Arizona, New Mexico, and Utah.
    * B. attracted thousands of settlers in the 1820s and 1830s with its promise of cotton production.
    C. attracted nearly twice as many female as male settlers in the early years.
    D. is correctly represented by all the above statements.

21. The American Colonization Society:
    * A. had the support of both proslavery and antislavery spokespeople.
    B. was formed in 1841.
    C. had the support of most black leaders.
    D. was opposed by Henry Clay, John Marshall, Daniel Webster, and James Madison.

22. Sojourner Truth:
    A. had been born a slave.
    B. spoke for women's rights and abolition.
    C. changed her name (from Isabella) after a mystical conversation with God.
    * D. is correctly represented by all the above statements.

23. The Grimké sisters:
    A. were freed slaves who became effective speakers for the American Anti-Slavery Society.
    B. argued in several popular books that slavery was beneficial to both races.
    * C. worked for women's rights as well as abolition.
    D. were antislavery propagandists who hid their gender by using male pseudonyms.

24. William Lloyd Garrison:
    A. supported the use of physical violence.
    * B. was accused by slaveholders of stirring up the unrest that led to Nat Turner's insurrection.
    C. opposed immediate emancipation.
    D. was the most prominent southern abolitionist.

25. The American Anti-Slavery Society:
    A. advocated the violent overthrow of slavery.
    * B. conceded that each state could legislate its own domestic institutions (including slavery).
    C. opposed equal rights for blacks.
    D. is correctly represented by all the above statements.

26. The American Anti-Slavery Society split over the issue of:
    * A. women's rights.
      B. colonization.
      C. financial compensation for slave owners.
      D. biblical interpretation.

27. The debate over slavery:
      A. moved Methodists and Baptists to take an antislavery position.
      B. moved Methodists and Baptists to take a proslavery position.
    * C. split Methodists and Baptists into northern and southern denominations.
      D. was generally ignored by Methodists and Baptists until the Civil War.

28. Who said, "I stole this head, these limbs, this body from my master and ran off with them"?
    * A. Frederick Douglass
      B. William Lloyd Garrison
      C. Sarah Grimké
      D. Sojourner Truth

29. In the early 1830s a plan of gradual emancipation and colonization was debated and narrowly defeated in the state legislature of:
      A. Georgia.
      B. North Carolina.
      C. Tennessee.
    * D. Virginia.

30. George Fitzhugh's major proslavery argument was that:
      A. slavery was justified in the Bible.
    * B. southern slavery was better for workers than the "wage slavery" of northern industry.
      C. blacks were the product of a separate creation.
      D. blacks and whites could not live together without risk of race war except for slavery.

Essay Questions

1. How important was slavery to the economy of the Old South? Discuss its effects on agriculture, industry, and any other relevant aspects of the South.

2.   Describe white society in the Old South. What myths have been associated with its various groups? In each case, what was the reality?

3.   Evaluate the goals, methods, and leadership of the abolitionist movement. Which of the methods were most effective? Why?

4.   Describe the southern defense of slavery before and after 1830. How did this change affect the intellectual life of the Old South?

5.   What roles did religion, folklore, and family life play in the lives of slaves?

Matching Questions

A)   studied the chemistry of soils to improve their productivity
B)   antislavery editor murdered in Illinois
C)   wrote *Cannibals All! or, Slaves Without Masters*
D)   presidential candidate of Liberty party
E)   wrote *American Slavery as It Is: Testimony of a Thousand Witnesses*
F)   allegedly plotted slave rebellion in South Carolina
G)   edited *The Liberator*
H)   founded antislavery society in New York
I)   major Alabama industrialist
J)   most celebrated "conductor" of the Underground Railroad

D   1. James G. Birney
C   2. George Fitzhugh
G   3. William Lloyd Garrison
B   4. Elijah Lovejoy
I   5. David Pratt
A   6. Edmund Ruffin
H   7. Arthur Tappan
J   8. Harriet Tubman
F   9. Denmark Vesey
E   10. Theodore Dwight Weld

Chapter 16

THE CRISIS OF UNION

This chapter covers political developments from the election of 1848 through the secession of the lower South and the period prior to Lincoln's inauguration. It includes the controversy over the expansion of slavery in western lands, the development of the Compromise of 1850, assertions of manifest destiny on the world scene, the controversy over Kansas, the Lincoln-Douglas debates, and the election of 1860.

Chapter Outline

   I. Quarrels arising from the conquest of Mexican territory in the Southwest
      A. The Wilmot Proviso
      B. Calhoun's resolutions in reaction to the Proviso
      C. Other proposals to deal with slavery in the territories
         1. Extension of the Missouri Compromise line
         2. Popular, or squatter, sovereignty
      D. Controversy over admission of Oregon as a free state

  II. The push for California statehood
      A. California gold rush
      B. The mining frontier
      C. Zachary Taylor as president
      D. Taylor calls for admission of California as a free state

 III. The Compromise of 1850
      A. Clay's compromise package of eight resolutions
      B. Calhoun's response
      C. Webster's plea for union
      D. Seward's response for the abolitionists
      E. The Committee of Thirteen proposes an "Omnibus Bill"
      F. Taylor's death
      G. Fillmore supports the Clay compromise
      H. The Douglas strategy of six (later five) separate bills
      I. Terms of the Compromise

       J. Reaction to the Fugitive Slave Law
          1. Terms of the law
          2. *Uncle Tom's Cabin*

IV. The election of 1852
    A. The Democrats turn to Franklin Pierce
    B. Free Soilers promote John P. Hale
    C. Whigs turn to Winfield Scott and his martial glory
    D. Pierce the victor

V. Foreign adventures
    A. Efforts to expand southward
       1. Early efforts to capture Cuba
       2. The Ostend Manifesto
    B. Achievements of American diplomacy in the Pacific
       1. Opening of China to Americans
       2. Perry's expedition to Japan
    C. The Gadsden Purchase of 1853

VI. The Kansas-Nebraska Crisis
    A. Development
       1. Ideas for a transcontinental railroad
       2. Douglas's Nebraska bill leads to repeal of the
          Missouri Compromise
    B. Northern reactions to the extension of slavery
       1. Protests
       2. Strains on the political parties
          a. Creation of Republican party
          b. Effect on Whig party
    C. The "battle" for Kansas
       1. Efforts to promote settlement of Kansas by Free
          Soilers and pro-slavery forces
       2. The official pro-slavery government
       3. The counter-government in Topeka
       4. Violence in Lawrence and Pottawatomie
       5. The Sumner-Butler-Brooks clash in Congress

VII. The election of 1856
    A. The American and Whig parties nominate Fillmore
    B. The Republicans choose John Frémont as their first
       presidential candidate
    C. The Democrats nominate James Buchanan
    D. The campaign and Buchanan's election
    E. Nature of the Buchanan presidency

VIII. The Dred Scott decision
    A. Nature of the case
    B. Analysis of the court's decision
    C. Southern demands for a federal slave code

IX. Movements for Kansas statehood
    A. Governor Walker's efforts
    B. The Lecompton Constitution
    C. Buchanan's support for Lecompton
    D. Defeat of the proposal
    E. Postponement of Kansas statehood

X. Financial panic of 1857
    A. Causes and nature of the economic reversal
    B. Sectional reactions to the economic problems

XI. The Lincoln-Douglas senatorial contest in Illinois
    A. The candidates and their situation
    B. The Freeport Doctrine
    C. Douglas's efforts to bait Lincoln
    D. Results of the election

XII. Further sectional problems at the end of the decade
    A. John Brown's raid at Harper's Ferry
    B. The effects of Brown's raid and martyrdom

XIII. The election of 1860
    A. The Democratic convention eventually nominates Douglas
    B. The southern Democrats nominate Breckenridge
    C. The Republican convention nominates Lincoln and adopts a platform
    D. The Constitutional Union Party formed to support Bell and preservation of the Union
    E. Nature of the campaign
    F. Outcome of the election

XIV. Secession begins
    A. Secession of states of the Deep South
    B. Buchanan's reactions to secession
    C. Problems of federal property in the seceded South
    D. Last efforts to compromise

Lecture Ideas

1. Divide the class up into groups, and after a general lecture on the various causes that led up to the Civil War, let each group research and report on their findings. See David M. Potter's *The Impending Crisis, 1848–1861* (1976), Kenneth M. Stampp's *American in 1857* (1990), and *The Causes of the American Civil War*, edited by Edwin C. Rozwenc (2nd ed., 1972).

2. Harriet Beecher Stowe's *Uncle Tom's Cabin*, one of the most popular and important books of the 1850s, could be the subject of an instructive lecture; a good source would be Thomas F. Gossett's *Uncle Tom's Cabin and American Culture* (1985), which discusses, among other things, how Stowe came to write the book, the organization of the novel, its picture of slave life, and its reception in the North and South.

True/False Questions

T   1. Congress never passed the Wilmot Proviso.

T   2. In the mining frontier of the Far West, women often enjoyed greater opportunities than back East.

T   3. The Republican party was created in 1854 by the merging of several antislavery groups.

T   4. The author of *Uncle Tom's Cabin* was Harriet Beecher Stowe.

T   5. The Pottawatomie Massacre was part of the conflict between proslavery and antislavery forces in Kansas.

T   6. One-fifth of the gold seekers who went to California in 1849 died within six months.

T   7. In 1857 Kansas had only 200 slaves, and most people there were antislavery.

F   8. Stephen Douglas was one of the most extreme proslavery and states' rights advocates in the Democratic party.

F   9. The Republican platform in 1860 promised to end slavery in the southern states.

F   10. By February 1861, eleven southern states had withdrawn from the Union.

Multiple-Choice Questions

1. The Wilmot Proviso sought to:
   A. assure protection of slavery in Texas.
   * B. forbid slavery in any of the lands acquired through the Mexican War.
   C. keep slavery out of all territories of the United States.
   D. apply the principle of popular sovereignty to all future territories of the United States.

2. Popular sovereignty:
   A. was endorsed by the Whig party.
   B. was first proposed by President Polk.
   C. would let Congress decide the issue of slavery on a state-by-state basis.
   * D. would allow the people of each territory to decide the issue of slavery.

3. Which of the following would have been least likely to join the Free Soil party?
   A. Massachusetts Whigs
   B. members of the Liberty party
   * C. John C. Calhoun
   D. Van Buren Democrats

4. In the presidential election of 1848:
   A. the new Free Soil party carried most of the southern states.
   B. Zachary Taylor was the Democratic candidate.
   * C. Lewis Cass came in second place.
   D. California cast its first electoral votes for Martin Van Buren.

5. President Zachary Taylor wanted to admit California as a state immediately because he:
   A. was antislavery, and California had voted on a free-state constitution.
   B. was proslavery, and California had voted on a slave-state constitution.
   * C. wished to bypass the divisive issue of slavery in the territories.
   D. was afraid Mexico would make new claims on the area since gold had been discovered there.

6. During the debate over the Compromise of 1850, one senator
   made a conciliatory speech ("I wish to speak today, not
   as a Massachusetts man, not as a Northern man, but as an
   American. . . . I speak today for the preservation of the Union.")
   that was scorned by abolitionist leaders. That senator was:
   A. Henry Clay.
   B. Henry S. Foote.
   C. William H. Seward.
   * D. Daniel Webster.

7. President Taylor's death:
   * A. strengthened the chance for compromise in 1850.
   B. put proslavery Franklin Pierce in the White House.
   C. put antislavery William H. Seward in the White
   House.
   D. was caused by a heart attack he suffered on the Senate
   floor while speaking for the Compromise of 1850.

8. The Compromise of 1850:
   A. admitted Utah as a slave state.
   B. admitted Utah as a free state.
   C. outlawed slavery north of the line 36° 30' in the western
   territories.
   * D. abolished the slave trade in the District of Columbia.

9. The Fugitive Slave Law of 1850:
   A. was part of the Missouri Compromise.
   * B. denied a jury trial for alleged fugitives.
   C. was often opposed in the South.
   D. brought about the recapture of some 2500 escaped
   slaves.

10. The novel *Uncle Tom's Cabin*:
    * A. was perhaps the most effective piece of antislavery
    propaganda.
    B. alerted southerners to the plight of the slave, although the
    book was a commercial failure.
    C. was called "the greatest book of the age" by Senator A. P.
    Butler.
    D. is correctly represented by all the above statements.

11. The winner of the presidential election of 1852 was:
    A. Millard Fillmore.
    * B. Franklin Pierce.
    C. Winfield Scott.
    D. Martin Van Buren.

12. The Ostend Manifesto was:
    A. an agreement by the United States, Britain, and France to use their joint force to gain independence for Cuba.
    B. an attempt to gain Cuba as a colony for freed American slaves.
    * C. a diplomatic dispatch that suggested the United States might consider using force to take Cuba if Spain refused to sell it.
    D. an insult to the United States by Spain which became the basis for raids to take over Cuba.

13. During the 1840s and 1850s:
    A. several Chinese ports were opened to American trade.
    B. several Japanese ports were opened to American trade.
    C. American missionaries began to go to China in great numbers.
    * D. All the above statements are true.

14. The Gadsden Purchase of 1853:
    * A. was primarily for the purpose of a transcontinental railroad.
    B. was in the Northwest.
    C. was opposed by Jefferson Davis and other Southerners.
    D. is correctly represented by all the above statements.

15. Passage of the Kansas-Nebraska Act was a victory for:
    A. abolitionists.
    B. immigrant groups in America.
    * C. the concept of popular sovereignty.
    D. Southerners who wanted a transcontinental railroad to run west from New Orleans.

16. Stephen Douglas was more successful than Clay in getting the Compromise of 1850 passed because:
    A. he dropped the question of the slave trade in the District of Columbia.
    B. he could depend on a sympathy vote from supporters of deceased President Taylor.
    C. his support for popular sovereignty allowed many abolitionist senators to vote with him.
    * D. he split the issues into separate bills.

17. Charles Sumner:
    A. was a senator from South Carolina.
    B. made a slanderous proslavery speech on the Senate floor.
    * C. was attacked and beaten by the nephew of a man he insulted.
    D. is correctly represented by all the above statements.

18. In the election of 1856:
   * A. Republicans nominated their first presidential candidate.
   B. James Buchanan was the Republican presidential candidate.
   C. Stephen Douglas was the Democratic presidential candidate.
   D. John C. Frémont swept the Deep South states.

19. In its decision in *Dred Scott* v. *Sandford*, the Supreme Court:
   A. ruled that slaves who were taken to free states would be considered free.
   B. ruled that slaves who were taken to free territories would be considered free.
   C. upheld the constitutionality of the Missouri Compromise.
   * D. noted that blacks did not have federal citizenship and therefore could not bring suit in federal courts.

20. President Buchanan:
   A. supported the Lecompton Constitution because he opposed the spread of slavery.
   B. opposed the Lecompton Constitution because he favored the spread of slavery.
   C. opposed the Lecompton Constitution because he was politically dependent on northern congressmen.
   * D. supported the Lecompton Constitution because he was dependent on southern congressmen.

21. One important effect of the financial panic of 1857 was that:
   A. a new national banking system was adopted the next year to prevent a recurrence of the event.
   * B. the South was convinced of the superiority of its economic system.
   C. northern manufacturers were less hurt by the economic reverse than were southern farmers.
   D. an agreement was made to decrease the tariff in 1858 to prevent a further economic decline.

22. The Freeport Doctrine might be defined as the concept that:
   A. slavery could not be prohibited in a territory until that territory became a state.
   B. slavery was immoral and ought to be abolished in all territories of the United States.
   * C. even if slavery were permitted in a territory, the people could effectively end it by refusing to pass laws to sustain it.
   D. if blacks were freed from slavery, they must be given full legal and social equality.

23. The Whig party was effectively destroyed by stresses arising from:
    A. the defeat of Winfield Scott in 1852.
    * B. the passage of the Kansas-Nebraska Act.
    C. the proposed Lecompton Constitution.
    D. John Brown's raid at Harper's Ferry.

24. John Brown's raid at Harper's Ferry resulted in:
    * A. his execution for treason and inciting insurrection.
    B. panic in the North.
    C. a slave uprising in Virginia.
    D. some important mending of differences between North and South as each section saw the consequences of extremist actions.

25. At the 1860 Democratic convention in Charleston, South Carolina:
    A. northern delegates walked out when a proslavery plank was passed.
    * B. southern delegates walked out when a proslavery plank was defeated.
    C. delegates nominated Lewis Cass for the presidency.
    D. delegates nominated James Buchanan for reelection to the presidency.

26. In the presidential election of 1860:
    * A. Abraham Lincoln was the Republican candidate.
    B. Abraham Lincoln received more southern votes than either of the two Democratic candidates.
    C. John C. Breckinridge was the only candidate with solid support in both North and South.
    D. Stephen Douglas ran on a platform that said slavery was "an evil, not to be extended."

27. The candidate of the Constitutional Union party in the election of 1860 was:
    * A. John Bell.
    B. Stephen A. Douglas.
    C. William H. Seward.
    D. Alexander H. Stephens.

28. The first of the southern states to secede from the Union was:
    A. Alabama.
    B. Georgia.
    C. Mississippi.
    * D. South Carolina.

29. Faced with the secession of the southern states, President Buchanan:
   A. declared the southern states "in rebellion, and therefore in a state of war, against the United States."
   B. announced that he would regain control of federal property seized by the Confederacy.
   * C. argued that secession was illegal, but that he lacked the constitutional authority to coerce a state.
   D. offered his resignation in a last-ditch effort to preserve the Union.

30. The Crittenden Compromise proposed to:
   A. outlaw slavery in the United States after 1865.
   * B. guarantee continuance of slavery in the states where it then existed.
   C. guarantee that all new territories would be open to slavery.
   D. give slaves full representation rather than allow them to count for only three-fifths of a person.

Essay Questions

1. Explain the issues that led to the Compromise of 1850 and show how the Compromise was fashioned and passed.

2. "The Mexican War may accurately be blamed for causing the Civil War because it opened new wounds between the North and South as it spurred controversy over slavery in the territories acquired from Mexico." Do you agree or disagree? Explain.

3. What various solutions were proposed to deal with the problem of slavery in the territories?

4. At what point (if any) did the Civil War become inevitable? If you could change historical events, what would you do at that point to avoid war?

5. What caused the Civil War? (Your answer should *not* be simply a detailed chronology of events.)

Matching Questions

A) led American expedition to Japan
B) led Pottawatomie Massacre
C) elected president of the Confederate States of America
D) died in July 1850
E) caned Charles Sumner
F) author of Freeport Doctrine
G) argued that a congressional ban on slavery in the territories would violate the Fifth Amendment
H) Chief Justice for Dred Scott case
I) 1848 Free Soil presidential candidate
J) president before Franklin Pierce

E   1. Preston Brooks
B   2. John Brown
G   3. John C. Calhoun
C   4. Jefferson Davis
F   5. Stephen A. Douglas
J   6. Millard Fillmore
A   7. Matthew Perry
H   8. Roger B. Taney
D   7. Zachary Taylor
I   10. Martin Van Buren

Chapter 17

THE WAR OF THE UNION

This chapter traces the course of the Civil War from Fort Sumter to Appomattox. It covers problems of raising armies, diplomacy, emancipation, financing the war, and political maneuvering in wartime.

Chapter Outline

I. The end of the interim period
   A. Lincoln's hints
   B. The inauguration
   C. Presidential appointments
   D. The conflict begins
      1. Resupply of Fort Sumter
      2. The South's response
      3. Opening guns of the war
      4. Anderson's surrender
   E. Lincoln's initial steps of war
      1. Call for 75,000 militiamen
      2. Blockade of southern ports
   F. Secession of the upper South
      1. Departure of Virginia, Arkansas, Tennessee, and North Carolina
      2. Creation of West Virginia
   G. Other slave states remain in the Union
      1. Suspension of *habeas corpus* to hold Maryland
      2. Divided Kentucky
      3. The battle for Missouri

II. The personal agonies of war
   A. Lee's decision to join the Confederacy
   B. Pro-Union sentiment in the South

III. Balance of force
   A. The North's advantages
      1. Population
      2. Industry

        3. Farm production
        4. Transportation
    B. The South's advantage: strong military leaders
    C. Sea power, an important advantage for the North

IV. The first battle
    A. Winfield Scott's strategy for the North
    B. First Battle of Bull Run
        1. Basis for confrontation
        2. Military retreat
        3. Impact of battle
    C. The war's early phase
        1. Northern and southern strategies
        2. Naval actions
            a. Ironclad ships
            b. Union seizures along the southern coasts

V. Effort to build armies
    A. Lincoln's early calls for volunteers
    B. Confederate army recruitment
        1. Adoption of conscription
        2. Loopholes in Confederate conscription
    C. Union conscription
        1. Bounties offered
        2. Conscription and its exemptions
    D. Impact of conscription
        1. A spur to volunteers
        2. Exercise of central power in the South
        3. New York draft riots

VI. The war in 1862
    A. The West in the Civil War
        1. The Kansas-Nebraska border
        2. Western Indians
    B. Actions in the West
        1. Grant's move against Forts Donelson and Henry
        2. Battle of Shiloh
    C. McClellan's peninsular campaign
        1. McClellan's character
        2. His advance on Richmond
        3. Jackson's Shenandoah campaign
        4. Lee's attack on McClellan
        5. Appointment of Halleck as general-in-chief
    D. Second Battle of Bull Run

      E. Lee's invasion at Antietam
         1. McClellan's mistakes
         2. Lincoln's appointment of Ambrose Burnside
      F. Battle of Fredericksburg
      G. Assessment of the war at the end of 1862

VII. Emancipation
      A. The move for emancipation
         1. Lincoln's considerations
         2. Military actions of emancipation
         3. Lincoln's proposal for compensated emancipation
         4. Congressional actions against slavery
         5. Arguments for emancipation
         6. The preliminary Emancipation Proclamation
         7. Emancipation
         8. Effects of emancipation
      B. Blacks in the military
         1. Authorization for their use
         2. Blacks in military service
            a. The Massachusetts 54th Regiment
            b. Other black units
      C. The abolition of slavery

VIII. Women and the war
      A. Traditional restraints on women loosened
         1. Nurses
         2. Thrust into public roles
      B. War took toll on women's marital relationships

IX. The revolutionary impact of the war
      A. Power shift to the North
      B. Measures passed by the North

X. Financing the war
      A. Methods used in the North
         1. Increased tariff and excise taxes
         2. Income tax
         3. Issuance of greenbacks
         4. Bonds
      B. Confederate finances
         1. Import and export duties
         2. Direct tax on property
         3. Taxes on other items after 1863
         4. Bond issues
         5. Paper money

XI. Confederate diplomacy
    A. Importance of diplomacy to the Confederacy
    B. Early hopes of recognition
    C. The Mason and Slidell episode
    D. Confederate raiding ships

XII. Union politics
    A. Pressure of the Radicals
    B. Actions of the Democrats
    C. Lincoln's suspension of habeas corpus
        1. Constitutional issues
        2. Arrests
        3. Vallandigham case
    D. Democratic campaign of 1864
    E. Election results

XIII. Confederate politics
    A. Status of politics in the Confederate system
    B. Problems of states' rights in the Confederacy

XIV. Wearing down the Confederacy
    A. Appointment of Joseph E. Hooker to lead the North
    B. Battle of Chancellorsville (a Confederate victory)
    C. Grant's successful assault on Vicksburg
    D. Lee's unsuccessful invasion at Gettysburg
    E. Union victory at Chattanooga

XV. Defeat of the Confederacy
    A. Grant and Sherman to pursue the war
    B. The wilderness campaign
        1. Grant's strategy
        2. Siege of Petersburg
    C. Sherman's march through the South
        1. Sherman's pursuit of Johnston
        2. Davis replaced Johnston with John B. Hood
        3. Armies move in opposite directions
        4. Sherman's destruction of Georgia
        5. Sherman moves into South Carolina
    D. Lee's effort to escape the Petersburg siege
    E. Surrender at Appomattox (9 April 1865, Palm Sunday)
    F. Other Confederate forces surrender
    G. The occupation of Charleston
    H. The Civil War as the first modern war

Lecture Ideas

1. For an interesting lecture on women in the Civil War, see George C. Rable's *Civil Wars: Women and the Crisis of Southern Nationalism* (1989), Mary Elizabeth Massey's *Bonnet Brigades* (1966), and Drew G. Faust's *Mothers of Invention: Women of the Slaveholding South and the Civil War* (1996).

2. Lincoln's ideas on race and his eventual decision to emancipate the slaves would make a good lecture. Stephen B. Oates's *Our Fiery Trial* (1978) would be a good source. For additional materials, see two collections of documents: *Lincoln on Black and White*, edited by Arthur Zilversmit (1971), and *Lincoln's Decision for Emancipation*, edited by Hans L. Trefousse (1975).

3. For a lecture on black participation in the Civil War, a good source would be James M. McPherson's *The Negro's Civil War* (1965) and the appropriate chapter in McPherson's more recent *Battle Cry of Freedom* (1988), and Dudley Cornish's *The Sable Arm: Black Troops in the Union Army, 1861–1865* (1956).

4. Divide the class into groups and have them look into the Civil War regionally. Then have them present the war from the North, South, and West's perspective. See Phillip S. Paludan's *A People's Contest: The Union at War, 1861–1865* (1988), Emory Thomas's *The Confederate Nation 1861–1865* (1979), and Alvin Josephy's *The Civil War in the West* (1992).

5. A good overview of the military strategies of the North and the South is a must. See Herman Hattaway's *How the North Won: A Military History of the Civil War* (19783), Charles Royster's *The Destructive War: William Tecumseh Sherman, Stonewall Jackson, and the Americans* (1991), and Archer Jones's *Civil War Command and Strategy: The Process of Victory and Defeat* (1992).

6. A general lecture on Lincoln and the war could be very valuable in tying the whole topic of the Civil War together. See James M. McPhersen's *Abraham Lincoln and the Second American Revolution* (1990), Phillip S. Paludan's *The Presidency of Abraham Lincoln* (1994), and David Donald's *Lincoln* (1995).

True/False Questions

T   1. In his first inaugural address, President Lincoln said: "I am loath to close. We are not enemies, but friends. We must not be enemies. Though passion may have strained, it must not break our bonds of affection."

T   2. Four states joined the Confederacy after President Lincoln called on the loyal states to supply an army to put down the southern rebellion.

F   3. The mountainous region of Tennessee was among the most pro-Confederate areas in the South.

F   4. Federal troops were never able to capture Charleston, South Carolina, during the war.

T   5. Opposition to the draft provoked a week-long riot in New York City.

T   6. The Battle of Antietam marked the bloodiest single day of the Civil War.

T   7. For many American women, the Civil War was a liberating experience that marked a significant change in their status.

F   8. With the absence of southern congressman during the war, Republicans passed an act granting citizenship to African Americans.

T   9. "Copperheads" were members of the extreme fringe of the Peace Wing of the Democratic party.

T   10. Bull Run (Manassas) is in Virginia.

Multiple-Choice Questions

1. In his inaugural address, Abraham Lincoln emphasized:
    A. the moral wrongness of slavery.
  * B. the "perpetual" nature of the Union.
    C. the loyalty of Southerners as demonstrated in the War of 1812.
    D. economic development.

2. The Civil War began when:
   A. Union forces at Fort Sumter fired on nearby Confederate positions.
   B. Confederate forces at Fort Sumter fired on nearby Union positions.
   C. Union forces fired on Confederate troops stationed in Fort Sumter.
   * D. Confederate forces fired on Union troops stationed in Fort Sumter.

3. To keep Maryland in the Union, Lincoln:
   A. canceled state elections.
   * B. suspended the writ of habeas corpus.
   C. threatened to blockade the state.
   D. did all the above.

4. All the following slave states remained in the Union *except*:
   A. Delaware.
   B. Kentucky.
   C. Missouri.
   * D. Virginia.

5. At the beginning of the Civil War, the North:
   A. generated less farm production than the South.
   B. had about the same extent of railroad development as the South.
   C. produced almost 60 percent of the nation's manufactures.
   * D. had an edge of about four to one in potential manpower.

6. In the Civil War:
   A. over 600,000 Americans were killed or died of disease.
   B. 50,000 men lost an arm or a leg.
   C. one of every twelve adult white males served in the Confederate or Union army.
   * D. All the above statements are true.

7. The first real battle of the war:
   * A. was fought near Washington, D.C.
   B. was the Battle of Harper's Ferry.
   C. was a victory for the Union forces.
   D. resulted in the death of Gen. Albert S. Johnston.

8. Robert Anderson:
   * A. surrendered at Fort Sumter.
   B. was Lincoln's secretary of the treasury.

    C. was a Union soldier executed for spying on the United
       States.

    D. organized the first Union regiment to include both black
       and white soldiers.

9. Which of the following statements about conscription during the
   Civil War is *not* true?

    A. Only six percent of the Union army was drafted.

    B. In the South, plantation owners with 20 or more slaves
       were exempted from the draft.

  * C. The Union was the first side to use the draft.

    D. Those drafted could find a substitute or pay a fee rather
       than join the army.

10. Which one of the following was a Confederate general?

    A. Ambrose E. Burnside

    B. Joseph E. Hooker

  * C. Joseph E. Johnston

    D. George G. Meade

11. Naval actions:

  * A. were probably more important than land battles in late
       1861 and early 1862.

    B. included a fight between two ironclads, the Confederate
       Monitor and the Union *Merrimack.*

    C. included a fight between two ironclads, the Confederate
       Merrimack and the Union *Virginia.*

    D. were not important in the war until 1863.

12. Forts Donelson and Henry:

    A. were sites of two of the most important battles in the
       eastern theater before 1864.

    B. were important Union fortifications on the Great Lakes.

    C. fell to Robert E. Lee in 1863.

  * D. fell to Ulysses S. Grant in 1862.

13. The Battle of Shiloh:

  * A. was a story of missed opportunities.

    B. appeared at first to be a Union victory until southern
       reinforcements arrived.

    C. led to the appointment of Robert E. Lee as Gen. Joseph E.
       Hooker's replacement.

    D. allowed the Confederates to regain control of the
       Tennessee River.

14. The Anaconda strategy:
    A. was General P. G. T. Beauregard's strategy for southern victory.
    B. was General U. S. Grant's strategy for northern victory.
    C. assumed a quick end to the war.
    * D. included, among other things, a blockade of the southern coast.

15. Who commanded the Confederate troops at Antietam?
    A. Stonewall Jackson
    B. Albert S. Johnston
    * C. Robert E. Lee
    D. J. E. B. Stuart

16. Which of the following statements best describes the Civil War at the end of 1862?
    A. Union troops had a definite edge in the East.
    B. Confederate troops had a definite edge in the West.
    C. After the decisive victories at Fredericksburg and Antietam, Union officers anticipated a quick end to the war.
    * D. The war in the East was a virtual deadlock.

17. Lincoln justified his Emancipation Proclamation on the basis of:
    * A. military necessity.
    B. religion.
    C. racial superiority.
    D. John Locke's contract theory of government.

18. The Emancipation Proclamation:
    A. technically freed slaves only in the states that had remained loyal to the Union.
    B. offered slave owners financial compensation for the loss of their slaves.
    C. was based on the congressional power to confiscate the property of traitors.
    * D. ended any chance that Britain or France would support the Confederacy.

19. Which one of the following battles was a Union victory?
    A. Chancellorsville
    B. Fredericksburg
    * C. Gettysburg
    D. Second Manassas

20. The number of blacks in the Union army:
    A. was small, because a federal law prohibited free Negroes from carrying firearms.
    B. was reduced after Lincoln's Emancipation Proclamation.
    * C. was roughly 200,000, about 10 percent of the Union army's total manpower.
    D. fell after 1862.

21. Which of the following was *not* a significant source of money to finance the Union war effort?
    * A. the sale of public lands
    B. the sale of bonds
    C. increased tariffs and taxes
    D. new issues of paper money

22. Confederate finances:
    A. were in better shape than the Union's at the beginning of the war.
    B. were hurt during the war by a marked deflation of Confederate currency.
    C. depended mostly on various income and property taxes.
    * D. depended mostly on new issues of paper money.

23. Most of the Confederacy's diplomatic efforts were aimed at:
    * A. England.
    B. Egypt and India.
    C. South America.
    D. Spain.

24. Robert Smalls:
    A. warned Lincoln not to issue the Emancipation Proclamation until after a Union victory.
    B. was a Union general who freed slaves in upper South Carolina, Georgia, and Florida without proper authority.
    C. was a New York congressman who helped Lincoln write the Emancipation Proclamation.
    * D. was a slave who escaped with his family on a Confederate gunboat.

25. In the election of 1864:
    A. Andrew Johnson was the presidential candidate of the National Union party.
    * B. Democrats called for an immediate end to the war.
    C. Republicans called for an armistice.
    D. Radical Republicans supported Abraham Lincoln.

26. Alexander Stephens:
    - A. was the Confederacy's secretary of the treasury.
    - * B. was the vice-president of the Confederacy.
    - C. was the highest-ranking U.S. military official to resign his commission and join the Confederacy.
    - D. led the Confederate defense of New Orleans.

27. In the Confederate election year of 1863:
    - A. President Jefferson Davis was almost unanimously reelected.
    - B. President Jefferson Davis was reelected by a small margin.
    - * C. many men who opposed Jefferson Davis and secession were elected to the Confederate congress.
    - D. Robert E. Lee decided at the last minute not to run against Jefferson Davis.

28. Pickett's Charge, one of the greatest of the Confederacy's military failures, occurred in the Battle of:
    - * A. Gettysburg.
    - B. Chattanooga.
    - C. Chancellorsville.
    - D. Cold Harbor.

29. Sherman's march through Georgia and the Carolinas:
    - A. was hampered by the dogged persistence of Gen. Robert E. Lee.
    - B. was planned to divert attention from General McClellan's movements to the north.
    - C. proved to be the Union's biggest strategic error.
    - * D. resulted in the destruction of many southern towns and cities.

30. At Appomattox:
    - A. Jefferson Davis surrendered.
    - B. all the remaining Confederate forces surrendered.
    - C. Robert E. Lee was captured after one of the bloodiest battles of the war.
    - * D. General Grant allowed southern soldiers to keep their own horses and sidearms.

Essay Questions

1. What was the military strategy of each side at the start of the Civil War, and how and why did it change as the war continued?

2. List and describe briefly the reasons why the North won the Civil War. What were the North's strengths and advantages?

3. Account for the issuance of the Emancipation Proclamation, showing how it was both shrewd military and diplomatic strategy and an effort for humanitarian reform.

4. Describe domestic politics during the war, both North and South. What problems did Abraham Lincoln and Jefferson Davis face? How did they deal with these problems?

5. Why did the South lose the war? What were its weaknesses and disadvantages?

Matching Questions

A) Lincoln's second vice-president
B) killed at Chancellorsville by his own men
C) promoted sale of war bonds for Union
D) famous Copperhead
E) determined to "make Georgia howl" in 1864–1865
F) commanded black Massachusetts regiment
G) 1864 Democratic presidential candidate
H) vice-president of the Confederacy
I) led Union naval victories at New Orleans and Mobile
J) surrendered near Durham, North Carolina, on April 18, 1865

C	1.	Jay Cooke
I	2.	David Farragut
B	3.	Thomas Jackson
A	4.	Andrew Johnson
J	5.	Joseph E. Johnston
G	6.	George B. McClellan
F	7.	Robert Gould Shaw
E	8.	William T. Sherman
H	9.	Alexander Stephens
D	10.	Clement Vallandigham

Chapter 18

RECONSTRUCTION: NORTH AND SOUTH

This chapter covers the effects of the Civil War; Reconstruction under Lincoln, Johnson, and Congress; the impeachment of Johnson; the South during Reconstruction; Grant's administration; and the disputed election of 1876.

Chapter Outline

I. America after the Civil War
  A. Effects of the war on the nation as a whole
  B. Legislation to benefit northeastern businessmen and western farmers
    1. Morrill Tariff
    2. National Banking Act
    3. Subsidies for north-central transcontinental railroad
    4. Homestead Act of 1862
    5. Morrill Land Grant Act of 1862
  C. Devastation of the South during the war hampered later growth
    1. Much private and public property destroyed
    2. Confederate currency and bonds worthless
    3. $4 billion invested in labor—the slaves—wiped out
    4. Problems of postwar agriculture
  D. A transformed South
  E. Special problems of the freedmen
    1. Though free, the former slaves had little with which to make a living
    2. The Freedmen's Bureau
    3. Other relief agencies

II. Lincoln and Reconstruction
  A. Lincoln's lenient 10 percent plan
  B. Loyal governments appeared in Tennessee, Arkansas, and Louisiana, but were not recognized by Congress
  C. Arguments by Lincoln and Congress for authority over Reconstruction
  D. The stricter Wade-Davis bill

     E. Lincoln's philosophy of Reconstruction
     F. Lincoln's assassination

III. Johnson's plan for Reconstruction
     A. Johnson's philosophy of Reconstruction
     B. Johnson's plan
        1. Exclusion from pardon of those owning property worth over $20,000
        2. States must invalidate secession ordinances, abolish slavery, and repudiate Confederate debt
     C. Most southern states met all of Johnson's requirements

IV. Congress, in December 1865, refused to seat senators and congressmen from the southern states
     A. Southern states had elected to Congress many ex-Confederate leaders
     B. Southern states had passed repressive Black Codes

V. The critical year of 1866: Radical Republicans gain power
     A. Faced with southern intransigence, moderate Republicans drifted toward the Radicals
     B. The Radicals: who they were and how they planned to reconstruct the South
        1. Conquered provinces
        2. State suicide
        3. Forfeited rights
     C. Johnson began to lose battle with Congress
        1. Johnson's veto of bill to extend life of Freedmen's Bureau upheld by Senate
        2. Johnson's veto of Civil Rights Acts of 1866 overridden
        3. Johnson's veto of revised Freedmen's Bureau bill overridden
        4. Congress passed Fourteenth Amendment
           a. Supported Civil Rights Act of 1866
           b. The Amendment reaffirmed state and federal citizenship and contained important clauses: "privileges and immunities," "due process of law," and "equal protection of the laws"
     D. Johnson lost support of the American public
        1. Unsuccessful speaking tour of Midwest
        2. In election of 1866, Republicans won over two-thirds majority in each house

VI. Congressional Reconstruction
  A. Congress moved to protect its program from President Johnson
    1. Command of the Army Act
    2. Tenure of Office Act
  B. Military Reconstruction Act
  C. Second and Third Reconstruction Acts
  D. Congress protected its program from Supreme Court
  E. New governments established in southern states

VII. Impeachment and trial of Johnson
  A. Johnson removed Secretary of War Edwin Stanton in violation of Tenure of Office Act
  B. House of Representatives passed eleven articles of impeachment
  C. In Senate trial, vote to convict was one short
  D. Effects of impeachment on Radicals and Johnson

VIII. Republican rule in the South
  A. New governments established in southern states
  B. The work of the Union League
  C. Blacks in the Reconstructed South
    1. Feelings of nationalism
    2. Separate churches
    3. Black families
    4. Black schools
  D. Blacks in politics
    1. Introduced suddenly to politics, many rose to high positions
    2. Black influence in Reconstruction governments has been greatly exaggerated
  E. White Republicans in the South
    1. Carpetbaggers—northern Republicans who allegedly came south for political and economic gain
    2. Scalawags—southern white Republicans
  F. The Republican record
    1. Achievements of Republican governments
    2. Corruption of Republican governments

IX. White southerners reacted to Republican regimes by forming terrorist groups
  A. Formation of Ku Klux Klan
  B. Activities of Klan and similar anti-black, anti-Republican groups
  C. Prosecution under new federal laws ended most of these activities

X. Southern conservatives regained power
  A. Klan weakened black and Republican morale
  B. North was also concerned with westward expansion, Indians wars, and the economic and political questions of the tariff and currency
  C. Republican control of southern states began to collapse in 1869
  D. By 1876, Radical regimes survived only in Louisiana, Florida, and South Carolina

XI. Grant administration
  A. Positions of Democratic and Republican parties and the election of 1868
  B. Grant, an inept political leader, made many unwise appointments
  C. The problem of the government's debt
    1. Support for monetary expansion
    2. Support for monetary restriction
    3. Treasury began withdrawing greenbacks from circulation
  D. Scandals in Grant's administration
    1. Jay Gould and Jim Fisk tried to corner the gold market
    2. The Crédit Mobilier scandal
    3. Other scandals disclosed
  E. Republican reformers and the election of 1872
  F. Economic distress and the beginning of the Panic of 1873
  G. The Resumption Act of 1875

XII. The election of 1876
  A. Campaigns marked by few real issues and much mudslinging
  B. Disputed vote count in three southern states
  C. Congress formed special Electoral Commission to resolve problem
  D. The Compromise of 1877
  E. Some promises kept and many broken after Hayes took office
  F. The legacy of Reconstruction

Lecture Ideas

1. After you give a general overview of Reconstruction, divide the class up into two groups and have them research the issues of Presidential Reconstruction vs. Congressional Reconstruction. See Eric Foner's *Reconstruction: America's Unfinished Revolution* (1988), Peyton McCrary's *Abraham Lincoln and Reconstruction* (1978), and Michael L. Benedict's

A Compromise of Principle: Congressional Republicans and Reconstruction (1974).

2. A lecture on congressional efforts to reshape southern society would allow the students to see what attempts were made in this area. See Michael Perman's *The Road to Redemption: Southern Politics, 1869–1879* (1984) and *Reunion Without Compromise: The South and Reconstruction, 1865–1868* (1973), and T. Carter's *When the War Was Over: The Failure of Self–Reconstruction in the South, 1865–1877* (1985).

3. For a lecture on the role of African Americans in the early postwar years, see Leon Litwack's *Trouble in Mind: Black Southerners in the Age of Jim Crow* (1988) and Jay Mandle's *Not Slave, Not Free: The African American Economic Experience Since the Civil War* (1992).

True/False Questions

T   1. The most popular religious denomination among blacks in the postwar South was Baptist.

F   2. The Fifteenth Amendment was ratified during the Civil War.

T   3. "Scalawags" was the derogatory name given to native white Republicans in the South.

T   4. President Johnson opposed the extension of the Freedmen's Bureau.

F   5. Radical Republicans generally neglected the needs of black education in the South.

T   6. "Waving the bloody shirt" meant referring to the Civil War and the southern rebellion in order to discredit political opponents.

T   7. After the House of Representatives impeached President Johnson, the Senate failed to convict him by just one vote.

F   8. The Crédit Mobilier scandal led to the expulsion of several congressmen accused of embezzling most of the profits of black-owned businesses that they helped establish.

F   9. Democrats generally favored "sound" or "hard" monetary policies.

T   10. In the Compromise of 1877, Republicans promised to
            withdraw federal troops from Louisiana and South Carolina.

Multiple-Choice Questions

1. Slavery was abolished throughout the Union:
   * A. by the Thirteenth Amendment.
     B. by the Fourteenth Amendment.
     C. in 1863.
     D. in 1874.

2. At the end of the Civil War, the newly freed slaves were given:
     A. small plots of land confiscated from southern planters.
     B. forty acres and a mule.
   * C. medical and legal assistance from the Bureau of Refugees,
        Freedmen, and Abandoned Lands.
     D. five dollars for every year they had served in bondage.

3. During the Civil War, Congress passed:
     A. a number of laws designed to ease the transition of the
        southern states from the Confederacy back into the Union.
     B. the Morrill Tariff, which halved the average level of
        import duties.
   * C. the Homestead Act of 1862, which gave 160 acres to
        settlers who lived on the land for five years.
     D. the Pullen Agriculture Act, which set standards governing
        tenancy on small farms.

4. Under Lincoln's plan for Reconstruction:
     A. loyal governments appeared in five states, but Congress
        refused to recognize them.
     B. loyal governments were recognized by Congress in three
        southern states.
     C. 10 percent of elected officials in a state had to be black.
   * D. 10 percent of the 1860 voters had to take an oath of
        allegiance to the Union.

5. The Wade-Davis Bill:
     A. would have admitted representatives from Tennessee,
        Arkansas, and Louisiana to Congress in 1864.
   * B. was more stringent than Lincoln's plan for readmitting the
        southern states.
     C. would have granted congressional authority to Lincoln's
        Emancipation Proclamation.
     D. included the controversial "10 percent plan."

6. Abraham Lincoln was assassinated:
   A. just three months after the Civil War was over.
   B. by a crazed actor who thought Lincoln would be too lenient toward the South.
   * C. by John Wilkes Booth.
   D. All the above are true.

7. Andrew Johnson's based his plan for Reconstruction on:
   A. his strong belief in Negro suffrage.
   B. his "forfeited rights" theory.
   * C. a strict adherence to the Constitution; hence, since the Union was indestructible, the former Confederate states had never left it, and Reconstruction was therefore unnecessary.
   D. a strict adherence to the Constitution; hence, since the former Confederate states had left the Union, Congress could insist on great changes in those states before letting them reenter the Union.

8. Henry Wirz was executed after the Civil War because he had:
   A. helped John Wilkes Booth plan Lincoln's assassination.
   B. helped John Wilkes Booth escape from Ford's Theater.
   C. led a company of soldiers on a raid of Washington, D.C., in which several women and children were killed.
   * D. commanded the Confederate prison at Andersonville, Georgia, where many Union prisoners had died.

9. The states that had seceded were simply "out of their proper practical relation with the Union," and the nation's goal following the war was to return them to "their proper practical relation." This statement was made by:
   A. Andrew Johnson.
   * B. Abraham Lincoln.
   C. Thaddeus Stevens.
   D. Benjamin Wade.

10. Andrew Johnson's plan for Reconstruction:
    A. was closer to the Wade-Davis Bill than to Lincoln's plan.
    B. excluded from pardon all Southerners who did not own land.
    * C. required the southern states to ratify the Thirteenth Amendment.
    D. required Negro suffrage in the South.

11. "Black Codes" were designed by:
    A. Johnson and his cabinet to ensure the political rights of blacks.
    * B. southern legislatures to set blacks aside as a caste separate from whites and subject to special restraints.

    C. Republicans in Congress to ensure the economic rights of blacks.

    D. the Ku Klux Klan and similar groups as a plan of intimidation of the recently freed slaves.

12. Southern intransigence included all the following *except* the:

    A. election of many ex-Confederate leaders to Congress.

    * B. refusal of every southern states to ratify the Thirteenth Amendment.

    C. passage of laws that restricted the rights of blacks.

    D. requirement that blacks enter into strict annual labor contracts.

13. Radical Republicans:

    A. included Alexander H. Stephens and James G. Blaine.

    B. were, for the most part, motivated by hopes of personal economic gain.

    C. would have supported Lincoln's plan for Reconstruction had Lincoln lived.

    * D. gained strength in 1866.

14. The Civil Rights Act of 1866:

    A. had the support of President Johnson, who had urged Congress to pass such a measure.

    B. gave to adult black males the right to vote in local and state—but not national—elections.

    * C. was passed over Johnson's veto.

    D. was unconstitutional, according to most Radical Republicans.

15. The Fourteenth Amendment:

    A. guaranteed the right of former slaves to vote.

    B. forbade states to subject any person to "cruel and unusual punishment."

    * C. forbade states to deprive any person of life, liberty, or property without "due process of law."

    D. was vetoed by President Johnson.

16. In 1866:

    A. President Johnson was reelected by an extremely small margin.

    B. President Johnson was reelected president by a large margin.

    * C. Republicans won a majority of seats in each house of Congress, thus assuring that the congressional plan of Reconstruction would pass over Johnson's vetoes.

    D. Democrats still held a slight majority in Congress, but many Democrats were hesitant to support Johnson further.

17. Which of the following best describes the role of blacks in southern politics during Reconstruction?
    * A. About 600 blacks served in the state legislatures.
    B. Two black governors were elected.
    C. In most areas, black voters overwhelmed white voters for several years.
    D. Just two blacks were elected to Congress.

18. The House of Representatives found grounds to begin impeachment proceedings against President Johnson when he:
    A. kept vetoing the legislation of congressional Reconstruction.
    B. refused to appoint military commanders to head the five districts set up by Congress in the Military Reconstruction Act.
    * C. violated the Tenure of Office Act.
    D. pardoned thousands of former Confederates.

19. Among the accomplishments of Radical Reconstruction were all the following *except*:
    A. setting up the beginnings of state school systems.
    * B. relieving the freedmen from continued economic dependence on whites.
    C. rewriting state constitutions, introducing universal male suffrage, and instituting a more equitable apportionment of the legislatures.
    D. repairing some of the physical damage of the Civil War.

20. The Military Reconstruction Act:
    A. said that "no legal state government or adequate protection for life and property now exists in the rebel States."
    B. required southern states to accept black suffrage.
    C. required southern states to ratify the Fourteenth Amendment.
    * D. is correctly represented by all the above statements.

21. The Union League:
    A. was prosecuted under the Civil Rights Act of 1866 and forced to disband.
    B. established informal white militias to keep blacks from voting.
    C. was responsible for more violence than the Ku Klux Klan against blacks in Mississippi.
    * D. was a Republican group that, among other things, helped prepare former slaves to exercise their new right to vote.

22. Andrew Johnson was from the state of:
    A. Florida.

      B. Massachusetts.

      C. New York.

*   D. Tennessee.

23. Ulysses S. Grant:
    - A. was elected president in 1868 despite the heavy black Democratic vote.
    - B. brought confidence and honesty to a national government torn by Reconstruction.
    - * C. brought little political experience and judgment to the presidency.
    - D. pushed for civil service reform throughout his presidency.

24. Radical Reconstruction in the South:
    - A. ended in some Deep South states as early as 1867, and in all states by 1871.
    - B. ended in two states as early as 1869, but continued in some Deep South states until 1890.
    - * C. was over by 1877.
    - D. was ended by presidential proclamation in 1872.

25. The Joint Committee on Reconstruction:
    - A. was established in 1869.
    - B. was set up by President Johnson to offset growing congressional opposition to his policies.
    - C. was chaired by soon-to-be-president Ulysses S. Grant.
    - * D. recommended a new constitutional amendment—the Fourteenth—in part to remove all doubts about the constitutionality of the Civil Rights Act of 1866.

26. The so-called Mulligan letters:
    - A. revealed the extent of corruption of the "Whiskey Ring" in St. Louis.
    - * B. linked Republican James G. Blaine to shady railroad deals.
    - C. cost Horace Greeley the 1872 Republican presidential nomination.
    - D. revealed cases of vote fraud in three states in the election of 1876.

27. In the election of 1876:
    - A. Democrats and Republicans both favored stricter federal control of the South.
    - B. there were major contested vote counts in three western states.
    - * C. Rutherford B. Hayes was the Republican candidate.
    - D. James G. Blaine was the Republican candidate.

28. The Resumption Act, passed by Congress in 1875:
    A. finally reversed the postwar inflation that had stifled economic growth for almost a decade.
    B. called for the resumption of the policy of withdrawing greenbacks from circulation.
    * C. allowed for the redemption of greenbacks in gold.
    D. had the support of the National Greenback party.

29. The plan by Jay Gould and Jim Fisk to corner the gold market:
    A. led to the censure of several southern congressmen.
    B. led to the impeachment of Grant's secretary of war.
    * C. ended on "Black Friday" when President Grant ordered the selling of a large quantity of gold.
    D. led to the Panic of 1873.

30. The Electoral Commission, set up by Congress in January 1877:
    A. was designed to assure "a free ballot and a fair count" in future presidential elections.
    * B. consisted of fifteen members, five each from the House, the Senate, and the Supreme Court.
    C. found some instances of fraud in the 1876 election but decided that the election should stand.
    D. gave the electoral votes of Florida, Louisiana, and South Carolina to the Democrats.

Essay Questions

1. What were the major problems facing the nation in April 1865? What factors stood in the way of a solution to those problems?

2. Describe the plans for Reconstruction offered by Abraham Lincoln, Andrew Johnson, and Congress. What was the goal of each plan? How did each plan propose to accomplish its goal?

3. What problems did blacks in the South face after Emancipation? What attempts did the government make to solve these problems?

4. What were the major economic issues between 1868 and 1876?

5. How was the contested election of 1876 decided? Describe the political, racial, and sectional effects of the decision.

Matching Questions

A) elected lieutenant governor of Louisiana
B) senator from Massachusetts, a leading Radical Republican
C) Grant's secretary of state
D) secretary of war under Johnson until 1867
E) senator from Mississippi
F) Pennsylvania congressman, directed prosecution of President Johnson in Senate
G) Democratic presidential candidate in 1876
H) opposed Grant in 1872 presidential election
I) Georgian elected to U.S. Senate in 1865
J) said treason "must be made infamous and traitors must be impoverished"

C   1. Hamilton Fish
H   2. Horace Greeley
J   3. Andrew Johnson
A   4. Pinckney B. S. Pinchback
E   5. Hiram Revels
D   6. Edwin M. Stanton
I   7. Alexander H. Stephens
F   8. Thaddeus Stevens
B   9. Charles Sumner
G   10. Samuel J. Tilden

Chapter 19

NEW FRONTIERS: SOUTH AND WEST

This chapter covers economic and agricultural developments in the New South, the Bourbons, southern race relations, American Indian policy and the western frontiers of the miners, the cowboys, and the farmers.

Chapter Outline

   I. Prophets and goals of the New South
      A. Henry Grady and his New South speech
      B. The New South Creed

  II. Economic growth in the New South
      A. Textile mills
      B. Tobacco
         1. John Ruffin Green and Bull Durham
         2. The Dukes and the American Tobacco Company
      C. Other natural resources
         1. Coal and iron ore
         2. Lumber
      D. Miscellaneous products
      E. Two great forces at the turn of the century
         1. Petroleum
         2. Hydroelectric power

 III. Agriculture in the New South
      A. Seaman A. Knapp and the demonstration method of agricultural education
      B. Problems in southern agriculture
         1. Land ownership
            a. Sharecropping
            b. Tenant farming
         2. Credit—the crop-lien system

  IV. The political leaders of the New South
      A. Definition and evaluation of the term "Bourbon"

B. Bourbon ideology
    1. Allied politically with eastern conservatives
    2. Allied economically with eastern capitalists
C. Effects of Bourbon retrenchment
    1. Education
       a. Greatly reduced spending on education
    2. Convict leasing
    3. Repudiation of state debts
D. Achievements of the Bourbons
E. Opposition to the Bourbons

V. Blacks and the New South
A. Education
B. Flexibility in Bourbon race relations
    1. Negro voting
    2. Little strict segregation
C. Black disenfranchisement
    1. Purpose—to allow whites to divide politically
    2. The Mississippi plan
       a. Residence requirement
       b. Disqualification for conviction of certain crimes
       c. Poll tax and other taxes must be paid
       d. Literacy test (with understanding clause)
    3. Variations of the Mississippi plan (including the "grandfather clause")
    4. Effects of the Mississippi plan
D. Segregation in the South
    1. The Supreme Court
       a. The *Civil Rights Cases* (1883)
       b. *Plessy* v. *Ferguson* (1896)
    2. Southern states passed Jim Crow legislation
E. Lynchings of blacks
    1. Black response to racism and statutory segregation
       a. Accommodation
       b. Create independent culture and institutions
    2. Irony of segregation
       a. Economic opportunities
       b. Rise of black activism
F. Two black leaders
    1. Booker T. Washington and accommodation
    2. W. E. B. Du Bois and protest

VI. Reconciling Tradition with Innovation

VII. The settlement of the West
    A. The Great Plains slowed settlement
    B. Factors that increased settlement
    C. Immigrants in the West
    D. Exodusters
        1. Benjamin Singleton
        2. The exoduster experience
        3. Buffalo soldiers

VIII. The miner in the West
    A. The development of mining communities
    B. The great gold, silver, and copper strikes
    C. Western states admitted to the Union

IX. Indians in the West
    A. Indians, forced to cede lands to the government, war with the United States
        1. The Indian wars
        2. Chivington's massacre of 450 Indians at Sand Creek
    B. *Report on the Condition of the Indian Tribes*
        1. Decision to place Indians on reservations
        2. Agreements at Medicine Creek Lodge and Fort Laramie
    C. George Custer and the Battle of the Little Bighorn
    D. Continued Indian resistance
        1. Chief Joseph
        2. Wounded Knee
        3. The slaughter of the buffalo
    E. Reform of Indian policy
        1. Helen Hunt Jackson
        2. The Dawes Severalty Act
            a. Goal of the Dawes Act
            b. Effect of the Dawes Act

X. Cowboys in the West
    A. Early cattle raising in the West
    B. The great cattle drives
        1. Joseph McCoy and Abilene
        2. The role of railroad refrigeration
        3. The decline of the long drives
    C. The open-range cattle industry
    D. Range wars

XI. Farmers in the West
    A. The problem of land
       1. Homestead Act of 1862
       2. The Newlands Reclamation Act of 1901
    B. The problem of water
       1. Effects of the Newlands Act
       2. Other solutions
    C. Technological advances that aided farmers
    D. Western farms, large and small
    E. Pioneer women
    F. A violent culture

XII. The end of the frontier
    A. Frontier line no longer existed after 1890
    B. Frederick Jackson Turner and "The Significance of the Frontier in American History"

Lecture Ideas

1. Sharecropping is a subject that leads to a discussion on a variety of experiences for blacks after the Civil War. Give an overview of the sharecropping system and its economic, social, and political consequences. See Edward Royce *The Origins of Southern Sharecropping* (1993) and Roger L. Ransom and Richard Sutch's *One Kind of Freedom* (1977).

2. Give the class a research project on the Jim Crow laws. Ask them to define the term Jim Crow and describe life for the average black person under the Jim Crow system. See Leon Litwack's *Trouble in Mind: Black Southerners in the Age of Jim Crow* (1998) and C. Vann Woodward's classic *The Strange Career of Jim Crow* (1974).

3. Richard White's *"It's Your Misfortune and None of My Own"* (1991) is an interesting and fairly comprehensive history of the American West. For a lecture on the Indian wars, see Robert M. Utley's *The Indian Frontier of the American West, 1848–1890* (1984).

4. For a lecture on the role of women in the farmers' frontier, see Joanna L. Stratton's *Pioneer Women: Voices from the Kansas Frontier* (1981) and Julie Roy Jeffrey's *Women: The Trans-Mississippi West, 1840–1880* (1979).

5. A lecture detailing the myths of the Old American West will capture your students' imaginations. See Walter Nugent and Martin Ridge, eds., *The American West: The Readers* (1999) and Rodman W. Paul's *The Far West and the Great Plains in Transition* (1998).

True/False Questions

T   1. By 1900, lumbering in the South had surpassed textiles in value.

T   2. In the crop-lien system, farmers could grow little besides cotton or some other staple crop.

F   3. The term "Bourbon" celebrated the French origin of many New South leaders.

F   4. Louisiana's efforts to stop black voting reduced the number of black voters by almost 25 percent.

T   5. The number of cotton mills in the South more than doubled between 1880 and 1900.

F   6. The frontier Indian wars began in the early 1880s with skirmishes against the Cherokees.

T   7. The Indian wars effectively ended with the capture of Geronimo.

F   8. In the *Civil Rights Cases* (1883), the Supreme Court upheld the Civil Rights Act of 1875.

T   9. The great boom in the range-cattle trade did not last long because cattle drives were economically unsound.

F   10. Most western settlers purchased their land directly from the federal government through the Homestead Act (or its later revisions).

Multiple-Choice Questions

1. The major prophet of the New South Creed was:
   A. J. L. M. Curry.
   * B. Henry W. Grady.
   C. John Ruffin Green.
   D. Edmund Ruffin.

2. The New South Creed emphasized all the following *except*:
   A. industrialization.
   B. sectional peace.
   * C. women's rights.
   D. racial harmony.

3. The American Tobacco Company was:
   A. based in Dallas, Texas.
   B. second only to the Bull Durham Company in cigarette production at the turn of the century.
   * C. broken up by the Supreme Court in 1911.
   D. the first such government-owned company in the United States.

4. The "Pittsburgh of the South," so named because it was an iron center, was:
   * A. Birmingham, Alabama.
   B. Houston, Texas.
   C. Nashville, Tennessee.
   D. Rome, Georgia.

5. Seaman A. Knapp:
   * A. invented the demonstration method of agricultural education.
   B. was the progressive president of the University of Georgia.
   C. owned the Corsicana oil field in Texas (site of the famous Spindletop gusher).
   D. was the most famous of the "Buffalo Soldiers."

6. Sharecroppers and tenant farmers:
   * A. increased in number after the Civil War.
   B. were often so poor they had trouble making mortgage or tax payments on their land.
   C. were more common in the Upper South than in the Deep South.
   D. generally improved the land more than the owners would have done on their own.

7. Bourbons:
   A. were the leaders of the Republican party in the South after Reconstruction.
   B. opposed the growth of industry and business in the New South.
   * C. often favored convict leasing.
   D. generally honored state debts incurred during Reconstruction.

8. Who was the first president of the National Association of Colored Women?
   A. Ida B. Wells
   B. Ann Beston
   * C. Mary Church Terrell
   D. Mary Plunkett

9. The first great "cowtown" was:
   * A. Abilene, Kansas.
   B. St. Louis, Missouri.
   C. Dallas, Texas.
   D. Butte, Montana.

10. The Bourbons' policy toward race relations between Reconstruction and 1890:
    A. was strict; few blacks were allowed to vote and Jim Crow laws segregated almost all public places.
    * B. was flexible; many blacks voted, and most of the restrictive Jim Crow laws had not yet been passed.
    C. resulted in the almost-total disenfranchisement of blacks by 1880.
    D. was accurately reflected in the phrase "separate but equal."

11. By preventing blacks from voting and by enacting "Jim Crow" laws, the South:
    * A. embraced apartheid.
    B. helped mend the tension between the races.
    C. promoted economic harmony between whites and blacks.
    D. set in motion another Civil War.

12. The Mississippi plan of disenfranchisement included all the following *except* a:
    A. residency requirement.
    * B. provision disqualifying anyone who owned less than $300 in personal property.
    C. provision disqualifying those who had not paid their poll taxes.
    D. literacy requirement.

13. In the case of *Plessy* v. *Ferguson*, the Supreme Court:
    A. ruled that a federal Civil Rights Act could not extend to individual action.
    B. decided that segregation on railroad cars was illegal under the Fourteenth Amendment.
    * C. upheld a Louisiana segregation law.
    D. ruled that the Fourteenth Amendment's guarantee of "equal protection of the laws" applied to private businesses.

14. The lynching of blacks in the South:
    A. prompted the passage of a federal anti-lynching law in 1892.
    B. decreased just before the turn of the century, possibly because whites could control blacks through Jim Crow laws.
    * C. increased at about the same time that Jim Crow laws spread through the South.
    D. occurred at the same rate at the turn of the century as similar lynchings in the North.

15. Booker T. Washington:
    * A. was born of a slave mother and a white father.
    B. had a Ph.D. in history from Harvard and wrote several distinguished historical works.
    C. criticized W. E. B. Du Bois's "Atlanta Compromise" speech.
    D. is correctly represented by all the above statements.

16. Who said, "In all things that are purely social we can be as separate as the five fingers, yet one as the hand in all things essential to mutual progress"?
    A. George Washington Cable
    B. W. E. B. Du Bois
    C. Philip Sheridan
  * D. Booker T. Washington

17. Benjamin Singleton:
  * A. was an early promoter of black migration to the West.
    B. won a Congressional medal of Honor for his capture of Sitting Bull.
    C. invented the refrigerated railroad car.
    D. was elected "Readjuster" governor of Virginia in 1879.

18. "Exodusters" were:
    A. Chinese immigrants in California.
    B. Scandinavian immigrants in the West.
  * C. black Southerners who moved west.
    D. prostitutes who worked in the cowtowns.

19. The Comstock Lode was:
    A. just outside of Deadwood, South Dakota.
  * B. in Nevada.
    C. on land given to the Cherokee Indians in the 1830s.
    D. the site of the first uranium mine in the United States.

20. Six states were created from the western territories in the years 1889–1890. These states were *not* admitted before 1889 because:
  * A. Democrats in Congress were reluctant to create states out of territories that were heavily Republican.
    B. the lawlessness of many western towns discouraged Congress from admitting the territories as states.
    C. polygamy, as practiced by the Mormons in the West, was unacceptable to Congress.
    D. if large mining firms had been forced to pay state taxes, they would have had to close down.

21. Following the 1867 *Report on the Condition of the Indian Tribes,* Congress decided that the best way to end the Indian Wars was:
    A. to send in the army, under men such as George Custer, to break the morale of the Indians.
    B. systematically to kill most of the buffalo.

      C. to "Americanize" the Indians by offering them an education at the white man's schools.

*   D. to persuade the Indians to live on out-of-the-way reservations.

22. In the Battle of the Little Bighorn:

      A. General George Custer's troops were massacred by the Cherokee and Seminole Indians.

*   B. some 2500 Indians annihilated a detachment of 200 soldiers.

      C. Chief Red Cloud was captured and murdered.

      D. Sioux and Cheyenne Indians won a large chuck of the Montana Territory, which they kept for fourteen years.

23. Chief Joseph:

      A. was killed at the Battle of Wounded Knee.

*   B. was the peaceful and dignified leader of the Nez Percé Indians.

      C. signed the treaty allowing the federal government to "remove" the Indians to lands west of the Mississippi River.

      D. originated the Ghost Dance to bring on the day of the Indians' deliverance.

24. The Dawes Severalty Act:

      A. was designed to "Americanize" the Indians.

      B. gave individual Indians up to 160 acres of land that, for the Indians' protection, the government held in trust for 25 years.

      C. caused the Indians to lose over half of their land by 1934.

*   D. is correctly represented by all the above statements.

25. Which of the following statements about the cowboys' frontier is *not* true?

*   A. With two or three notable exceptions, blacks were not allowed to be cowboys.

      B. Texas longhorns were noted more for their speed and endurance than for their value as beef.

      C. Much of the cowboys' equipment had been passed on from Mexico.

      D. Cattle ranching had been common since colonial times.

26. *A Century of Dishonor*:
    A. was a best-selling novel about life in the western mining towns.
    B. told the story of four immigrant families who went west in the 1840s in search of a better life.
    C. exposed the prostitution industry of many western towns and led to reforms.
  * D. focused the nation's attention on the Indian cause.

27. Joseph Glidden:
    A. was a railroad man who reaped great profits from the early cattle drives.
  * B. invented barbed wire.
    C. made his fame as a buffalo hunter, slaughtering thousands of the animals.
    D. led the sheep ranchers against the cattlemen for control of western grazing lands.

28. The Newlands Reclamation Act of 1901:
    A. sold to settlers the lands created by clearing the timber from the western public lands.
    B. allowed the government to reclaim some of the land once given to railroads.
    C. authorized the government to begin a tremendous tree-planting project to reclaim part of the arid West.
  * D. provided funds for irrigation works.

29. The western frontier of the last half of the nineteenth century:
  * A. was often violent.
    B. had more women than men.
    C. generally had little ethnic or racial diversity.
    D. is correctly represented by all the above statements.

30. According to the superintendent of the census, the frontier line no longer existed after:
    A. 1875.
    B. 1880.
  * C. 1890.
    D. 1900.

Essay Questions

1. One of the goals of the New South prophets was a diversified agriculture. What factors stood in the way of this goal?

2. In what ways did the Bourbons' emphasis on economy affect the South?

3. Describe the pattern of race relations in the South from the end of Reconstruction to 1900.

4. One might say that the West actually consisted of three frontiers: the miners', the cowboys', and the farmers'. What problems did each of these groups face?

5. Describe the government's policy toward Indians. How did this policy develop over the years, and what were the main factors that influenced its development?

Matching Questions

A)   editor of the *Atlanta Constitution*
B)   made improved plow for Plains farmers
C)   Louisiana octoroon
D)   said "We refuse to surrender the leadership of this race to cowards and trucklers"
E)   founded American Tobacco Company
F)   philanthropist in area of education
G)   educated at Hampton Institute
H)   led massacre of 450 Indians at Sand Creek
I)   barbed-wire promoter
J)   author of *A Century of Dishonor*

H	1. J. M. Chivington
D	2. W. E. B. Du Bois
E	3. James Buchanan Duke
I	4. John W. Gates
A	5. Henry Grady
J	6. Helen Hunt Jackson
B	7. James Oliver
F	8. George Peabody
C	9. Homer Plessy
G	10. Booker T. Washington

Chapter 20

BIG BUSINESS AND ORGANIZED LABOR

This chapter discusses the advances in railroads and manufacturing, the captains of industry, workers in an industrialized America, and the growth of radicalism after the Civil War.

Chapter Outline

I. Economic effects of the Civil War
    A. Per-capita output decreased in the 1860s
    B. Recovery after the war
    C. Factors arising from the war that might have aided economic growth

II. The railroads
    A. Growth of railroads
    B. The transcontinental railroads
        1. Federal land grants and subsidies
        2. Pacific Railway bill (1862) authorized transcontinental line on north-central route
            a. Union Pacific Railroad
            b. Central Pacific Railroad
        3. Chinese labor
        4. First transcontinental railroad completed at Promontory Point
        5. Other transcontinental railroads
    C. Financing the railroads
        1. Western railroad finances
            a. The Crédit Mobilier Company
            b. Role of the federal government
        2. Eastern railroad finances
            a. Jay Gould
            b. Cornelius Vanderbilt

III. Manufacturing and inventions
    A. The growth of new industries and the transformation of old ones

    B. Two technological advances that changed people's lives
       1. Alexander Graham Bell and the telephone
       2. Thomas Alva Edison and the electric light

IV. Entrepreneurs
    A. John D. Rockefeller
       1. The Pennsylvania oil rush of 1859
       2. Rockefeller as oil refiner
       3. Growth of Standard Oil
       4. Rockefeller's organization of Standard Oil
    B. Andrew Carnegie
       1. Early ventures
       2. Carnegie and steel
       3. "The Gospel of Wealth"
    C. J. Pierpont Morgan
       1. Morgan and investment banking
       2. Morgan and railroads
       3. Morgan and steel
    D. Sears and Roebuck
       1. Problem of distribution
       2. Solution: mail-order

V. Workers in an industrialized America
    A. Social trends
       1. Continued inequalities
       2. Upward social mobility
    B. Working conditions
       1. Wages earned and hours worked
       2. Poor safety and health conditions in factories
    C. The change from personal working conditions to
       impersonal, contractual relationships

VI. Early worker protest
    A. Reasons for the slow growth of unions
    B. The Molly Maguires
    C. The Great Railroad Strike of 1877
       1. Reduction of wages was immediate cause
       2. The strikes spread across the country
       3. Failure of the strikes
    D. Dennis Kearney and the Workingmen's Party of California

VII. The rise of unions
    A. Unions in the 1850s and 1860s

B. The National Labor Union
  1. The first federation of unions
  2. Limitations and achievements

VIII. The Knights of Labor
  A. Founded in 1869 by Uriah S. Stephens
  B. Under Terrence V. Powderly, saw greatest success
    1. Successful strikes against the Union Pacific and Jay Gould's railroads
    2. Growth in membership
  C. Decline of the Knights of Labor
    1. Another strike against Jay Gould failed
    2. The Haymarket Affair
      a. Riot in Haymarket Square
      b. Trial and sentencing of anarchists
      c. Effects on Knights of Labor
  D. Achievements of Knights of Labor

IX. The American Federation of Labor
  A. Structure of the AFL
  B. Samuel Gompers
    1. Concern for concrete economic gains
    2. Gompers's leadership in the AFL
  C. Membership growth in the AFL

X. Two strikes that hurt the union movement
  A. The Homestead Steel Strike of 1892
    1. Reasons for the strike
    2. Battle between strikers and Pinkerton detectives
    3. Strike failed, union dead at Homestead
  B. The Pullman Strike of 1894
    1. Workers forced to live in town of Pullman
    2. Workers turned to Eugene Debs and the American Railway Union
    3. Strike tied up most midwestern railroads
    4. Mail cars attached to Pullman cars
    5. Debs jailed and the union called off the strike

XI. Socialism and the unions
  A. Daniel DeLeon and the Socialist Labor Party
  B. Eugene Debs and the Social Democrat Party
  C. The Socialist Party of America
    1. Debs in the presidential elections of 1904 and 1912
    2. Successes of the party
    3. Decline of the party

XII. The Industrial Workers of the World
   A. Origins of the IWW: western mining and lumber camps
   B. Goals of the IWW
      1. To include all workers, skilled and unskilled
      2. To replace the state with one big union
   C. Decline of the IWW
      1. Disputes within the group
      2. William D. "Big Bill" Haywood
      3. Mary "Mother Jones" Harris

Lecture Ideas

1. A lecture on the transformation of the American economy from agrarian to industrial following the Civil War could be very interesting to your students. You can start off by discussing the Civil War as a factor and continue with the change in business practices, rise of the captains of industry, market pressures, changing labor force, and so on. As a way of interaction in class, have your students break up into groups, select one of the major robber barons of the era, and research his life. After your introductory lecture on the rise of big business, have each group present and justify the philosophies of their selected robber baron. A good source for starting such a lecture would be Chapters 7–12 of Robert Heilbroner and Aaron Singer's *The Economic Transformation of America 1600 to the Present* (1994) and Robert H. Weibe's classic *The Search for Order* (1967).

2. The Transcontinental Railroad, if presented in a comprehensive lecture, allows you to cover a vast range of topics for this period. A general lecture allows for a discussion on business practices, the role government plays in the economy, the expansion of the West, the impact on the Native Americans, the role of the labor force—including the use of immigrant laborers, and the impact on the environment. A good point of discussion after your lecture would be to show the film *The American Experience: The Iron Rail*. A good Web resource is www.nps.gov/gosp/research/articles_index.html. Additionally, you can look in David Howard Bain's *Empire Express: Building the First Transcontinental Railroad* (1999).

3. The rise of national unions in America is essential to an understanding of society and big business in the late nineteenth and early twentieth centuries. Develop a comparison of the National Labor Union, Knights of Labor, American Federation of Labor, and the International Workers of the World. Focus on their leadership, philosophies, goals, and effectiveness as you survey each union's experiences. You can

discuss each union's position on immigrants, blacks, women, and unskilled workers. A good solid source for building this lecture is Foster Rhea Dulles and Melvyn Dubofsky's *Labor in America* (1999). A good comparison of the Knights and AFL is Gerald Grob's *Workers and Utopia* (1961). For a history of the IWW, see Melvin Dubofsky's *We Shall Be All: A History of the IWW* (1969).

4. An effective lecture on this topic should also include how industrialization impacted the working class in the United States. Be sure to include a discussion on how it affected where and how the working class worked, where they lived, and the accompanying social, political, and economic expectations. A good source on this topic is Herbert Gutman's *Work, Culture, and Society in Industrializing America* (1976). Another good resource is David Montgomery's *The Fall of the House of Labor* (1987).

True/False Questions

T   1. The first transcontinental railroad was completed at Promontory, Utah.

T   2. The 1860s was the only decade in the mid- to late-nineteenth century in which per capita output decreased.

T   3. Cornelius Vanderbilt made most of his money in railroads.

F   4. The number of inventions registered at the U.S. Patent Office remained fairly constant through the nineteenth century.

F   5. Andrew Carnegie was an outspoken opponent of Darwinism.

F   6. The Foran Act made it illegal for federal or state government workers to join labor unions.

T   7. The "sand lot" incident in San Francisco in 1877 led to animosity against Chinese immigrants.

F   8. The Haymarket Affair took place in St. Louis.

T   9. Anarchists oppose all forms of government.

T   10. American labor unions, unlike their European counterparts, seldom allied themselves with socialists.

Multiple-Choice Questions

1. From the end of the Civil War to the turn of the century:
   * A. the value of manufactures increased sixfold.
   B. farm production declined.
   C. average wages and earnings declined.
   D. All the above took place.

2. The growth of the railroads:
   A. was a major cause of the economic expansion at the end of the nineteenth century.
   B. resulted in an increase in total mileage from about 30,000 miles in 1860 to almost 200,000 in 1900.
   C. was greatest in the decade of the 1880s.
   * D. is correctly represented by all the above statements.

3. A transcontinental railroad was *not* built before the Civil War because:
   A. the Appalachian Mountains presented great engineering problems.
   B. Congress refused to consider federal subsidies for a private railroad.
   * C. North-South sectional differences prevented Congress from selecting a route.
   D. many southern states used the states' rights argument to reject federal aid for railroads.

4. The first transcontinental railroad:
   A. was completed in 1885.
   * B. was built by the Central Pacific and the Union Pacific Railroads.
   C. followed a southern route through Texas and the Arizona and New Mexico Territories.
   D. led to the bankruptcy of "Commodore" Vanderbilt.

5. Mary "Mother Jones" Harris promoted all of the following causes *except*:
   A. higher wages.
   B. shorter hours.
   C. restrictions on child labor.
   * D. temperance.

6. The California "Big Four":
  * A. were railroad investors.
    B. owned the largest mining companies in the West.
    C. controlled the National Bell Telephone Company.
    D. included Jay Gould and Cornelius Vanderbilt.

7. The Pennsylvania oil rush:
  * A. outweighed, in economic importance, the California gold rush of a decade before.
    B. gave J. Pierpont Morgan his start in business.
    C. ended the monopoly in petroleum production that Oklahoma had enjoyed for a quarter of a century.
    D. is correctly described by all the above statements.

8. Which of the following best accounts for the success of Standard Oil?
    A. Its scientists found new technical processes for refining oil more efficiently.
    B. It bought out the Erie Railroad in order to keep transportation charges low.
    C. It was one of the first companies to invest heavily in advertising.
  * D. Its corporate structure—known as "vertical integration"—allowed the company to grow tremendously.

9. Holding companies:
  * A. are firms that control the stock of other companies.
    B. were outlawed in New Jersey in 1888.
    C. allowed J. Pierpont Morgan to build a monopoly in the oil shipping business.
    D. were declared unconstitutional by the Supreme Court in 1868.

10. Andrew Carnegie:
    A. used much of the fortune he inherited from his father to drill his first oil well.
    B. paid almost $500 million for J. Pierpont Morgan's railroad interests.
  * C. made money in many areas, including oil, railroads, iron and steel, and bridge building.
    D. is correctly described by all the above statements.

11. What industry was "the first big business, the first magnet for the great financial markets, and the first industry to develop a large-scale management bureaucracy"?
   A. oil
 * B. railroads
   C. steel
   D. telephone/telegraph

12. Thomas Alva Edison invented:
 * A. the first successful incandescent light bulb.
   B. the air brake for trains.
   C. the (heavier-than-air) airplane.
   D. all the above.

13. Of the following, which one was most associated in the public mind with the "money trust"?
   A. Andrew Carnegie
 * B. J. P. Morgan
   C. John D. Rockefeller
   D. Richard Sears

14. The first billion-dollar corporation was:
   A. National Bell Telephone.
   B. Northern Pacific Railroad.
   C. Standard Oil.
 * D. United States Steel.

15. All the following accompanied industrialization between 1865 and 1914 *except*:
   A. a rise in real wages and earnings.
   B. a change from personal working relationships to impersonal, contractual relationships.
 * C. fewer women and children in the work force.
   D. poor safety and health conditions in factories.

16. The Molly Maguires:
   A. were named for the daughter of George Maguire, the owner of a Pennsylvania coal field.
   B. accomplished their goals of better wages and working conditions for miners through peaceful arbitration.
 * C. aimed to right the perceived wrongs against Irish coal workers.
   D. was the first major labor organization for western miners.

17. The Great Railroad Strike of 1877:
    A. was led by Samuel Gompers.
    B. won higher wages for railroad workers.
    C. did not have the support of the public at first, but as the strike (and its violence) spread, so did public sympathy for the strikers.
    * D. ended when the workers, who lacked organized bargaining power, returned to work.

18. The Workingmen's Party of California:
    A. was the political wing of the National Labor Union.
    * B. was based on anti-Chinese sentiment.
    C. campaigned (unsuccessfully) for restrictions on Mexican immigration.
    D. ended when the 1877 railroad strike ushered in better working conditions.

19. The National Labor Union:
    A. opposed the eight-hour day for employees of the federal government.
    B. opposed reforms such as cooperatives and equal rights for women and blacks in favor of simply bargaining with employers to get the best working conditions and wages possible.
    C. was led by Alfred Chandler.
    * D. was the first major federation of trade unions.

20. The greatest growth of the Knights of Labor took place:
    A. in 1875, when the federal government outlawed the use of violence against union members.
    * B. in the mid-1880s, when the union had several successful strikes against the railroads.
    C. under the leadership of Uriah S. Stephens.
    D. as a result of the Great Railroad Strike of 1877.

21. The Knights of Labor declined for all the following reasons *except*:
    A. a strike against Jay Gould in 1886 failed.
    * B. Uriah S. Stephens, its president, died in 1879.
    C. the Haymarket Affair discredited the union.
    D. its leadership was devoted more to reform than to the nuts and bolts of organization.

22. The Haymarket Affair:
    A. was started by the Knights of Labor.
    B. led to the passage of the Foran Act of 1885.

    C. marked the beginning of the Federation of Organized Trades and Labor Unions.

* D. was blamed, probably unfairly, on seven anarchist leaders.

23. The American Federation of Labor:
    * A. was concerned more with concrete economic gains than with social or political reforms.
    B. was formed in 1869 but experienced most of its growth in the early years of the twentieth century.
    C. was a federation of industrial unions; craft unions could not join until 1948.
    D. could claim as members almost half of all industrial workers in 1900.

24. Who said, "At no time in my life have I ever worked out a definitely articulated economic theory"?
    * A. Samuel Gompers
    B. William D. Haywood
    C. Terence V. Powderly
    D. Uriah S. Stephens

25. The Homestead Strike:
    A. involved workers at the Homestead Tobacco Company.
    * B. took place in Pittsburgh.
    C. was a victory for the union.
    D. is correctly represented by all the above statements.

26. The Pullman Strike ended:
    A. when Pullman hired Pinkerton detectives to harass the striking workers.
    B. despite President Grover Cleveland's support for the union.
    * C. after mail cars were attached to Pullman cars.
    D. when strike leader Samuel Gompers became ill and could no longer support the strikers' morale.

27. In *In re Debs*, the Supreme Court:
    A. overturned the conviction of Eugene Debs for destroying private property.
    B. upheld the conviction of Eugene Debs for destroying private property.
    C. overturned the conviction of Eugene Debs for inciting a riot.
    * D. upheld the conviction of Eugene Debs for violating a court injunction forbidding the obstruction of interstate commerce or of the transportation of the mails.

28. Daniel DeLeon:
    A. was the attorney general of Illinois who obtained an injunction against the striking Pullman employees.
    B. was convicted of throwing a bomb at strikers outside the Pullman plant.
    C. published an antisocialist paper in the 1890s.
  * D. was the leading figure in the Socialist Labor party.

29. Which of the following statements about the Socialist Party of America is *not* true?
  * A. Its support was confined to industrial workers in the Northeast.
    B. In 1912 the party's presidential candidate received almost 900,000 votes.
    C. It was plagued by disagreements over America's participation in World War I.
    D. It elected mayors in 33 American cities.

30. The Industrial Workers of the World:
  * A. had its origin in the mining and lumber camps of the West.
    B. was less radical than the American Federation of Labor.
    C. ended suddenly when its 1912 textile strike in Lawrence, Massachusetts, filed to win any concessions for the workers.
    D. ended in 1903 when the organization's officers were convicted of embezzling most of its funds.

31. William D. "Big Bill" Haywood:
    A. led a private army against striking miners in Colorado.
    B. was elected mayor of Milwaukee in 1910.
    C. served as editor of *The People*, the organ of the Socialist Labor party.
  * D. was the leader of the "Wobblies."

Essay Questions

1. What factors account for the dramatic growth in business after the Civil War?

2. Trace the development and completion of the first transcontinental railroad.

3. Describe Andrew Carnegie's philosophy concerning big business growth and how this reflected the wisdom of some Americans.

4. What factors shaped the growth of labor unions during this period?

5. Compare the aims and achievements of the Knights of Labor, the American Federation of Labor, and the Industrial Workers of the World.

Matching Questions

A) founded Standard Oil
B) president of the Homestead Steel Works
C) Knights of Labor leader
D) wrote "The Gospel of Wealth"
E) presidential candidate of the Socialist Party of America
F) a founder of mail-order business
G) "prince of railroad 'robber barons'"
H) organized Workingmen's Party of California
I) labor organizer executed for murder
J) consolidated steel industry into the United States Steel Corporation

D   1. Andrew Carnegie
E   2. Eugene V. Debs
B   3. Henry Clay
G   4. Jay Gould
I   5. Joe Hill
H   6. Dennis Kearney
J   7. J. Pierpont Morgan
C   8. Terrence V. Powderly
A   9. John D. Rockefeller
F   10. Alvah Roebuck

Chapter 21

THE EMERGENCE OF URBAN AMERICA

This chapter covers the growth of cities in late-nineteenth-century America, the new immigration, education, the influence of Darwinian thought in the social sciences and literature, and social reforms.

Chapter Outline

I. The American city in the late nineteenth century
   A. The growth of cities
      1. Cities in the West
      2. Transportation and industry as factors of growth
      3. Elevators allowed cities to grow vertically
      4. Streetcars and bridges allowed cities to grow horizontally
   B. City politics
   C. The attraction of the cities

II. Immigration to America
   A. Immigrants a major force in the growth of cities
      1. Numbers of immigrants
      2. Ethnic neighborhoods
      3. Reasons for coming to America
   B. A new wave of immigration
      1. After 1890, most immigrants from southern and eastern Europe
      2. Difference in culture, language, and religion
   C. Ellis Island
   D. Immigrant life
      1. Working conditions
      2. Living conditions
   E. The nativist response
      1. New immigrants viewed as a threat
      2. The American Protective Association
      3. Immigration restriction
         a. Early laws excluded "undesirables"
         b. Chinese immigrants excluded in 1882

III. Popular culture
    A. Wild West shows
    B. Vaudeville
    C. Outdoor recreation
    D. Saloon culture
    E. Working women and leisure
    F. Spectator sports

IV. Education and the professions
    A. Public education
        1. Increases in spending for schools
        2. Secondary schools
    B. Vocational Training
        1. Booker T. Washington and Calvin M. Woodward
        2. Vocational training in high schools
        3. Agricultural and mechanical colleges
        4. Demonstration agents for agricultural education
    C. Higher education
        1. Increases in college attendance
        2. Women in higher education
        3. Graduate schools

V. The rise of professionalism
    A. Education for professionals
    B. Licensing of professionals
    C. Associations for professionals

VI. Theories of social change
    A. Charles Darwin's *Origin of Species* (1859)
    B. Social Darwinism
        1. Herbert Spencer's *System of Synthetic Philosophy*
        2. Tenets of Social Darwinism
        3. William Graham Sumner
    C. Reform Darwinism
        1. A challenge to Social Darwinism
        2. Lester Frank Ward and his Dynamic Sociology

VII. Realism in the social sciences
    A. "Scientific" history
    B. Sociology
        1. Albion W. Small and his *General Sociology*
        2. Move from abstract theories to concrete studies of human relations

      C. Economics
         1. Move from abstract theories to concrete studies
         2. The research of the new economists

VIII. Realism in philosophy
      A. William James and pragmatism
         1. The meaning and value of ideas is in their practical consequences
      B. John Dewey and "instrumentalism"
         1. Ideas as instruments
         2. Progressive education

IX. Realism in literature
      A. Local color
         1. Reasons for its popularity
         2. Early practitioners
      B. Literary realism
         1. Mark Twain
         2. William Dean Howells
         3. Henry James
      C. Literary naturalism
         1. Introduction of scientific determinism into literature
         2. Stephen Crane
         3. Jack London
         4. Theodore Dreiser

X. Social criticism in the late nineteenth century
      A. Henry George's *Progress and Poverty*
      B. Henry Demarest Lloyd's *Wealth against Commonwealth*
      C. Thorstein Veblen's *The Theory of the Leisure Class*

XI. The social gospel
      A. Community service and care for the unfortunate
      B. Religious reformers
         1. Washington Gladden
         2. Walter Rauschenbusch
            a. *Christianity and the Social Crisis*
            b. A theological basis for the social gospel movement
      C. The Roman Catholic church and reform
         1. Pope Pius IX's *Syllabus of Errors* hindered support for reform
         2. Pope Leo XIII's *Rerum novarum* more liberal
         3. American Catholics remained isolated from reform movements

XII. The settlement house movement
   A. Definition of settlement houses
      1. Jane Addams's Hull House most famous
      2. Other settlement houses
   B. Accomplishments of settlement houses
   C. Criticism of settlement houses

XIII. The women's suffrage movement
   A. Women in the work force
   B. Susan B. Anthony wanted Fourteenth Amendment to include women
   C. Split in the movement
      1. National Woman Suffrage Association promoted many feminist causes
      2. American Woman Suffrage Association promoted only women's suffrage
   D. National American Woman Suffrage Association
      1. Leadership
      2. Accomplishments
         a. Nine western states had full suffrage by 1912
         b. Fewer and later successes in East
   E. Other women's reform organizations

XIV. Toward a welfare state
   A. Regulation of business by states
   B. The "due process of law" clause of the Fourteenth Amendment
      1. "Person" read to include corporations
      2. Doctrine of "substantive due process"
      3. Cases arising from these
   C. "Liberty of contract" cases
   D. Tensions between laissez-faire doctrines and growing sense of reform

Lecture Ideas

1. For a lecture on the influence of Darwinian thought on various aspects of American life, consider Paul F. Boller's *American Thought in Transition: The Impact of Evolutionary Naturalism, 1865–1900* (1969) and Richard Hofstadter's *Social Darwinism in American Thought* (rev. ed., 1975).

2. Divide the class up into different groups and assign each group an aspect of the various forces at work in American society at the end of the nineteenth century. The groups should look at industrialization,

224 / Chapter 21: The Emergence of Urban America

immigration, urbanization, and so on. See Charles N. Glaab and
A. Theodore Brown's *A History of Urban History* (1983), Walter
Nugent's *Crossings: The Great Transatlantic Migrations, 1870–1914*
(1992), and Daniel Rodgers's *The Work Ethic in Industrial America*
(1978).

3. For a lecture on the rise of the urban boss and the urban political
   machine, see Alexander B. Callow's *The City Boss in America* (1976)
   and John M. Allswang's *Bosses, Machines, and Urban Voters* (1986).

4. For a lecture on the everyday life of Americans at the end of the
   nineteenth century, see Thomas J. Schlereth's *Victorian America*
   (1991).

5. Luc Sante's *Low Life: Lures & Snares of Old New York* (1991), an enter-
   taining and instructive look at urban culture in the late nineteenth
   century, would be a good source for a lecture on that topic.

True/False Questions

T   1. The spread of mass transit was a major factor in the
             growth of the suburbs.

F   2. Most Asian immigrants entered the United States at
             Charleston, South Carolina, rather than at Ellis Island.

T   3. Local colorists expressed the nostalgia of an urbanizing
             and industrializing people.

T   4. Saloons were the poor man's social clubs during the late
             nineteenth century.

F   5. Dumbbell tenements gave city dwellers substantially
             healthier and more comfortable living conditions.

F   6. The peak decade of immigration was the 1890s.

T   7. "Padrones" were hiring agents who secured jobs for
             immigrants in return for a share of their wages.

T   8. The modern American graduate school is based on the
             model of German universities.

F   9. Major league baseball, integrated in the 1880s, was the
             first professional sport to treat blacks and whites equally
             (at least on the field).

F 10. Elizabeth Cady Stanton argued that Susan B. Anthony's push for voting rights was "biologically and morally misguided."

Multiple-Choice Questions

1. Which area had the greatest proportion of people living in cities?
   A. the Midwest
   B. the Northeast
   C. the South
   * D. the Pacific coast

2. Chicago's Hull House was designed to assist:
   A. abused wives.
   B. alcoholics and drug addicts.
   * C. slum dwellers.
   D. unwed mothers.

3. Urban political bosses:
   * A. often were the biggest source of assistance for city dwellers.
   B. brought efficient, scandal-free government to America's growing cities.
   C. tended to scorn immigrants in the cities.
   D. are correctly represented by all the above statements.

4. After 1890, most immigrants were:
   A. from northern and western Europe.
   * B. Jews and Catholics.
   C. of Teutonic and Celtic origin.
   D. from Mexico.

5. Ellis Island:
   A. was opened in 1892.
   B. averaged 5,000 immigrants a day in 1907.
   C. was used mainly to process new immigrants, not to comfort or assist them.
   * D. is correctly represented by all the above statements.

6. The American Protective Association:
   A. was a group of pharmaceutical companies that began a sanitation campaign in New York City.
   B. was mainly an anti-Semitic organization.
   * C. was strongest in the upper Mississippi Valley.
   D. campaigned for a stronger navy.

7. The exclusion of Chinese immigrants:
    A. came only after the exclusion of immigrants from southern and eastern Europe.
    B. came only after the exclusion of immigrants from northern and western Europe.
    C. was opposed by white workers in the Far West.
   * D. was first authorized with a ten-year suspension.

8. The Morrill Acts of 1862 and 1890:
    A. restricted Chinese immigration.
    B. placed severe quotas on "new immigrants" from Europe.
    C. established vocational schools aimed at giving job skills to immigrants.
   * D. established and funded land-grant colleges.

9. All the following became more common between the Civil War and the turn of the century *except*:
    A. graduate schools.
    B. the licensing of practitioners in certain professional fields.
   * C. core curricula of prescribed courses at major colleges and universities.
    D. public schools.

10. Women's access to higher education:
   * A. improved shortly after the Civil War.
    B. was practically nonexistent until the 1920s.
    C. was resisted most strongly by western state universities.
    D. came quickest in the South.

11. Herbert Spencer:
   * A. coined the phrase "survival of the fittest."
    B. was the influential president of Harvard University.
    C. invented the modern game of basketball.
    D. was the first person to earn a Ph.D. from an American university.

12. A strict Social Darwinist would object to all the following *except*:
    A. the graduated income tax.
    B. sanitation and housing regulations.
   * C. a governmental policy of laissez-faire in regard to business.
    D. regulation of medical quacks.

13. William Graham Sumner:
    A. wrote "The Gospel of Wealth," a Social Darwinist justification for accumulated wealth.
    B. was one of the most outspoken opponents of Darwinism in America.

    *   C. argued in his book *Folkways* that social conditions were set by tradition or custom, not by reason or natural laws.

        D. wrote *System of Synthetic Knowledge.*

14. The main idea of Reform Darwinism was that:
    A. humans, made in the image of God, should not be included among the animals when discussing Darwinism.
    B. government should not interfere with business.
    * C. cooperation, not competition, would best promote progress.
    D. man continued to evolve according to Darwin's principles of natural selection.

15. According to Albion W. Small, sociology was the:
    A. study of theories of how a society might function in certain conditions.
    * B. scientific analysis of social phenomena with emphasis on groups in society.
    C. study of the evolution of human society.
    D. historical analysis of social relations in the past.

16. An early leader of the social gospel movement was:
    * A. Washington Gladden.
    B. De Wit Talmadge.
    C. Silas Lapham.
    D. Henry Ward Beecher.

17. The author of *Pragmatism: A New Name for Some Old Ways of Thinking* was:
    * A. William James.
    B. Henry James.
    C. Henry Adams.
    D. Herbert Baxter Adams.

18. According to proponents of progressive education:
    * A. children should study many subjects as a way of enlarging their personal experience.
    B. children should learn strict habits and standards of behavior early in life.
    C. schools were for academic education; moral and cultural education should come from the family and community.
    D. elementary school children should be segregated by gender.

19. The subject of *Wealth against Commonwealth* was:
    A. the American Tobacco Company.
    * B. Standard Oil.
    C. corruption in the banking system.
    D. corruption in the stock market.

20. William Dean Howells:
    * A. was an important literary critic.
    B. opposed literary realism.
    C. wrote "The Celebrated Jumping Frog of Calaveras County."
    D. wrote *Innocents Abroad*.

21. Stephen Crane and Jack London belonged to a literary
    movement called:
    * A. naturalism.
    B. romanticism.
    C. local color.
    D. socialist fiction.

22. The author of *Sister Carrie* was:
    * A. Theodore Dreiser.
    B. Henry James.
    C. Carrie Meeber.
    D. Mark Twain.

23. *Progress and Poverty* argued that:
    A. government assistance for the poor was wrong.
    * B. nobody had the right to the value that accrued from
      the land.
    C. the "single-tax" idea was immoral and probably
      unconstitutional.
    D. the Catholic Church was wrong in its views on modernization.

24. Thorstein Veblen:
    * A. wrote about "conspicuous consumption" and
      "conspicuous leisure."
    B. wrote *An American Tragedy*.
    C. argued that too many industrial experts were becoming
      business managers.
    D. defended the productive efficiency of big business against
      its critics.

25. The acknowledged intellectual head of the social gospel
    movement in America was:
    A. Henry Adams.
    B. John Carter.
    * C. Walter Rauschenbusch.
    D. Calvin M. Woodward.

26. Pope Leo XIII's *Rerum novarum*:
    A. declared erroneous such ideas as liberalism and rationalism.
    * B. expressed a new Catholic doctrine condemning the poverty and degradation caused by capitalism.
    C. forbade workers to join labor unions.
    D. condemned women's suffrage.

27. Which of the following statements best describes the status of women's suffrage at the turn of the century?
    A. Women could vote in a few northeastern cities, but no state had adopted women's suffrage.
    * B. Several states, all in the West, had adopted women's suffrage.
    C. Women could generally vote in presidential and other national elections, but not in local or state elections.
    D. Women's suffrage was confined to the South.

28. The National Consumers League:
    A. organized boycotts to lower food prices.
    B. was secretly supported by several of the large retailers it allegedly tried to regulate.
    * C. sought to make the public aware of labor conditions.
    D. promoted a laissez-faire approach to business.

29. In 1869, the women's movement split on the issue of:
    A. whether to grant suffrage to black as well as white women.
    B. the role of women in the religious professions.
    C. the political involvement of settlement houses in women's rights.
    * D. whether or not the movement should concentrate on female suffrage to the exclusion of other feminist causes.

30. The stance of the Supreme Court in the late nineteenth century on liberty of contract could best be described as favorable toward:
    A. all workers.
    B. union workers.
    C. immigrant workers.
    * D. business.

Essay Questions

1. Describe the growth of the movement for women's rights in this period. What accomplishments were made? What obstacles held the movement back?

2. How did immigration to America change in the latter half of the nineteenth century, and what was the response to that change?

3. Compare Social Darwinism and Reform Darwinism. What were the basic assumptions of each movement?

4. How did late-nineteenth-century American literature reflect the impact of Darwinian thought?

5. Among the responses to urbanization was the rise of the social gospel and settlement houses. Describe each of these, showing what problems each tried to correct and how they went about their tasks.

Matching Questions

A) chief spokesperson for Reform Darwinism
B) developed safety elevator
C) Mark Twain
D) New York City political boss
E) wrote *Wealth against Commonwealth*
F) started Hull House
G) headed Wild West show
H) wrote *Varieties of Religious Experience*
I) wrote *Looking Backward, 2000–1887*
J) "Give me your tired, your poor / Your huddled masses yearning to breathe free"

F   1. Jane Addams
I   2. Edward Bellamy
C   3. Samuel Langhorne Clemens
G   4. William Cody
H   5. William James
J   6. Emma Lazarus
E   7. Henry Demarest Lloyd
B   8. Elisha Graves Otis
D   9. George Washington Plunkitt
A   10. Lester Frank Ward

Chapter 22

GILDED-AGE POLITICS AND AGRARIAN REVOLT

This chapter covers Gilded-Age politics, the issues of the currency, tariffs, and civil service reform, the discontent of farmers, the rise of agrarian political movements, and the triumph of metropolitan and industrial values.

Chapter Outline

I. Gilded-Age politics
   A. The traditional view of Gilded-Age politics
      1. Mediocre political leaders
      2. Few real differences between political parties
      3. Factors shaping Gilded-Age politics
         a. Americans, remembering the Civil War, were hesitant to take clear-cut stands
         b. Parties evenly divided
         c. No "strong" chief executive in Gilded Age
      4. Alliance between politics and business
      5. Voter turnout extremely high
      6. Cultural conflicts between ethnic and religious groups shaped political parties
      7. Immigration and politics
      8. Prohibition and politics
   B. State and local initiatives
      1. Role of state governments
      2. Use of the court system

II. The administration of Rutherford B. Hayes
   A. Civil service reform
      1. Republican party split between Stalwarts and Half-Breeds
      2. The removal of Chester A. Arthur and Alonzo Cornell
   B. Limiting the role of government

III. The administrations of James A. Garfield and Chester A. Arthur
  A. Garfield as president
    1. Election of 1880
    2. Garfield's assassination
  B. Arthur as president
    1. Arthur and reform
      a. Prosecution of the Star Route Frauds
      b. Pendleton Civil Service Act (1883)
    2. Attempts to lower tariff

IV. The first administration of Grover Cleveland
  A. Election of 1884
    1. Republicans
      a. James G. Blaine and the "Mulligan letters"
      b. Rise of the Mugwumps
    2. Democrats
      a. Grover Cleveland and early career of reform
      b. Cleveland and the potential scandal of an illegitimate child
    3. Last-minute blunders by Blaine
  B. Cleveland as president
    1. Cleveland and civil service reform
      a. Promised support for Pendleton Act
      b. But he removed many Republican officeholders
    2. Cleveland and the public treasury
      a. 81 million acres of public land restored to federal government
      b. Opposition to pension raids on Treasury
    3. Cleveland and railroad regulation—the Interstate Commerce Commission
    4. Cleveland and the tariff
      a. Annual message of 1887 devoted entirely to tariff
      b. Bill for modest tariff reduction died in Congress

V. The administration of Benjamin Harrison
  A. Election of 1888
    1. Tariff was main issue
    2. Corruption and the phony "Murchison letter"
    3. Cleveland won popular vote, but lost election in electoral college
  B. Harrison as president
    1. Many federal officeholders removed on partisan grounds

       2. Pensions for Union veterans doubled
       3. Sherman Anti-Trust Act, 1890
       4. Sherman Silver Purchase Act, 1890
       5. McKinley Tariff of 1890
    C. Midterm elections of 1890
       1. Great Republican losses
       2. Reasons for Republican losses

VI. The farm problem and agrarian protest movements
    A. The diversity of farm interests
    B. Decline in commodity prices
       1. Domestic overproduction
       2. International competition
    C. Railroads and middlemen
       1. High railroad rates
       2. Little bargaining power
    D. High tariffs
    E. Debt
       1. Crop liens and land mortgages
       2. Forced to grow cash crops

VII. The Grange
    A. Oliver H. Kelley founded the Grange in 1867
       1. Membership in the Grange
       2. Goals of the Grange
    B. "Granger Laws"
       1. Regulation of railroad and warehouse rates
       2. Supreme Court upheld warehouse regulation in
         Munn v. *Illinois* (1877)
    C. Decline of the Grange
       1. Failure of economic ventures
       2. The Independent National (Greenback) party

VIII. The Farmers' Alliance
    A. The growth of the Alliance
    B. The Texas Alliance
       1. Charles W. Macune
       2. Alliance exchanges
    C. Farm politics
       1. The subtreasury plan
       2. In West, third-party successes
       3. In South, influenced Democratic party

   D. Leaders of farm movement
      1. Mary Elizabeth Lease
      2. "Sockless Jerry" Simpson
      3. Tom Watson

IX. The Populist party
   A. Formed in Cincinnati in May 1891
   B. Omaha Platform
      1. Finance
      2. Transportation
      3. Land
   C. Election of 1892
      1. James B. Weaver as Populist presidential candidate
      2. Weaver received over a million popular votes, carried four states

X. The economy and the silver solution
   A. An inadequate currency
   B. The depression of 1893
      1. Worker unrest
         a. In 1894, 750,000 workers on strike
         b. Millions unemployed
         c. Coxey's Army marched on Washington
   C. Midterm elections of 1894
      1. Republican victories
      2. Populists elected thirteen to Congress
   D. Depression focused attention on currency issue
      1. Repeal of the Sherman Silver Purchase Act
      2. Silver notes issued to build gold reserve

XI. The election of 1896
   A. Candidates and positions
      1. Republicans nominated William McKinley on gold-standard platform
      2. Democrats nominated pro-silver William Jennings Bryan after his "cross of gold" speech
      3. Rather than split silver vote, Populists also nominated Bryan
   B. Victory for McKinley
      1. Bryan carried most of the West and South
      2. Bryan unable to attract votes of midwestern farmers and eastern workers

XII. The new era
- A. The triumph of metropolitan and industrial America over rural and agrarian America
- B. New gold discoveries ended the depression
- C. The coming of the Spanish-American War ended much controversy over tariffs and the currency

Lecture Ideas

1. An introductory lecture on the Gilded Age is a great way to start this chapter. Focus in on the politics of the age. See Mark W. Summers's *The Gilded Age* (1997) and Robert Cherny's *American Politics in the Gilded Age* (1997).

2. Give a general overview of the agrarian revolts in this period. Then divide the class into two distinct groups, the defenders of the Populist Movement and the opponents of the Populist Movement. See the classic by Richard Hofstadter's *The Age of Reform* (1955), Michael Kazin's *The Populist Persuasion* (1998), and Robert C. McMath's *American Populism: A Social History* (1993).

3. For a lecture on the election of 1896 and William Jennings Bryan as "reformer," see John A. Garraty's "William Jennings Bryan" (*American Heritage*, Dec. 1961). Also useful is Paul W. Glad's *McKinley, Bryan, and the People* (1964). Louis W. Koenig's "The First Hurrah" (*American Heritage*, April 1980) tells how Bryan's 1896 campaign changed the way future presidential hopefuls would run for office.

True/False Questions

F   1. Benjamin Harrison was assassinated by Charles Guiteau, a deranged office seeker.

F   2. James Garfield was the first southerner to be elected president since the Civil War.

F   3. Grover Cleveland was known as "the continental liar from the state of Maine."

F   4. Mugwumps tended to oppose civil service reform.

T   5. The Grand Army of the Republic was an organization of Union veterans.

T   6. Farmers were generally hurt by the high tariff.

F   7. The Farmers' Alliances were strongest in the Midwest and Northeast.

T   8. The Farmers' Alliances accepted female and black members.

T   9. One of the biggest problems farmers faced was falling commodity prices, caused in part by overproduction.

T   10. In 1896, the Republican party supported the gold standard.

Multiple-Choice Questions

1. The one issue on which there were clear-cut divisions between Democrats and Republicans in the Gilded Age was:
   A. immigration.
   B. civil service reform.
   C. the regulation of big business.
   * D. the tariff.

2. Which of the following was *not* a factor in shaping Gilded-Age politics?
   A. Politics was seen more as a way to get elected than a way to press certain issues.
   * B. Business remained separate from politics.
   C. In national politics, neither party could keep both a majority in Congress and a president in the White House.
   D. None of the presidents in this period could be described as a strong leader.

3. Which of the following would most likely have been a Gilded-Age Republican?
   A. a southern white
   B. a Jewish immigrant
   * C. a prohibitionist
   D. an atheist

4. Which of the following would most likely have been a Gilded-Age Democrat?
   A. a New England Protestant
   * B. a German immigrant
   C. a nativist
   D. an African American

5. In *Munn v. Illinois*, the Supreme Court upheld:
    A. labor unions' right to organize.
    B. the philosophy that corporations were artificial people.
  * C. the right of state and local governments to regulate industry essential to the public welfare.
    D. the anarchist right to form protest political parties.

6. The Stalwarts:
    A. were a faction in the Democratic party.
    B. generally favored a lenient southern policy.
  * C. were led by Roscoe Conkling.
    D. were also known as the "Half-Breeds."

7. Which of the following best describes Rutherford B. Hayes and civil service reform?
    A. Hayes was able to get several civil service reform bills through Congress.
    B. Hayes was against civil service reform, but Congress passed several bills over his vetoes.
    C. Hayes was against civil service reform, but he signed several bills for political expediency.
  * D. Hayes was unable to get civil service legislation through Congress, but he set up his own rules for merit appointments.

8. Chester A. Arthur was:
    A. elected to the presidency with less than half of the popular vote.
    B. the first president since Lincoln to die in office.
    C. elected to the presidency despite untrue rumors concerning gambling debts circulated by the Democrats just before the election.
  * D. connected with the New York Customs House corruption before he became president.

9. The so-called "Mongrel Tariff" of 1883:
    A. raised the average duty on imports by about 5 percent, less of an increase than President Arthur supported.
  * B. lowered the average duty on imports by about 5 percent, less of a decrease than President Arthur supported.
    C. raised the average duty on imports by about 25 percent, almost exactly what President Arthur wanted.
    D. lowered the average duty on imports by about 25 percent, almost exactly what President Arthur wanted.

10. The Pendleton Civil Service Act:
    * A. provided for appointment to a number of government jobs on the basis of competitive exams.
      B. was signed into law by James Garfield.
      C. was vetoed as "an unconstitutional intrusion of government into the private sphere" by Benjamin Harrison.
      D. set up the first racial quotas for government service jobs.

11. During the campaign for the presidential election of 1884, many prominent Republican leaders and supporters left the party because:
      A. they would not vote for a woman as vice-president.
      B. the "Mugwumps" had gained power within the party.
    * C. letters were discovered linking candidate James G. Blaine to the railroads.
      D. the party refused to take a firm stand on the tariff.

12. Grover Cleveland:
    * A. was the first Democrat elected to the White House after the Civil War.
      B. said that "just as the people support the government, so should the government support the people."
      C. refused to fire federal workers on partisan grounds.
      D. is correctly represented by all the above statements.

13. The Interstate Commerce Act:
    * A. was created to regulate railroads.
      B. was passed over Cleveland's veto.
      C. was overturned by the Supreme Court in *Wabash Railroad v. United States*.
      D. is correctly represented by all the above statements.

14. Which of the following was a Democrat?
      A. Chester A. Arthur
      B. James G. Blaine
      C. James Garfield
    * D. Winfield Scott Hancock

15. Benjamin Harrison was elected president:
      A. in a campaign waged mainly on the issue of currency reform.
    * B. although he received fewer popular votes than the loser, Grover Cleveland.

    C. despite publication of the "Mulligan letters" linking him to the railroads.

    D. in the only Gilded Age campaign not marred by dirty tricks and personal attacks on the candidates.

16. Which of the following was named father of an illegitimate child?
    - A. Chester A. Arthur
    - * B. Grover Cleveland
    - C. James Garfield
    - D. John Sherman

17. The election of 1890 revealed:
    - A. a contentment on the part of the American people.
    - B. a need for a strong three-party system.
    - * C. a deep-seated unrest in the farming communities of the South and the West.
    - D. a deep hatred for American politics.

18. Which of the following was *not* a factor in the decline of commodity prices during the Gilded Age?
    - A. Much new land had been brought into cultivation, increasing production.
    - B. Innovations in transportation brought American farmers more into competition with farmers around the world.
    - * C. The Sherman Silver Purchase Act decreased the amount of silver purchased by the government and therefore caused deflation and lower prices.
    - D. Debt-ridden farmers produced more than the market would support at good prices.

19. Passage of the "Granger Laws":
    - * A. laid a foundation for stronger legislation to follow.
    - B. proved very effective in the short term.
    - C. split the Grange Alliance.
    - D. helped the urban workers of the Northeast.

20. In the case of *Munn* v. *Illinois*, the Supreme Court:
    - * A. upheld a law involving warehouse regulation.
    - B. overturned "Granger Laws" in that state.
    - C. upheld the constitutionality of the Bland-Allison Act.
    - D. allowed the Farmers' Alliance to have separate organizations for Negro members.

21. The Independent National party:
    * A. was more commonly known as the Greenback party.
    B. won five states in the presidential election of 1888.
    C. drew most of its support from nativists in New England.
    D. appealed mainly to immigrant voters in the Northeast.

22. The subtreasury plan:
    A. promoted deflation by withdrawing silver certificates from circulation.
    B. was passed by Congress in 1890.
    * C. allowed farmers to secure low-interest government loans.
    D. is correctly represented by all the above.

23. Mary Elizabeth Lease:
    A. founded the Patrons of Husbandry (the Grange).
    * B. advised farmers to "raise less corn and more hell."
    C. was the presidential candidate of the Greenback party in 1892.
    D. wrote the 1892 Omaha platform for the People's party.

24. "Sockless Jerry" Simpson:
    A. was secretary of agriculture under Harrison.
    B. was the economist whose books influenced passage of the Bland-Allison Act and the Sherman Silver Purchase Act.
    C. was a leading union veteran and, for a time, pension commissioner.
    * D. was a Kansas Alliance leader.

25. All the following were included in the 1892 Omaha Platform of the People's party *except*:
    * A. halting the free and unlimited coinage of silver.
    B. increasing the amount of currency in circulation.
    C. nationalizing the railroads.
    D. implementing the subtreasury plan.

26. In the presidential election of 1892, the Populist candidate:
    A. won.
    B. came in second.
    C. did best in the Northeast.
    * D. won 22 electoral votes.

27. The group that benefited most from the Depression of 1893 in the elections of 1894 was the:
    A. Democrats.
    * B. Republicans.
    C. farmers.
    D. labor unions.

28. "You shall not crucify mankind upon a cross of gold!" This statement was made by:
    * A. William Jennings Bryan.
    B. William McKinley.
    C. Grover Cleveland.
    D. Thomas E. Watson.

29. In the presidential election of 1896, William Jennings Bryan:
    A. was the candidate of the Populist party.
    B. carried most of the states in the West and South.
    C. could not win the votes of urban workers in the Northeast.
    * D. is correctly described by all the above statements.

30. One theme of Gilded Age politics was the:
    * A. triumph of urban-industrial interests.
    B. triumph of rural-agricultural interests.
    C. rise of the common man.
    D. extension of government into the private sphere.

Essay Questions

1. Describe Gilded-Age politics. What were the main issues? What factors influenced voters to be either Republican or Democrat?

2. Describe the controversy over civil service reform in the Gilded Age. Which groups favored such reforms? What types of reforms did they achieve?

3. What problems did American farmers face in 1890?

4. What were the main planks of the 1892 Omaha Platform of the Populist party? How would these provisions have helped solve the problems the farmers faced?

5. "By the end of the Gilded Age, the values of a metropolitan and industrial America had triumphed over those of a rural and agrarian America." What evidence supports this statement?

Matching Questions

A) Populist presidential candidate in 1892
B) coauthor of *The Gilded Age*
C) founded the Grange
D) elected to two nonconsecutive terms as president
E) devised the subtreasury plan
F) McKinley's campaign manager
G) Democratic presidential candidate in 1896
H) Garfield's vice-president
I) husband of "Lemonade Lucy"
J) led march on Washington, D.C., to demand that the federal government provide jobs for the unemployed

H   1. Chester A. Arthur
G   2. William Jennings Bryan
D   3. Grover Cleveland
J   4. Jacob S. Coxey
F   5. Mark Hanna
I   6. Rutherford B. Hayes
C   7. Oliver H. Kelley
E   8. Charles W. Macune
B   9. Charles Dudley Warner
A   10. James B. Weaver

Chapter 23

AN AMERICAN EMPIRE

This chapter covers American expansion and foreign policy from the Civil War through the administration of Theodore Roosevelt.

Chapter Outline

I. Toward the new imperialism
    A. Reasons for American expansion
        1. Markets
        2. Naval power
            a. Alfred Thayer Mahan's *The Influence of Sea Power upon History*
            b. Expansion of navy
        3. Racial thought
            a. Social Darwinism
            b. John Fiske's *American Political Ideas*
            c. Josiah Strong's *Our Country*
    B. William Seward and the purchase of Alaska
    C. Expansion in the Pacific
        1. Samoa
            a. Treaty of 1878
            b. After 1889, tripartite protectorate over Samoa
        2. Hawaii
            a. Boom in sugar production
            b. American influence in economy and government
            c. Queen Liliuokalani opposed Americans
            d. Americans rebel, proclaim Republic of Hawaii

II. The Spanish-American War
    A. "Cuba libre"
        1. Rebellion broke out in Cuba
        2. American view of Cuban revolt
            a. Similar to American Revolution
            b. "Butcher" Weyler
            c. Yellow journalism
         3. Cleveland refused to intervene

    B. Pressures for war
        1. McKinley elected on platform endorsing Cuban independence
        2. Spain offered Cuba autonomy in return for peace
        3. de Lôme letter
        4. Explosion of the *Maine*
        5. Spain authorized McKinley to dictate settlement
        6. U.S. actions
           a. Declared Cuba independent
           b. Teller Amendment: U.S. does not want Cuban territory
           c. Blockade of Cuba
        7. War with Spain (April 1898)
        8. Summary of reasons for war
    C. Campaigns
        1. Philippines
           a. George Dewey
           b. Captured Manila Bay
        2. Cuba
           a. Condition of armies
           b. Theodore Roosevelt and the "Rough Riders"
    D. End of war
        1. Terms of peace
           a. Spain gave up Cuba
           b. U.S. would acquire Puerto Rico
           c. The Philippines question
        2. Annexation of the Philippines
           a. Little desire for Philippines before war
           b. McKinley's reasons for annexation
           c. Other areas in Pacific annexed at this time
           d. Opposition to Treaty of Paris
           e. Filipino insurrection against United States
           f. Anti-imperialist thought

III. Organizing the new acquisitions
    A. Philippines
        1. Philippines Government Act: made Philippines an unorganized territory
        2. Jones Act set up elected legislature, affirmed U.S. intentions to grant independence
        3. Tydings-McDuffie Act offered independence in ten years

    B. Puerto Rico
       1. Foraker Act set up civil government
       2. Jones Act granted U.S. citizenship
    C. "Insular Cases": Constitution does not follow the flag
    D. Cuba
       1. Trouble with Cuban rebels
       2. Platt Amendment restricted Cuban independence
       3. Continued American intervention in Cuba

IV. China
    A. Imperial rivalries in China
    B. Open Door Policy (1899)
    C. The Boxer Rebellion (1900)
    D. Summary of America's China policy

V. Roosevelt's "big stick" diplomacy
    A. TR's rise
       1. Early years
       2. Election of 1900
          a. W. J. Bryan against McKinley (and TR)
          b. Issues, especially imperialism
       3. McKinley assassinated
       4. TR's character
    B. Panama Canal
       1. Early treaties hindered canal efforts
       2. America moved for a canal
          a. Agreements and problems with Colombia
          b. Rebellion in Panama
       3. America built the canal
          a. Isthmian Canal Commission created
          b. Resentment in Colombia
    C. Roosevelt Corollary
       1. Economic crisis in Dominican Republic invited foreign intervention
       2. Roosevelt Corollary to the Monroe Doctrine
       3. Specific actions in Dominican Republic
    D. Russo-Japanese War and aftermath
       1. Background
       2. TR sponsored peace settlement (Treaty of Portsmouth)
       3. Concern over Japanese strength near the Philippines

   4. Fear of "yellow peril" at home
      a. Discrimination against Japanese in California
      b. "Gentlemen's Agreement" restricted Japanese immigration
   E. Roosevelt mediated settlement in Morocco
   F. "Great White Fleet" showed off America's strength
   G. Roosevelt's foreign policy assessed

Lecture Ideas

1. A lecture on American imperialism is essential. Discuss the origins of American imperialism, America's justification and implementation of this policy, and the political and economic causations and results. See Emily S. Rosenberg's *Spreading the American Dream* (1982), Walter Lefeber's *The New Empire* (1998), and Anders Stephanson's *Manifest Destiny: American Expansionism and the Empire of Right* (1995).

2. Give a brief a lecture outlining how America put itself into a position to build the Panama Canal. Then have your class research the issue of the Panama Canal. Groups should look at how the United States went about building it, how successful it was, and what the status of the Canal is today. See David McCullough's *The Path Between the Seas* (1977) and Walter LeFeber's *The Panama Canal* (1978).

3. A good follow-up lecture on American imperialism would be a discussion on American imperialism in the Philippines. See Stuart Creighton Miller's *"Benevolent Assimilation": The American Conquest of the Philippines, 1899–1903* (1979), Richard Welch's *Response to Imperialism: The United States and the Philippine-American War, 1899–1902* (1979), and Stanley Karnow's *In Our Image: America's Empire in the Philippines* (1989).

4. A good way to end this chapter is on a discussion of the Anti-Imperialists. Be sure to include their main philosophies, who they were, and if they had any impact on American imperialist policy. See Robert L. Beisner's *Twelve Against Empire: The Anti-Imperialists, 1898–1900* (1985).

True/False Questions

F   1. William McKinley said that President Roosevelt had "no more backbone than a chocolate eclair."

F   2. The United States purchased Alaska from Great Britain.

T   3. Between 1875 and 1890, sugar from Hawaii could enter the United States duty free.

T   4. Spain conceded to practically all of the American demands concerning Cuba before the United States declared war.

F   5. Joseph Pulitzer, as editor of the *San Francisco Chronicle*, wrote against American interventionist policies at the turn of the century.

T   6. Theodore Roosevelt helped lead the "Rough Riders" in the Cuban campaign of the Spanish-American War.

T   7. "The White Man's Burden" was a pro-expansionist poem written by Rudyard Kipling.

T   8. "Butcher" Weyler was the nickname given to the Spanish general who detained insurrectionary Cubans in *reconcentrado* centers.

T   9. A French company dug a canal part of the way through Panama in the 1880s.

T   10. The United States agreed to pay $10 million plus $250,000 a year for the Panama Canal Zone.

Multiple-Choice Questions

1. John Fiske:
   * A. wrote *American Political Ideas*, a book that stressed the superior character of Anglo-Saxon peoples and institutions.
      B. was one of the earliest government officials to speak out against imperialism.
      C. used Darwinian concepts to show how American expansionism hurt the people of the areas America annexed.
      D. was a minister who added the sanction of religion to the expansionists' argument.

2. The United States wanted to acquire some control over the Pacific island groups of Samoa and Hawaii:
      A. because of oil deposits found there.
      B. despite Secretary of State William Seward's urgings for Americans to resist the expansionist impulse.
   * C. because the islands offered strategic locations for naval bases.
      D. despite the Treaty of Washington (1871), which ceded the islands to the Russians.

3. Queen Liliuokalani:
    A. was forced by Americans living in Hawaii to grant a constitutional government for the islands in 1899.
    B. welcomed American sugar planters to Hawaii.
    C. was an American pretender to the Hawaiian throne.
  * D. opposed the Americanization of Hawaii.

4. One of Spain's oldest colonies, Cuba:
    A. was the showcase of Spanish culture.
    B. meant very little to the Spanish.
    C. was the key port in the Spanish empire.
  * D. was a major export market for the mother country.

5. Who said, "Speak softly, and carry a big stick"?
    A. William Jennings Bryan
    B. Grover Cleveland
  * C. Theodore Roosevelt
    D. William H. Taft

6. The term "yellow journalism" arose from the:
    A. use of native reporters in the press coverage of the battles in the Philippines.
    B. press coverage of the trials of three Cuban officials who were accused of accepting bribes in the form of gold shipments from insurrectionists.
  * C. circulation war between two New York newspapers.
    D. use of propaganda in underground newspapers published by the Cuban insurrectionists.

7. The de Lôme letter:
    A. revealed the location of Spanish troops in Cuba.
    B. was the first of the Cuban insurrectionists' overtures for peace.
    C. blamed the destruction of the battleship *Maine* on Spanish agents.
  * D. referred to President McKinley as a weak and cowardly leader.

8. The battleship *Maine*:
    A. exploded as it left Miami for Cuba.
  * B. became a battle cry in the Spanish-American War.
    C. carried arms to the Cuban insurrectionists.
    D. disappeared at sea with no trace, but newspaper reporters claimed that Spain had ordered it sunk.

9. America went to war with Spain because of all the following *except*:
    A. the buildup of public pressure for war.
    * B. Spain's refusal to discuss terms for peace.
    C. alleged Spanish mistreatment of Cuban civilians.
    D. Americans tended to compare the Cuban insurrection with their own American Revolution.

10. The publisher of the *New York Journal* was:
    A. Henry W. Grady.
    * B. William Randolph Hearst.
    C. Charles Foster Kane.
    D. Frederick Jackson Turner.

11. The Teller Amendment:
    A. was added to an army appropriation bill in 1901.
    B. called for universal suffrage in America's new possessions.
    C. was defeated in the Senate.
    * D. disclaimed any American designs on Cuban territory.

12. In the Spanish-American War:
    A. America's victory could be attributed in large part to expert preparation.
    * B. more American soldiers died from disease than battle.
    C. the American victory in the decisive battle at Santiago depended on assistance from German forces.
    D. America finally settled the question of freedom of the seas.

13. The first major victory for American forces in the Spanish-American War was at:
    A. San Juan Hill.
    B. Santiago.
    * C. Manila Bay.
    D. Havana.

14. The treaty ending the Spanish-American War:
    * A. was opposed by most Democrats and Populists.
    B. was ratified in the Senate over the protests of William Jennings Bryan.
    C. provided for Spain to pay to the United States $10,000 for each American soldier killed in the war.
    D. provided for Hawaiian autonomy.

15. Which one of the following supported America's annexation of the Philippines?
    * A. Albert J. Beveridge
    B. Andrew Carnegie
    C. Samuel Gompers
    D. William James

16. Emilio Aguinaldo:
    * A. was the Filipino rebel leader.
    B. led the Spanish forces at San Juan Hill.
    C. was installed as Cuba's governor in 1898.
    D. was the martyred leader of the Cuban rebellion.

17. Who was president when the United States acquired the right to build a canal across Panama?
    A. Grover Cleveland
    B. William Jennings Bryan
    C. William McKinley
    * D. Theodore Roosevelt

18. When the United States and Colombia could not agree on a price for the Canal Zone:
    A. the matter was submitted to an international board for arbitration.
    B. Roosevelt sent the army to Colombia to force Colombian leaders to accept the American offer.
    * C. the Colombian province of Panama rebelled against Colombia.
    D. Colombian leaders offered the deal to the British.

19. The Platt Amendment:
    A. granted U.S. citizenship to inhabitants of Puerto Rico.
    B. arranged for a Cuban election to decide the issue of annexation.
    * C. sharply restricted the independence of Cuba's new government.
    D. set up the Army Yellow Fever Commission under Dr. Walter Reed.

20. Which president sent the "Great White Fleet" around the world in a show of America's naval strength?
    A. Grover Cleveland
    B. Benjamin Harrison
    C. William McKinley
    * D. Theodore Roosevelt

21. The Open Door policy:
    A. allowed a certain number of Chinese immigrants to the United States each year in return for special trading rights with China.
    B. allowed Cubans to enter the United States, and Americans to enter Cuba, freely.
    * C. proposed that foreign powers keep the China trade open to all nations on an equal basis.
    D. pledged economic aid to struggling Latin American republics.

22. The Boxer Rebellion took place in:
    A. 1883.
    * B. 1900.
    C. Mexico.
    D. Puerto Rico.

23. Theodore Roosevelt:
    A. had a Ph.D. in chemistry.
    B. was the first southern-born president since the Civil War.
    C. was a Democrat.
    * D. loved the outdoors and was, for a brief time, a cowboy.

24. In the election of 1900:
    A. Theodore Roosevelt ran for president against William Jennings Bryan.
    B. Theodore Roosevelt ran for president against William McKinley.
    * C. Democrats questioned America's policy of annexation.
    D. Republicans questioned America's policy of annexation.

25. The Hay-Herrán Treaty:
    A. ended the Spanish-American War.
    B. ended the insurrection in the Philippines.
    * C. concerned America's right to build a canal in Panama.
    D. failed to pass the United States Senate.

26. In the "Insular Cases," federal judges decided that:
    * A. protection of the American constitution does not necessarily extend to all subjects of the American empire.
    B. citizens of America's new possessions should be allowed to choose their own form of government.
    C. "the Constitution follows the flag."
    D. the president could not grant independence to America's new possessions without congressional approval.

27. The Roosevelt Corollary:
    A. encouraged American bankers to help finance the shaky Latin American governments.
    * B. stated that the United States could intervene in the affairs of Western Hemisphere countries to forestall the intervention of other powers.
    C. rescinded most of the provisions of the Monroe Doctrine.
    D. justified American intervention in the Far East.

28. As a result of Japan's show of strength in the Russo-Japanese War:
    A. America was quick to send money and support troops to aid Russia.
    B. Congress voted financial and military aid to Korea to help prevent a Japanese invasion of the Korean peninsula.
    C. Congress lifted the limitations it had previously set on Japanese immigration.
    * D. Americans began to doubt the security of the Philippines.

29. In the so-called Gentlemen's Agreement, President Roosevelt:
    * A. stopped the flow of Japanese immigrants to America.
    B. acknowledged Japan's dominance of Korea.
    C. agreed not to bring American armed forces into the Russo-Japanese War.
    D. agreed to help finance the Russian effort to seize Korea from the Japanese.

30. Roosevelt's intervention in the Russo-Japanese War and the Moroccan dispute:
    A. strained America's relations with Russia.
    * B. won Roosevelt the Nobel Peace Prize of 1906.
    C. involved the use of armed forces without the consent of Congress.
    D. weakened his image around the world.

Essay Questions

1. What were the reasons for American expansionism at the turn of the century? What justifications did Americans offer for expansionism?

2. How did Hawaii become part of the United States?

3. Describe the steps leading to America's war with Spain in 1898. Was war justified?

4. What effect did American ownership of the Philippines have on U.S. foreign policy?

5. What was the Open Door policy, and how did it come about?

Matching Questions

A) secretary of state; called Spanish-American War "a splendid little war"
B) Democratic presidential candidate in 1900
C) wrote *Our Country: Its Possible Future and Its Present Crisis*
D) American military governor in Cuba after Spanish-American War
E) elected vice-president in 1900
F) owned "The Yellow Kid"
G) proposed to return Queen Liliuokalani to Hawaiian throne
H) wrote *The Influence of Sea Power Upon History*
I) acquired Alaska for the United States
J) captured Manila Bay

B 1. William Jennings Bryan
G 2. Grover Cleveland
J 3. George Dewey
A 4. John Hay
F 5. William Randolph Hearst
H 6. Alfred Thayer Mahan
E 7. Theodore Roosevelt
I 8. William H. Seward
C 9. Josiah Strong
D 10. Leonard Wood

Chapter 24

THE PROGRESSIVE ERA

This chapter covers the antecedents and main features of progressivism and the domestic policies of the administrations of Roosevelt, Taft, and Wilson.

Chapter Outline

I. Elements of progressive reform
    A. Paradoxes in progressivism
        1. Progressivism as a "more respectable" populism
        2. Elements of conservatism in progressivism
    B. Antecedents to progressivism
        1. Populism
        2. The Mugwumps
        3. Socialism
    C. The muckrakers

II. Features of progressivism
    A. Greater democracy
        1. Direct primaries
        2. The initiative, referendum, and recall
        3. Popular election of senators
    B. "The gospel of efficiency"
        1. Frederick W. Taylor and *The Principles of Scientific Management*
        2. Shorter ballots
        3. New ideas for municipal government—commission system and the city-manager plan
        4. Robert La Follette and the "Wisconsin Idea"
    C. Corporate regulation
        1. Alternative solutions to the problems of big business
        2. The trend toward regulation
    D. Social justice
        1. Labor laws
            a. Child labor
            b. The Supreme Court and state labor laws

      2. Prohibition
   E. Public service functions of government

III. Roosevelt's progressivism—first term
   A. Trusts
      1. Roosevelt thought effective regulation better than attempts to restore competition
      2. Decision in *United States* v. *E. C. Knight* (1895) held manufacturing to be intrastate activity
      3. Supreme Court ordered the Northern Securities Company dissolved
   B. Anthracite coal strike of 1902
      1. Workers struck for more pay and fewer hours
      2. Mine owners closed mines
      3. Roosevelt threatened to take over the mines, forcing the owners to submit to arbitration panel
   C. More trust cases
      1. Overall, brought about 25 antitrust suits
      2. In *Swift and Company* v. *United States* (1905), the Supreme Court overturned its holding in the *Knight* case
   D. Antitrust and regulatory legislation of 1903
      1. An act created the Bureau of Corporations
      2. The Elkins Act made it illegal to take as well as give railroad rebates

IV. Roosevelt's progressivism—second term
   A. The election of 1904
   B. The Hepburn Act of 1906 gave the Interstate Commerce Commission power to set maximum rates
   C. Movement to regulate food processors and makers of drug and patent medicines
      1. Campaign against patent medicines
      2. Upton Sinclair's *The Jungle* and meat packers
      3. The Meat Inspection Act (1906)
      4. The Pure Food and Drug Act (1906)
   D. Conservation
      1. Roosevelt withdrew some 172 million acres of timberlands
      2. Other accomplishments in conservation
   E. The election of 1908
      1. Roosevelt handpicked William Howard Taft as his successor
      2. Taft won over Democratic candidate William Jennings Bryan

V. Taft's progressivism
   A. Taft's early career
   B. Tariff reform
      1. Taft wanted lower tariff
      2. Instead, tariff raised many rates
      3. Fearful of party split, Taft backed new tariff
   C. Ballinger-Pinchot controversy
      1. When Chief of Forestry Gifford Pinchot discovered possible corrupt dealings by Secretary of the Interior Richard Ballinger, he went public with his accusations
      2. Fired by Taft for insubordination
      3. Tarnished Taft's image as progressive
   D. The Taft-Roosevelt break
      1. Taft's administration brought suit against United States Steel, against Roosevelt's wishes
      2. Review of accomplishments of Taft's administration
      3. Although Roosevelt won most Republican state primaries, Taft controlled party machinery and won nomination
      4. Roosevelt became the nominee of the Progressive party

VI. The election of 1912
   A. The rise of Woodrow Wilson
   B. Campaign
      1. Roosevelt shot
      2. Taft had no chance
      3. Roosevelt's "New Nationalism"
         a. Influence of Herbert Croly
         b. Hamiltonian means to achieve Jeffersonian ends
      4. Wilson's "New Freedom"
         a. Influence of Louis Brandeis
         b. Restoration of an economy of small-scale competitive units
   C. Election figures—victory for Wilson
   D. Significance of the election of 1912
      1. A high-water mark for progressivism
      2. Brought Democrats back into effective national power
      3. Brought Southerners back into national and international affairs
      4. Altered the character of the Republican party

VII. Wilson's progressivism
   A. Relied more on party politics than popular support to pass reforms

    B. Underwood-Simmons Tariff (1913)
       1. Lowered average duty by about one-fifth
       2. To replace lost revenue, began income tax
    C. The Glass-Owen Federal Reserve Act (1913)
       1. Allowed reserves to be pooled
       2. Made currency and bank credit more elastic
       3. Lessened concentration of reserves in New York
    D. Wilson and trusts
       1. The Clayton Anti-Trust Act of 1914
          a. Outlawed price discrimination, "tying" agreements, interlocking directorates in large corporations, and the practice whereby a corporation buys up the stock of its competitors to gain control of the market
          b. Farm labor organizations exempted
       2. Federal Trade Commission
    E. Wilson and social justice
       1. Little legislation before 1916
       2. La Follette Seamen's Act (1915)
    F. Progressivism for whites only
       1. Wilson's racial attitudes
       2. Spread of uncompromising racists in Wilson's government
    G. A resurgence of progressivism
       1. Wilson added to his progressive record to form a broad base of support for 1916 election
       2. Farm reforms (credit and education)
       3. Federal Highways Act (1916) subsidized state highway departments
       4. Labor reform
          a. Keating-Owen Act (1916) excluded from interstate commerce goods manufactured by children under fourteen
          b. Adamson Act (1916) provided for eight-hour day for railroad workers
    H. Under Wilson, progressivism became a movement for positive government

VIII. Paradoxes of progressivism
    A. Disfranchisement of blacks
    B. Decisions made more by faceless policy-makers
    C. Decline in voter participation

Lecture Ideas

1. Progressivism is the place to begin your lectures for this chapter. Start with a definition and build from there. Describe who the progressives were, what their major objectives were, and their ultimate legacy upon the American reform spirit and American history overall. Once you have done this, divide the class up into groups and have them research in more detail a particular aspect of the progressive movement. See Steven J. Diner's *A Very Different Age* (1998), Alan Dawley's *Struggles for Justice* (1991), and Morton White's *Social Thought in America: The Revolt Against Formalism* (1975).

2. For a comparison of Theodore Roosevelt and Woodrow Wilson—a comparison that should be instructive in explaining certain progressive ideas—see John Milton Cooper, Jr.'s *The Warrior and the Priest* (1983), which compares the two on both domestic and foreign policies. Also useful would be John Blum's *The Progressive Presidents* (1980), and Michael McGerr's *The Decline of Popular Politics* (1986).

3. For a lecture on the original efficiency expert, see Spencer Klaw's "Frederick Winslow Taylor: The Messiah of Time and Motion" (*American Heritage*, Aug. 1979) or the first chapter of Samuel Haber's *Efficiency and Uplift* (1964). Also see Robert Kanigel's *The Best Way: Frederick Winslow Taylor and the Enigma of Efficiency* (1997) and Samuel P. Hayes's *Conservation and the Gospel of Efficiency* (1969).

4. Gerald H. Carson's "Who Put the Borax in Dr. Wiley's Butter?" (*American Heritage*, Aug. 1956) would be a good source for a lecture on the Pure Food and Drug Act. A good approach to the Meat Inspection Act would be to focus on the politics involved in progressive legislation; see "USDA Government Inspected" in *After the Fact*, by James West Davidson and Mark Hamilton Lytle (3rd ed., 1992).

True/False Questions

T   1. Among the antecedents to Progressivism were Populism, Socialism, and the Mugwumps.

T   2. Theodore Roosevelt gave muckrakers their name.

T   3. In *Swift and Company v. United States*, the Supreme Court put forth the "stream of commerce" doctrine.

F   4. The first regular federal income tax was made necessary by the low rates of the Tariff of 1902.

F   5. William Howard Taft finished second in the presidential election of 1912.

F   6. Woodrow Wilson was elected president in 1908.

F   7. Federal money for farm demonstration agents was approved in the Adamson Act.

T   8. Theodore Roosevelt considered the Federal Trade Commission to be the cornerstone of his program for big business.

T   9. The phrase "square deal" is associated with Theodore Roosevelt.

F   10. William H. Taft achieved the most significant tariff reduction of any progressive president.

Multiple-Choice Questions

1. The author of *The Shame of the Cities* was:
   - A. George F. Baer.
   - B. Ray Stannard Baker.
   - C. Henry Demarest Lloyd.
   - * D. Lincoln Steffens.

2. The subject of *Wealth Against Commonwealth* was:
   - * A. Standard Oil.
   - B. municipal corruption.
   - C. child labor.
   - D. urban transportation.

3. Frederick W. Taylor:
   - A. was an Oregon reformer responsible for many progressive measures enacted there.
   - * B. wrote *Principles of Scientific Management*.
   - C. was the progressive editor of *Arena*.
   - D. was founder of the National Child Labor Committee.

4. The commission plan of city government was first adopted in:
   - A. Atlanta, Georgia.
   - B. Durham, North Carolina.
   - * C. Galveston, Texas.
   - D. Springfield, Missouri.

5. The originator of the "Wisconsin Idea" of efficient government
    was:
    A. Lewis Hine.
    B. Hiram Johnson.
    C. Florence Kelley.
    *   D. Robert M. La Follette.

6. Which of the following best describes the method used by most
    progressives to solve the problem of economic power and its
    abuses?
    A. adopt a socialist program of public ownership
    B. follow the principles of laissez-faire government
    *   C. regulate big business
    D. allow business to work out its own destiny

7. Progressives concerned with social justice called for:
    A. prohibition.
    B. regulations on the hours of work for women.
    C. stricter building codes and factory inspection acts.
    *   D. all the above.

8. The Seventeenth Amendment:
    *   A. authorized the popular election of U.S. senators.
    B. gave women the right to vote.
    C. called for direct primaries.
    D. authorized the federal income tax.

9. The title of the novel that described the terrible conditions of the
    meat-packing industry was:
    A. *Chicago.*
    B. *The Great American Fraud.*
    *   C. *The Jungle.*
    D. *Maggie.*

10. During the anthracite coal strike:
    *   A. President Theodore Roosevelt won support for his use of
        the "big stick" against big business.
    B. thousands of striking miners marched on Washington,
        starting a riot that lasted three days.
    C. President Theodore Roosevelt threatened to use the army
        to force strikers back to work.
    D. arbitrators awarded the miners all their demands.

11. In the area of conservation, Theodore Roosevelt:
    A. believed strongly that natural resources should be preserved but felt that this was a matter for state, not federal, action.
    B. angered many conservationists by his appointment of Gifford Pinchot, a businessman with no experience in conservation, as head of the Division of Forestry.
    * C. used the Forest Reserve Act to withdraw over 170 million acres of timberland from logging.
    D. vetoed a bill authorizing a National Conservation Commission.

12. William Howard Taft:
    * A. was Roosevelt's choice as his successor.
    B. was described by many journalists as "the ultimate politician."
    C. found solid support from voters only in the South and Southwest.
    D. was, in the Republican tradition, opposed to a lower tariff.

13. President Taft's domestic policies generated a storm of controversy:
    A. overseas.
    B. within the Democratic Party.
    C. within the Progressive Party.
    * D. within his own party.

14. The Ballinger-Pinchot controversy:
    A. resulted in the immediate dismissal of Secretary of the Interior Richard A. Ballinger for his involvement in corrupt land dealings.
    B. proved to the public that Taft supported the conservation of America's resources.
    * C. contributed to the growing rift between Taft and Roosevelt.
    D. is correctly represented by all the above statements.

15. In the case of *Lochner* v. *New York*, the Supreme Court:
    A. upheld a Utah law limiting miners to eight-hour workdays.
    B. ordered the breakup of the "beef trust."
    C. ordered the breakup of the American Tobacco Company.
    * D. voided a state-legislated ten-hour day because it violated workers' "liberty of contract."

16. As president, Taft:
    A. was able to unite a faction-ridden Republican party with his towering personality.
    B. opposed both the Sixteenth and Seventeenth Amendments.
    C. brought fewer than one-third the number of antitrust suits prosecuted under Roosevelt.
*   D. withdrew more public lands in four years than Roosevelt had in nearly eight.

17. The Hepburn Act of 1906:
    A. was the first federal law regulating labor standards.
*   B. authorized the Interstate Commerce Commission to set maximum rates for railroads.
    C. in effect outlawed the Northern Securities Company.
    D. is correctly described by all the above statements.

18. In the presidential election of 1912, William Howard Taft:
*   A. was the Republican candidate.
    B. campaigned for his "Bull Moose" program.
    C. named George W. Norris as his vice-presidential running mate.
    D. All the above are correct.

19. Woodrow Wilson was:
*   A. a professor and college president.
    B. the leading Roman Catholic politician at the turn of the century.
    C. the progressive governor of Oregon.
    D. influenced mainly by Populist reformers.

20. Which candidate was shot during the 1912 presidential campaign?
    A. Eugene V. Debs
*   B. Theodore Roosevelt
    C. William H. Taft
    D. Woodrow Wilson

21. Theodore Roosevelt's "New Nationalism":
*   A. meant that government intervention, once identified with business interests, should be used to achieve democratic goals.
    B. was a conservative philosophy of a limited role of government.
    C. called for the breakup of all monopolies.
    D. meant that the federal government should concern itself with problems of social justice and let big business take care of itself.

22. The election of 1912:
    A. gave the Democrats effective national power for the first time in over half a century.
    B. signaled the return of Southerners to national and international affairs for the first time since the Civil War.
    C. altered the character of the Republican party, making it more conservative.
    * D. is correctly described by all the above statements.

23. Louis D. Brandeis:
    * A. influenced Wilson's New Freedom.
    B. led the conservative opposition to federal labor laws.
    C. was Theodore Roosevelt's vice-presidential running mate in 1912.
    D. was president of the Tennessee Coal and Iron Company.

24. To get support for his progressive reforms, Wilson:
    A. usually took his case directly to the people, as he did not trust Congress.
    B. acted through a bipartisan coalition of progressives.
    * C. relied on the party loyalty of Democrats.
    D. could not rely on most Democratic congressmen to stick with him.

25. The Underwood-Simmons Tariff:
    A. raised the average tariff and hence was supported by Wilson.
    B. raised the average tariff and hence was opposed by Wilson.
    C. lowered the average tariff and hence was opposed by Wilson.
    * D. lowered the average tariff and hence was supported by Wilson.

26. The Clayton Anti-Trust Act:
    A. was more lenient toward big business than was the Sherman Anti-Trust Act.
    * B. outlawed price discrimination and interlocking directorates.
    C. was originally opposed by labor union leaders.
    D. was considered by Theodore Roosevelt as the crowning achievement of his administration.

27. In his first term as president, Wilson:
    A. refused to support an amendment for women's suffrage.
    B. allowed the spread of racist practices in the federal government.
    C. withheld support from federal child-labor legislation.
    * D. did all the above.

28. Wilson's program of reform for farmers:
    A. was overwhelmingly rejected by Congress.
    B. included the subtreasury plan, which finally passed in Congress over two decades after the Populists first proposed it.
    * C. included the Warehouse Act of 1916 and the Federal Farm Loan Act.
    D. was based on the idea that farmers should help themselves rather than look to the government for assistance.

29. The Federal Reserve Act:
    A. made currency and bank credit more elastic.
    B. was the first major banking and currency reform in half a century.
    C. lessened the power of the huge New York banks.
    * D. is correctly represented by all the above statements.

30. In the progressive period:
    A. reformers were generally pessimistic about finding solutions to social ills.
    B. voter turnout increased.
    * C. many groups—blacks, the poor, the unorganized—had little influence.
    D. All the above statements are true.

Essay Questions

1. Describe the five major themes of progressive reform.

2. Which of the progressive presidents was the most progressive? Which was the least progressive? Explain.

3. What changes did progressivism bring to America? How was America different in 1920 from what it had been in 1900 because of progressivism?

4. In what ways was the election of 1912 significant?

5. "From its beginning to its end, the progressive movement was, more than anything else, paradoxical." What evidence could be used to support this statement?

Matching Questions

A)   the original "efficiency expert"
B)   Democratic presidential candidate in 1904
C)   wrote *The Jungle*
D)   Socialist party presidential candidate
E)   Progressive party presidential candidate in 1912
F)   influenced New Nationalism with *The Promise of American Life*
G)   wrote *Congressional Government*
H)   wrote *Wealth Against Commonwealth*
I)   chief justice of the United States in 1920s
J)   first Jewish member of the Supreme Court

J   1. Louis D. Brandeis
F   2. Herbert Croly
D   3. Eugene V. Debs
H   4. Henry Demarest Lloyd
B   5. Alton B. Parker
E   6. Theodore Roosevelt
C   7. Upton Sinclair
I   8. William H. Taft
A   9. Frederick W. Taylor
G   10. Woodrow Wilson

Chapter 25

AMERICA AND THE GREAT WAR

This chapter covers foreign affairs in Wilson's administration, the war in Europe, American neutrality and preparedness, America's entry into the war, domestic affairs during World War I, Wilson's Fourteen Points and his fight for the Versailles Treaty, and the transition from war to peace in America.

Chapter Outline

I. Wilson's foreign policy
   A. Idealistic diplomacy
      1. Secretary of State William Jennings Bryan
      2. God expected America to advance democracy and moral progress
   B. Mexico
      1. Gen. Victoriano Huerta established military dictatorship
      2. Incident at Tampico allowed Wilson to intervene
      3. The downfall of Huerta
      4. Mexican bandits
      5. Carranza's more liberal Mexican government
   C. In Caribbean, America marines helped put down disorders

II. An uneasy neutrality
   A. The beginning of the war
      1. Assassination of Austrian Archduke Franz Ferdinand
      2. The European system of alliances
         a. Central Powers (Germany, Austria-Hungary, Italy)
         b. Triple Entente (France, Great Britain, Russia)
   B. America's initial reaction
      1. Wilson urged Americans to be neutral
      2. Many immigrants for the Central Powers
      3. Old-line Americans for the Allies
      4. Role of propaganda

C. American neutrality strained
   1. Financial assistance to Allies
   2. Freedom of the seas
      a. Importance of sea power in European war
      b. British ordered ships carrying German goods via neutral ports to be stopped
   3. German submarine warfare
      a. Germans declared a war zone around the British Isles and threatened to sink any ships there
      b. German sinking of two ships divided the administration on a course of action
      c. *Lusitania* sunk; among 1,198 dead were 128 Americans
      d. America protested through a series of notes
      e. Unwilling to risk war, Secretary of State William Jennings Bryan resigned (June 1915)
   4. *Arabic* pledge
   5. Mediation efforts
   6. Peace advocated in Congress
   7. Germany promised not to torpedo merchant or passenger ships
D. The debate over preparedness
   1. Sinking of the *Lusitania* contributed to demands for a stronger army and navy
      a. National Security League organized
      b. Wilson's war preparation plans announced
      c. Some were against preparedness
   2. The army strengthened
   3. The navy strengthened
   4. Revenue Act of 1916
E. Election of 1916
   1. Republicans nominated Charles Evans Hughes
   2. Democrats nominated Wilson again
   3. Wilson campaigned on peace and a progressive platform
   4. Hughes was ambiguous on foreign policy and behind Wilson on social issues
   5. Wilson won in close race
F. Wilson's last efforts for peace
   1. Wilson asked each side to state its war aims
   2. Wilson said that America should share in laying the foundations for lasting peace
   3. Germany announced its new policy of unrestricted submarine warfare

4. Wilson broke diplomatic relations with Germany
5. Wilson decided to arm U.S. merchant ships
6. The Zimmermann telegram

III. America's entry into the war
   A. Declaration of war
   B. Reasons for war
   C. America's early role in the war
      1. American contributions to Allied naval strategy
         a. Convoy system
         b. Mine field across North Sea
      2. Liberty Loan Act helped finance British and French war efforts
      3. Token army of under 15,000 men under John J. Pershing sent to France
      4. Selective Service Act

IV. The home front
   A. Regulation of industry and the economy
      1. Lever Food and Fuel Control Act of 1917
      2. War Industries Board
         a. Most important of all mobilization agencies
         b. Under direction of Bernard Baruch, directed almost all of America's economy
   B. A new labor force
      1. African Americans
         a. The "Great Migration"
         b. Northern race riots
      2. Women
         a. Types of war work
         b. Effects temporary
      3. Organized labor
   C. Mobilizing public opinion—the Committee on Public Information
      1. Headed by George Creel
      2. "Expression, not repression"
   D. Civil liberties
      1. Public opinion, aroused to promote war, turned to "Americanism" and witch-hunting
      2. Espionage and Sedition Acts
         a. More than 1,000 convictions
         b. In *Schenck* v. *United States* and *Abrams* v. *United States*, Supreme Court upheld acts

V. America in the war
    A. Until 1918, American troops played only a token role
    B. The "race for France"
        1. By November 1918 over two million men in Europe
        2. Allied victories kept Germans out of France
        3. Second Battle of the Marne (July 15)
        4. By November Germany was retreating all along the front
    C. Intervention in Russia
    D. Wilson's plan for peace
        1. The Fourteen Points
            a. Open diplomacy
            b. Freedom of the seas
            c. Removal of trade barriers
            d. Reduction of armaments
            e. Impartial adjustment of colonial claims
            f. Evacuation of occupied lands
            g. National self-determination
            h. Polish access to the sea
            i. A League of Nations
        2. Allies accepted Fourteen Points as basis for peace, but demanded reparations for war damages
        3. Armistice signed on November 11, 1918

VI. Wilson's fight for the peace
    A. Wilson's domestic strength was declining
        1. The unraveling of his progressive coalition
        2. Democrats lose in the elections of 1918
        3. Wilson failed to invite any prominent Republicans to assist in the negotiations
    B. The negotiations in Paris
    C. The League of Nations
        1. For Wilson, the most important point
        2. Article X pledged members to consult on military and economic sanctions against aggressors
        3. Organization of the League
        4. "Round Robin" showed Republican opposition
        5. Amendments adopted to Wilson's plan
    D. Other negotiations
        1. France pushed for several harsh measures against Germany
            a. Territorial concessions
            b. Reparations

2. Problems with Wilson's principle of national self-determinism
3. Methods for resolving issues
    a. Use of committees of experts
    b. Use of plebiscites
4. The issue of reparations
    a. France wanted to use demands for reparations to cripple Germany
    b. Wilson agreed to clause where Germany accepted responsibility for war and thus for its costs
    c. Reparations Committee ultimately decided that Germany owed $33 billion

VII. Wilson's fight for the treaty
    A. Opposition in Senate
        1. The irreconcilables
        2. The reservationists
    B. Henry Cabot Lodge began his attack on the treaty
    C. Wilson took his case to the American people
        1. Delivered 40 addresses in 22 days
        2. Suffered stroke on October 2
        3. Now he refused to compromise on treaty
    D. The Senate vote on the Versailles Treaty
        1. On the treaty with reservations, Wilsonians and irreconcilables combined to defeat ratification
        2. On the treaty without reservations, reservationists and irreconcilables combined to defeat ratification
    E. The official end of the war by joint resolution of Congress

VIII. From war to peace
    A. The Spanish flu
    B. Economic transition
        1. Postwar boom
        2. Labor unrest
            a. In 1919, four million workers on strike
            b. Strike at U.S. Steel
            c. Boston Police Strike
    C. Racial friction
        1. The "Red Summer" of 1919
        2. Twenty-five race riots, with many deaths and injuries
    D. The Red Scare
        1. Fear of a social revolution (like Russia's)
        2. Most violence was the work of the lunatic fringe, but many Americans saw it all as "Bolshevism"

3. Role of A. Mitchell Palmer, attorney general, in promoting the Red Scare
4. The Red Scare began to evaporate by the summer of 1920

Lecture Ideas

1. To give your class a good understanding of American diplomatic relations on the eve of World War I, deliver a lecture on Wilson's foreign policy. See Lloyd E. Ambrosius's *Woodrow Wilson and the American Diplomatic Tradition* (1987), Arthur S. Link's *Woodrow Wilson: Revolution, War, and Peace* (1979), Frederick S. Calhoun's *Power and Principle: Armed Intervention in Wilsonian Foreign Policy* (1986), and Thomas J. Knock's *To End All Wars: Woodrow Wilson and the Quest for a New World Order* (1992).

2. Divide the class up into groups and have them research and report on the conditions and aspects of America on the domestic front during World War I. The groups should focus in on the economy, the role of women, the impact on other minorities, preparedness, civil liberties, and so on. See Robert H. Zieger's *America's Great War: World War I and the American Experience* (2000), Nail A. Wynn's *From Progressivism to Prosperity: World War I and American Society* (1986), Paul L. Murphy's *World War I and the Origin of Civil Liberties* (1979), and Frances R. Early's *A World Without War: How U.S. Feminists and Pacifists Resisted World War I* (1997).

3. It would do the class good for you to give a lecture on the fight for the League of Nations. See John Milton Cooper's *Breaking the Heart of the World: Woodrow Wilson and the Fight for the League of Nations* (2001), Ralph A. Stones's *The Irreconcilables* (1970), and Herbert Margulies's *The Mild Reservationists and the League of Nations* (1989).

4. In your lecture on World War I, you could describe how history textbooks in other countries describe American involvement in that conflict. *As Others See Us: International Views of American History*, edited by Donald W. Robinson (1969), is a good source for such information.

True/False Questions

T   1. Many immigrant groups in the United States supported the Central Powers in the European War.

T   2. For the early years of the war, all war reports coming to the United States had to be "cleared" through England.

272 / Chapter 25: America and the Great War

F   3. In the presidential election of 1916, Republicans used the slogan "He kept us out of war" to discredit Wilson.

F   4. The Zimmermann Telegram, sent to the Mexican government from the White House, was intercepted by the Germans.

F   5. "Four-Minute Men" were a special-operations unit of the U.S. Army.

T   6. The peace movement included Jane Addams, William Jennings Bryan, and Robert La Follette.

T   7. Nearly half a million southern blacks moved northward during the war years.

F   8. The percentage of women in the labor force in the 1920s was nearly double what it had been before World War I.

F   9. Former president Theodore Roosevelt was one of the biggest supporters of the League of Nations.

F   10. President Wilson suffered a temporarily incapacitating stroke in France while negotiating the peace treaty.

Multiple-Choice Questions

1. Which of the following statements best describes the diplomatic stance of Woodrow Wilson and William Jennings Bryan?
    A. America must, above all else, protect American interests around the world.
    B. America must not interfere in the affairs of other nations.
  * C. God expected America to spread democracy and moral progress throughout the world.
    D. America should prove its might wherever and whenever possible.

2. Concerning U.S. action in the Caribbean, President Wilson:
    A. firmly renounced the policies of Taft's "dollar diplomacy."
    B. announced that "American investments will be supported with American force to ensure American prosperity."
    C. argued that the United States should recognize any government that exercised de facto power.
  * D. kept marines in Nicaragua and sent marines to Haiti and the Dominican Republic.

3. Pancho Villa:
    A. was captured and executed by American forces in 1914.
    B. led the Mexican forces against an unsuccessful invasion by American marines and sailors at Vera Cruz.
    C. led the rebellion against Mexican President Porfirio Díaz.
*   D. killed a number of Americans in an attempt to provoke American intervention in Mexico.

4. All the following were members of the Triple Entente except:
*   A. Austria-Hungary.
    B. France.
    C. Great Britain.
    D. Russia.

5. When news of the European war first reached the United States:
    A. President Wilson immediately called on Congress to build up America's military strength.
    B. most old-line Americans were sympathetic to the Central Powers.
    C. Irish-Americans leaned toward support for the Allies.
*   D. most high government officials were pro-British.

6. President Wilson's response to the sinking of the *Lusitania*:
    A. was to sever diplomatic ties with Germany.
    B. included a speech in which he said that if Germany was responsible for the killing of any more Americans, then a state of war would exist between the United States and Germany.
    C. was conciliatory.
*   D. was a series of notes demanding that Germany stop such actions and pay reparations.

7. President Wilson's secretary of state resigned in 1915 because:
*   A. he thought Wilson's note to Germany denouncing the sinking of the *Lusitania* would draw America closer to war.
    B. he discovered that the *Lusitania* had carried a cargo of arms and ammunition.
    C. he disapproved of Wilson's conciliatory stance toward Germany.
    D. Wilson refused to sign the "*Arabic* pledge."

8. In the case of *Schenck v. United States*, the Supreme Court:
   A. struck down as unconstitutional the Lever Act, which had created the Food and Fuel Administrations.
   * B. upheld the conviction of a man who had circulated pamphlets against the draft.
   C. ruled that labor organizations as such did not fall under the jurisdiction of the War Industries Board.
   D. overturned the Espionage and Sedition Acts.

9. The Revenue Act of 1916:
   * A. was primarily to raise money to pay for war preparations.
   B. hit farmers and low-income Americans the hardest.
   C. was vetoed by President Wilson.
   D. is correctly represented by all the above statements.

10. In the presidential election of 1916, the Republicans:
    A. nominated Theodore Roosevelt.
    * B. lost by a small margin.
    C. nominated Woodrow Wilson.
    D. won by a large margin.

11. The Zimmermann Telegram:
    * A. asked for help from Mexico in the case of war between Germany and the United States.
    B. announced Germany's decision to wage unrestricted submarine warfare.
    C. announced the addition of three countries to the Central Powers.
    D. caused the United States to break diplomatic relations with Germany.

12. The congressional resolution for war:
    A. came quickly in response to the sinking of the *Lusitania*.
    * B. passed overwhelmingly.
    C. was divided strictly along party lines.
    D. included a provision that the United States would accept only an unconditional surrender from Germany.

13. The Food Administration:
    A. was headed by labor lawyer Frank P. Walsh.
    * B. taught Americans to plant "victory gardens" and to use leftovers wisely.
    C. used strict guidelines and coercive authority to achieve its goals.
    D. is correctly represented by all the above statements.

14. The most important of all the mobilization agencies was the:
    A. Fuel Administration.
    B. Emergency Fleet Corporation.
    C. United States Shipping Board.
  * D. War Industries Board.

15. George Creel:
    A. was the energetic leader of the War Labor Policies Board.
  * B. said that the best way to influence public opinion on the war was "expression, not repression."
    C. was the first and most celebrated conviction under the Espionage Act of 1917.
    D. was convicted under the "clear and present danger" doctrine.

16. Under the Espionage and Sedition Acts of 1917–1918:
    A. there were 25 prosecutions and 10 convictions.
    B. speaking and writing against Germany and Italy became a crime.
  * C. criticism of government leaders or war policies became a crime.
    D. censorship was aimed more at "middle America" than at socialists or other radicals.

17. The largest American action of the war was:
  * A. the Meuse-Argonne offensive.
    B. the Second Battle of the Marne.
    C. at Château-Thierry.
    D. just inside the German lines, near Metz.

18. The emphasis of Wilson's plan for peace was to:
    A. crush the military strength of the Central Powers.
    B. demand that the Central Powers pay the Allied nations for war damages.
    C. settle the issue of trade barriers.
  * D. ensure a lasting peace.

19. Some 8000 American troops landed in Russia in 1918:
    A. to help end the German occupation of Russia's eastern frontier.
  * B. when Russia signed a separate peace treaty with Germany.
    C. when Russia threatened to fight for the Central Powers.
    D. to fight the pro-Bolshevik "White" Russians.

20. In the mid-term elections of 1918:
    * A. Democrats lost control of both houses of Congress.
    B. labor, eastern businessmen, and western farmers expressed support for Democratic policies.
    C. Republican victories in the South were offset by heavy losses in the Northeast.
    D. Wilson asked voters to elect progressive candidates of either party.

21. To what did Wilson refer when he spoke of "the heart of the League"?
    A. the League of Nations army, which would enforce peace
    B. the Permanent Court of Justice, which would rule on international disputes
    * C. Article X, which would pledge members to consult on military and economic sanctions against aggressors
    D. the Assembly, which would allow each League member an equal voice

22. On the question of reparations:
    A. Wilson agreed with French and English officials that Germany should have to pay only for civilian damages.
    B. Wilson finally agreed that the German people should not be further humiliated by having to pay for the entire cost of the war.
    C. Germany finally agreed to pay just over $3 million.
    * D. French and British officials took a much harsher stance toward Germany than Wilson initially wished to.

23. When the Versailles Treaty came before the Senate:
    A. the Senate refused to ratify the treaty; it was not ratified until the reservationists' amendments had been added, in 1920.
    * B. Wilsonians refused to vote for an amended treaty.
    C. the Senate ratified it almost immediately, although several senators had wanted changes.
    D. the Senate refused to ratify it, and the United States remained technically at war with Germany until the end of World War II.

24. Which of the following groups in the Senate was the *smallest*?
    A. Wilsonians (favoring the Treaty of Versailles)
    B. reservationists (favoring the Treaty of Versailles with some changes limiting American participation in the League of Nations)

*   C. irreconcilables (completely opposing the Treaty of Versailles because of the provisions for the League of Nations)

D. The Wilsonians, reservationists, and irreconcilables were roughly equal in numbers.

25. The Spanish Flu epidemic:
    A. struck the United States in 1913.
    *   B. killed five times the number of Americans as died of combat deaths in France.
    C. ended suddenly in 1914.
    D. is correctly represented by all the above statements.

26. William Z. Foster is best associated with:
    A. Boston Police strike of 1919.
    B. Homestead strike of 1892.
    C. racial rioting during World War I.
    *   D. U.S. Steel strike of 1919.

27. The 1919 police strike in Boston:
    A. began when several officers protested their long hours and small pay by calling in sick.
    B. was settled when both sides agreed to submit to an arbitration panel.
    *   C. inadvertently launched a presidential career.
    D. launched the career of J. Edgar Hoover.

28. A race riot in which 38 people were killed and over 500 injured took place in July 1919 in:
    A. Albany, New York.
    B. Birmingham, Alabama.
    *   C. Chicago, Illinois.
    D. Detroit, Michigan.

29. The Red Scare of 1919–1920 reflected the:
    A. massive steel strikes around Chicago and in western Pennsylvania.
    B. tremendous growth of the Socialist party during World War I.
    *   C. impact of the Bolshevik Revolution in Russia and the actions of a "lunatic fringe" in the United States.
    D. demobilization of the American army.

30. The Red Scare of 1919–1920 was directed against:
    A. the Ku Klux Klan.
    B. blacks.
    C. labor unions.
    *   D. socialists and communists.

Essay Questions

1. Why did America enter the war in Europe when it did? Why did it not enter before?

2. Describe Wilson's Fourteen Points, discussing not only the details but the overall philosophy behind them as well.

3. Describe the economic mobilization on the American home front.

4. Why did the reservationists and the irreconcilables oppose the Treaty of Versailles? How effective was their opposition?

5. How and why were civil liberties curtailed during World War I? What was the effect of these curtailments?

Matching Questions

A) Massachusetts governor at time of Boston police strike
B) U.S. attorney general, led Red Scare
C) Wilson's first secretary of state
D) Wilson's second secretary of state
E) leading reservationist concerning League of Nations
F) head of Committee on Public Information
G) head of War Industries Board
H) Republican presidential candidate in 1916
I) World War I general
J) jailed for encouraging draft resistance

G   1. Bernard Baruch
C   2. William Jennings Bryan
A   3. Calvin Coolidge
F   4. George Creel
J   5. Eugene V. Debs
H   6. Charles Evans Hughes
D   7. Robert Lansing
E   8. Henry Cabot Lodge
B   9. A. Mitchell Palmer
I   10. John J. Pershing

Chapter 26

THE MODERN TEMPER

This chapter covers the defensive mood of the 1920s (nativism, the Klan, fundamentalism, and Prohibition), the new morality, the women's movement, the "New Negro," the influence of science on social thought, and the influence of modernism in literature and art.

Chapter Outline

I. The defensive mood of the 1920s
  A. America seemed to be changing, and these changes posed a threat to the older orthodoxies
  B. Nativism
    1. Sacco and Vanzetti
      a. Arrested for robbery and murder
      b. Their main crime might have been their political beliefs
      c. Executed despite public demonstrations on their behalf
    2. Immigration restriction
      a. Influence of racist pseudo-scientific studies
      b. New immigration quota law in 1924 favored old immigration from northern and western Europe
      c. New law allowed unrestricted immigration from Western Hemisphere countries
  C. The new Ku Klux Klan
    1. Unlike predecessor, devoted to "100% Americanism"
    2. The founding and early years of the new Klan
    3. Decline of the Klan
  D. Fundamentalism
    1. *The Fundamentals* (1910)
    2. William Jennings Bryan and other leaders against the teaching of evolution
    3. The Scopes Trial in Dayton, Tennessee
      a. The Tennessee antievolution law and the civil boosters of Dayton
      b. Bryan, Clarence Darrow, and the trial

        4. Death of Bryan and the decline of fundamentalism

  E. Prohibition

        1. Reasons for push for Prohibition

        2. Early prohibition movements

        3. Eighteenth Amendment ratified in 1919

        4. Problems of enforcement

           a. Illegal stills and rum-running

           b. Speakeasies

        5. Organized crime

           a. Prohibition gave new source of income

           b. Al Capone

        6. Decision to continue enforcement of Prohibition

II. The Roaring Twenties

  A. Defensive temper of the 1920s partly a reaction to social and intellectual revolution

  B. The Jazz Age

  C. F. Scott Fitzgerald chronicled the revolution

III. The new morality

  A. A revolution in manners and morals

  B. Growing awareness of Sigmund Freud's theories prompted discussion of sex

  C. Sex in books, magazines, and movies

  D. By 1930, the revolution was fading

  E. New views of marriage

        1. Roles within the family change

        2. Rise in divorce rate

IV. The women's movement

  A. Suffrage

        1. Margaret Sanger and birth control

           a. *The Woman Rebel*

           b. First family-planning clinic

           c. *Birth Control Review*

        2. Alice Paul and the militant movement

        3. Carrie Chapman Catt and the National Suffrage Association

        4. Woodrow Wilson finally endorsed the "Anthony Amendment"

        5. Nineteenth Amendment ratified in 1920

  B. The Equal Rights Amendment

        1. Promoted by Alice Paul and the Woman's party

        2. Introduced in Congress in 1923

        3. Congress did not adopt amendment until 1972; it then failed ratification

C. Working women
   1. Increases in number of voting women
   2. Most still in traditional occupations
   3. More opportunities for leisure and recreation

V. The "New Negro"
   A. In the Great Migration, nearly 1 million of the South's native blacks moved north
   B. Harlem Renaissance
      1. A rediscovery of black folk culture and an emancipation from the genteel tradition
      2. Writers of the Harlem Renaissance
   C. Negro nationalism
      1. Promoted black cultural expression and black exclusiveness
      2. Marcus Garvey the leading spokesman
   D. The NAACP
      1. Organized in 1910
      2. Main strategy of NAACP was legal action
      3. NAACP's attack on lynching
   E. Black political strength
      1. Oscar DePriest elected to Congress (first Negro congressman from the North)
      2. Successful fight against confirmation of John J. Parker for Supreme Court

VI. Science and social thought
   A. Isaac Newton's universe had been an ordered one with absolute standards; an infinite progress in knowledge seemed possible
   B. The work of Albert Einstein showed that everything is relative
   C. Werner Heisenberg's Uncertainty Principle indicated that human knowledge of the universe is limited

VII. The modernist movement in literature and art
   A. Features of modernism
   B. Modernism in art
   C. Modernism in literature
      1. Ezra Pound
      2. T. S. Eliot
      3. Gertrude Stein
      4. F. Scott Fitzgerald
      5. Ernest Hemingway

    D. The southern renaissance
       1. The Fugitives
       2. Thomas Wolfe
       3. William Faulkner

Lecture Ideas

1. An overview of the 1920s focusing in on America domestically will set up this chapter and Chapter 27. Lecture on all aspects of America in the 1920s (except presidential politics and the presidential synthesis). Be sure to include race, women, culture, prohibition, and others. See Lynn Bumenil's *The Modern Temper: America in the 1920s* (1995), David J. Goldberg's *Discontented America: The United States in the 1920s* (1999), and William E. Leuchtenburg's *The Perils of Prosperity* (1953).

2. The Scopes Trial allows you to divide your class in half and debate the merits of the case. Evolution versus creationism should make for a lively debate using the Scopes Trial to teach the issues as seen in that day plus a general lesson on courts and court procedures. You might even consider conducting a mock trial. See Edward Larson's *Summer for the Gods* (1997), Ray Ginger's *Six Days or Forever?* (1958), and Jeffrey P. Moran's *Scopes Trial: A Brief History with Documents* (2002).

3. A good source for a lecture on the tensions between old and new American values in the twenties is Charles Eagles's "Urban-Rural Conflict in the 1920s" (*The Historian*, Autumn 1986).

4. For a lecture on the New Negro, see the second chapter of Nathan Huggins's *Harlem Renaissance* (1971) for cultural aspects and the second chapter of Theodore G. Vincent's *Black Power and the Garvey Movement* (1971) for political aspects. For the New Woman, see part one of William H. Chafe's *The American Woman* (1972).

True/False Questions

F   1. The Ku Klux Klan of the 1920s was mainly a southern rural organization.

T   2. In the 1920s, people of Latin American descent became the fastest-growing ethnic minority in the United States.

T   3. By the time of the Prohibition Amendment, about three-quarters of the American people already lived in areas that were legally "dry."

F   4. Most fundamentalist victories came in the old Puritan strongholds of New England.

T   5. An obsession with sex permeated much of the literature and popular media of the 1920s.

F   6. The divorce rate declined in the 1920s.

T   7. The major American proponents of modernist literature lived in Europe.

F   8. "Flappers" was the slang word for illegal drinking establishments in the 1920s.

F   9. The NAACP favored militant protests over legal challenges as a way to end racial discrimination.

F   10. The culture of modernism emphasized order and certainty.

Multiple-Choice Questions

1. Nicola Sacco and Bartolomeo Vanzetti were:
   - A. convicted of bombing eight army supply trucks.
   - * B. two Italian-born anarchists sentenced to death and executed even though there was doubt as to their guilt.
   - C. finally exonerated of the charges of payroll robbery and murder.
   - D. murdered by members of the Ku Klux Klan.

2. The immigration quota laws passed in the 1920s:
   - A. favored immigrants from southern and eastern Europe.
   - * B. favored immigrants from northern and western Europe.
   - C. set strict limits on immigration from Mexico.
   - D. rescinded the "Gentlemen's Agreement" accepted during Theodore Roosevelt's administration.

3. The Ku Klux Klan of the 1920s was based mainly on:
   - * A. "100 percent Americanism."
   - B. prohibition.
   - C. fundamentalist religious beliefs.
   - D. antiblack rhetoric.

4. Who said, "When the hordes of aliens walk to the ballot box and their votes outnumber yours, then that alien horde has got you by the throat"?
   A. Clarence Darrow
   B. Ruth Benedict
   * C. William J. Simmons
   D. Moorefield Storey

5. The author of *Main Street*, a novel about the banality of small-town life, was:
   A. Sherwood Anderson.
   B. Countee Cullen.
   C. James Weldon Johnson.
   * D. Sinclair Lewis.

6. Which of the following statements about fundamentalists is *not* true?
   A. Their antimodernist attack often focused on Darwinism.
   * B. They stressed that the Bible should be studied in light of modern scholarship.
   C. They argued that the Bible could not be reconciled with evolution.
   D. Their belief was based, in part, on a literal interpretation of the Bible.

7. The Scopes trial:
   A. pitted William Howard Taft, former U.S. president and confessed agnostic, for the prosecution against fundamentalist Clarence Darrow for the defense.
   * B. concerned a state law that prohibited the teaching of evolution in public schools.
   C. marked the beginning of a large fundamentalist movement in America.
   D. is correctly represented by all the above statements.

8. Who insisted during the Scopes trial that a "great fish" had actually swallowed Jonah, that Joshua literally made the sun stand still, and that the world was created in 4004 B.C.?
   * A. William Jennings Bryan
   B. John T. Scopes
   C. Morris Shepard
   D. David C. Stevenson

9. The Volstead Act concerned:
   A. racial violence.
   B. organized crime.

C. immigration.

* D. prohibition.

10. The Amendment to the Constitution that barred the manufacture or sale of intoxicating liquors was ratified in:
    A. 1911.
    * B. 1919.
    C. 1928.
    D. 1932.

11. Which one of the following is associated with Dayton, Tennessee?
    * A. the Scopes Trial
    B. F. Scott Fitzgerald
    C. the lynching of three Italian anarchists
    D. Ernest Hemingway

12. The Wickersham Commission (1931):
    A. recommended that Congress pass a law forbidding the teaching of evolution.
    B. recommended that Congress pass an equal rights for women law.
    C. investigated Ku Klux Klan atrocities.
    * D. reported that enforcement of prohibition was ineffective.

13. The novel *This Side of Paradise* concerned:
    A. immigrant life in New York City.
    B. the lax enforcement of prohibition.
    * C. student life at Princeton.
    D. fundamentalist attacks on modernism.

14. Carrie Chapman Catt was best known for her achievements promoting:
    A. modernist art.
    B. prohibition.
    * C. women's suffrage.
    D. racial reforms.

15. Alice Paul:
    * A. was the militant head of the National American Woman Suffrage Association's Congressional Committee.
    B. was the pseudonym of Sylvia Jenkins, author of many stories in *Paris Nights* and other pulp magazines.
    C. wrote *The American Family*, a sociological study of the effects of the new morality on family life.
    D. was the main character in James Branch Cabell's novel *Jurgen*.

16. Which Amendment to the Constitution gave women the right to vote?
    A. Seventeenth
    B. Eighteenth
    * C. Nineteenth
    D. Twentieth

17. Congress adopted the Equal Rights Amendment in:
    A. 1912.
    B. 1921.
    C. 1931.
    * D. 1972.

18. Which of the following statements best describes working women in the 1920s?
    * A. The number of employed women rose.
    B. The number of employed women declined.
    C. Women were finally able to break into many formerly "male" occupations.
    D. A woman was finally elected president of the American Federation of Labor.

19. The movement of southern blacks to the North:
    A. was called the "Great Migration."
    B. created a steady growth of black political influence.
    C. involved nearly a million African Americans by 1930.
    * D. is correctly represented by all the above statements.

20. The author of *Cane*, considered by many to be the greatest single work of the Harlem Renaissance, was:
    A. Claude McKay.
    * B. Jean Toomer.
    C. DuBose Heyward.
    D. Langston Hughes.

21. The Universal Negro Improvement Association:
    A. sponsored black artists and writers.
    * B. was led by Marcus Garvey.
    C. promoted Booker T. Washington's idea of racial peace through accommodation.
    D. was the forerunner of the National Association for the Advancement of Colored People (NAACP).

22. Which one of the following was *not* known primarily as a jazz musician?
    A. King Oliver
    B. Jelly Roll Morton
    C. Louis Armstrong
    * D. Claude McKay

23. Judge John J. Parker:
    A. was backed by the NAACP for a seat on the Supreme Court.
    * B. failed to win confirmation to the Supreme Court, partly because the NAACP campaigned against him.
    C. retired from the Supreme Court in 1917 to lead the NAACP's legal attack on segregation.
    D. was killed by a bomb planted in his car by white supremacists.

24. Margaret Sanger is best associated with:
    A. equal rights for women.
    B. Prohibition.
    * C. birth control issues.
    D. income tax amendment.

25. Young single women participated in urban amusements for a variety of reasons *except*:
    A. adventure.
    B. autonomy.
    * C. profit.
    D. escape.

26. *The Waste Land*, a difficult poem that became the favorite of many modernist readers because of its sense of disillusionment and its suggestion of a burnt-out civilization, was written by:
    A. Franz Boas.
    * B. T. S. Eliot.
    C. Ezra Pound.
    D. Gertrude Stein.

27. Three of the following four novels were written by the same author. Which was not?
    A. *A Farewell to Arms*
    B. *For Whom the Bell Tolls*
    C. *The Old Man and the Sea*
    * D. *The Great Gatsby*

28. *The Sun Also Rises*:
    A. was an epic poem by Carl Sandburg that portrayed the patriotism of the American people through history.
   * B. described a group of Americans seeking fulfillment in Europe.
    C. was Ezra Pound's poetic justification of the excesses of the 1920s.
    D. told the story of a black sharecropping family that moved to Chicago in the 1920s.

29. The novels of Ernest Hemingway:
   * A. depicted the cult of athletic masculinity and a desperate search for life.
    B. portrayed utopian communities in a socialist society.
    C. attacked the corruption of machine politics in the large cities.
    D. traced the philosophical connections between twentieth-century America and eighteenth-century England.

30. The "Anthony Amendment" concerned:
   * A. women's suffrage.
    B. prohibition.
    C. religion in society.
    D. immigration restrictions.

Essay Questions

1. Describe the defensive temper of the 1920s. What factors contributed to it?

2. What were the political and cultural manifestations of a new sense of identity among blacks in the 1920s?

3. How did the scientific work of Albert Einstein and Werner Heisenberg influence American thought?

4. "The major theme in American society in the 1920s was the theme of newness." Defend this statement.

5. Describe the influence of modernism in literature.

Matching Questions

A) wrote *This Side of Paradise*
B) wrote *Look Homeward, Angel*, an autobiographical novel that described the author's youth in North Carolina
C) wrote "Rose is a rose is a rose is a rose"
D) wrote "The Love Song of J. Alfred Prufrock"
E) black congressman, elected from Chicago in 1928
F) as governor of Texas, eliminated textbooks that upheld Darwinism
G) developed principle of uncertainty
H) leading birth control advocate
I) leader of Negro nationalism
J) founder of KKK

E   1. Oscar DePriest
D   2. T. S. Eliot
F   3. Miriam Ferguson
A   4. F. Scott Fitzgerald
I   5. Marcus Garvey
G   6. Werner Heisenberg
H   7. Margaret Sanger
J   8. William J. Simmons
C   9. Gertrude Stein
B   10. Thomas Wolfe

Chapter 27

REPUBLICAN RESURGENCE AND DECLINE

This chapter covers the transformation of progressivism, domestic affairs in the administrations of Harding, Coolidge, and Hoover, the Republican prosperity of the 1920s, and the first three years of the Depression.

Chapter Outline

I. The transformation of progressivism
    A. Wilson's progressive coalition had dissolved by 1920
        1. Disillusionment over World War I
        2. Organized labor unhappy over strikes of 1919–1920
        3. Farmers dissatisfied with wartime price controls
        4. Intellectuals disillusioned by prohibition and anti-evolution movements
        5. Many of progressivism's major goals had been reached
    B. Progressivist impulse transformed to move for good government and public services

II. Harding's administration
    A. The election of 1920
        1. Warren Harding won the Republican nomination after the convention deadlocked
        2. James Cox won the Democratic nomination
        3. Victory for Harding, with 60 percent of the popular vote
    B. Harding as president
        1. Appointments included good and bad choices
        2. Harding lacked self-confidence as president
        3. Policies of Andrew Mellon
            a. Tax reductions for the rich
            b. A higher tariff
        4. Harding named conservative advocates of big business to head major regulatory agencies
    C. Corruption in Harding's administration
        1. Scandals of the Ohio Gang

        2. The Teapot Dome scandal
           a. Albert Fall of the Interior Department allowed private companies to exploit government-owned oil deposits
           b. Harding troubled by the scandals
        3. Harding's death spared him from public disgrace
        4. Recent assessments of Harding

III. The rise of Calvin Coolidge
    A. Became president at Harding's death
    B. Coolidge's character
    C. Election of 1924
        1. Coolidge, who controlled the party machinery, won the Republican nomination
        2. John W. Davis named candidate of divided Democratic party
        3. Progressive, Farmer-Labor, and Socialist parties named Robert La Follette
        4. Landslide victory for Coolidge; La Follette polled largest vote ever for third-party candidate

IV. Republican prosperity in the 1920s
    A. Much of prosperity fueled by growth of consumer-goods industries
        1. Motion pictures
        2. Radio broadcasting
    B. Advances in transportation
        1. Airplanes
           a. Industry foundered after World War I
           b. Acts providing government subsidies for manufacturers
           c. Amelia Earhart
        2. Automobiles
           a. Provided market for steel, glass, rubber, textiles, oil, and so forth
           b. Salient example of mass production

V. Coolidge's administration
    A. Economic stabilization
        1. Herbert Hoover (secretary of commerce) and "associationalism"
           a. Hoover's *American Individualism* (1922)
           b. Standardization in industry and business
           c. Promoted trade associations
        2. Supreme Court upheld trade associations

  B. Agricultural policies
    1. Agriculture still weak in the 1920s
    2. Commodity-marketing associations
    3. The American Farm Bureau Federation represented corporate attitudes of commercial farmers
    4. The Farm Bloc
        a. A coalition of western Republican and southern Democratic congressmen
        b. Legislation to aid farmers
    5. The McNary-Haugen bill
        a. Plan to dump surplus crops on world market to raise prices on home market
        b. Vetoed by Coolidge
  C. Labor policies
    1. Employers used various devices to keep out unions
        a. "American plan"—the open shop allowed employers not to hire unionists
        b. "Yellow-dog" contracts—workers forced to agree not to join union
        c. "Industrial democracy" and "welfare capitalism"— offered workers alternatives to unions
    2. Union membership declined in 1920s
    3. Gastonia strike of 1929

VI. Hoover's administration
  A. Election of 1928
    1. Republicans nominated Herbert Hoover
    2. Democrats nominated Alfred Smith
    3. Similarities in Republican and Democratic platforms
    4. The images of the candidates
    5. Victory for Hoover
  B. Hoover as progressive and humanitarian
  C. For farmers, Hoover endorsed the Agricultural Marketing Act, which supported farm cooperatives
  D. The Hawley-Smoot Tariff raised duties to all-time high
  E. The economy out of control
    1. The Florida real-estate boom
    2. Increased speculation in the stock market
    3. The stock market peaked on September 3, 1929

VII. Hoover in the Depression
  A. The stock market had its worst day on October 29
  B. Hoover's first action was to express hope, though wages fell and unemployment rose

    C. Reasons for the crash
       1. Economic factors
       2. Governmental policies
       3. The gold standard
    D. The human toll of the Depression
    E. Hoover's attempts at recovery
       1. Asked businessmen to let profits suffer before purchasing power
       2. Increased opportunities for credit
       3. The "Hooverization" of America
       4. Hoover kept to his philosophy of voluntarism
    F. In elections of 1930 Republicans lost control of both houses of Congress
    G. More attempts at recovery
       1. The Reconstruction Finance Corporation, to keep financial institutions open
       2. Glass-Steagall Act increased loan opportunities
       3. Federal Home Loan Act provided financing for home mortgages
       4. The Emergency Relief and Construction Act provided funds for public works programs

VIII. Protests against Hoover's policies
    A. Farmers
       1. Legislative programs brought farmers little relief
       2. Farmers protested by striking and blocking delivery of produce
    B. Communists
       1. Some successes
          a. Share Croppers Union in Alabama
          b. National Mine Workers' Union in Kentucky
       2. No significant increase in party membership
    C. Veterans
       1. Congress in 1924 had voted veterans' bonus payable in 1945
       2. The Bonus Expeditionary Force marched on Washington demanding immediate payment of the bonus
       3. Congress rejected their demands, but many veterans stayed in Washington
       4. Army used to evict veterans

Lecture Ideas

1. One way to show the emphasis on business during the 1920s would be to discuss Bruce Barton's *The Man Nobody Knows*, a best-seller that described Jesus Christ as a successful businessman (which was considered an extreme compliment). See Leo P. Ribuffo's "Jesus Christ as Business Statesman" (*American Quarterly*, June 1981), Roland Marchand's, *Creating the Corporate Steel: The Rise of Public Relations and Corporate Imagery in American Big Business* (1998), and James Gilbert's *Designing the Industrial State* (1972).

2. Divide the class up into three groups and assign each group a president to research who served in the 1920s. Then have group presentations highlighting each president. See John Hick's *Republican Ascendancy* (1960), Robert Ferrell's *The Strange Deaths of Warren G. Harding* (1996) and *The Presidency of Calvin Coolidge* (1998), and David Bruner's *Herbert Hoover* (1979).

3. A lecture on the Stock Market Crash of 1929 and the Great Depression is a must. See Robert McElvaines's *The Great Depression* (1983), David Kennedy's *Freedom of Fear* (1999), John Garraty's *The Great Depression* (1987), Michael Bernstein's *The Great Depression* (1989), and John K. Galbraith's *The Great Crash, 1929* (1955).

True/False Questions

F   1. The biggest scandal under President Hoover was the "Teapot Dome" affair of 1930.

F   2. Warren G. Harding was shot by the assassin Charles Guiteau.

T   3. According to Calvin Coolidge, the president should passively defer to Congress.

T   4. The Hawley-Smoot Tariff raised import duties to an all-time high.

F   5. Businessmen flew "Hoover flags" to show their support for the president's hands-off approach to the Depression.

F   6. The federal government refused to assist the young aircraft industry in the 1920s.

F   7. Robert La Follette said, "The chief business of the American people is business."

T   8. "Parity," as used in this chapter, refers to farm prices.

T   9. More than any previous president, Hoover got the government involved in efforts to relieve the effects of economic depression.

F   10. Politically, Democrats suffered most from the stock market crash and the beginning of the Depression.

Multiple-Choice Questions

1. The progressive coalition that elected Woodrow Wilson president dissolved by 1920 for all the following reasons *except*:
   * A. many of the progressive reforms still seemed unattainable.
   B. intellectuals became disillusioned because of popular support for prohibition and the antievolution movement.
   C. radicals and pacifists became disenchanted with America's entrance into the Great War and the war's aftermath.
   D. the middle class became more interested in business than reform.

2. The result in the presidential election of 1920 might be attributed to:
   A. the smear campaign directed against Democratic candidate A. Mitchell Palmer.
   * B. the fact that Americans in the 1920s were "tired of issues, sick at heart of ideals, and weary of being noble."
   C. Southerners who expressed their displeasure at President Wilson's policies by voting Republican.
   D. all the above.

3. The "Ohio Gang":
   A. rivaled Charlie Chaplin in box office receipts in the 1920s.
   * B. was a group of President Harding's friends who were named to political office.
   C. was a group of angry young men in a short story by Sinclair Lewis about the consumer culture.
   D. hosted the first national radio program.

4. The tariff policy of the early 1920s:
   A. made it easier for other nations to sell to the United States.
   * B. made it harder for other nations to sell to the United States.
   C. made it easier for other nations to repay their war debts.
   D. led Americans to cut back on loans and investments abroad.

5. Harding's secretary of the treasury:
   A. favored retaining the high wartime level of taxation in order to build up the public treasury.
   * B. favored a reduction of the high wartime level of taxation, but mainly for the rich.
   C. favored a reduction of the high wartime level of taxation, but mainly for the poor and middle class.
   D. persuaded Congress to drop the personal income tax instituted under Wilson.

6. On the issue of regulating big business, President Harding:
   A. showed his support for regulation by pressuring Congress to pass stricter laws.
   * B. named conservative advocates of big business to head the Interstate Commerce Commission and the Federal Trade Commission.
   C. and his administration brought a record number of suits against corporations.
   D. named Robert La Follette, a former leading progressive, to head a government commission to investigate unfair business practices.

7. The biggest scandal of the Harding administration:
   A. led to an attempt to impeach Harding that fell just four votes short of success in the House of Representatives.
   B. concerned a corrupt U.S. customs official who had regularly allowed Chinese imports into the country duty free.
   C. was the impeachment of the attorney general for fraudulent handling of German assets seized after World War I.
   * D. involved the leasing of government-owned oil deposits to private companies.

8. In the 1924 presidential election:
   A. Robert M. La Follete barely won the nomination of a faction-ridden Republican party.
   B. the Democratic candidate almost upset the Republican candidate.
   * C. Calvin Coolidge swept both the popular and electoral votes by decisive majorities.
   D. A. Mitchell Palmer was the Democratic candidate.

9. John W. Davis:
    * A. was the Democratic presidential candidate in 1924.
    B. invented the radio.
    C. starred in *The Jazz Singer*.
    D. was the first head of the Federal Communications Commission.

10. Coolidge's administration was marked by:
    A. a continuation of the post-World War I economic slump.
    B. continued tax breaks for the lower and middle classes at the expense of the upper class.
    * C. prosperity.
    D. the creation of the Internal Revenue and Tariff Commission, which drastically reformed taxation formulas and duty lists.

11. The arrival of the modern motion picture was marked by a 1915 movie based on Thomas Dixon's novel *The Clansman*. This movie was:
    * A. *Birth of a Nation*.
    B. *Sons of the South*.
    C. *Adam's Children*.
    D. *The Wilderness*.

12. The rise of the automobile:
    * A. was aided by Henry Ford's mass-production innovations.
    B. encouraged the sprawl of suburbs and sparked real-estate booms.
    C. quickened the good-roads movement.
    D. All the above statements are true.

13. As secretary of commerce, Herbert Hoover:
    A. endorsed strict laissez-faire policies to allow businesses to govern themselves.
    * B. supported the trade-association movement.
    C. pushed for stricter regulation of big business in order to protect individual Americans.
    D. supported trust-busting legislation and Justice Department lawsuits.

14. In the 1920s, farm prices:
    A. kept at their high wartime levels.
    B. kept at their low wartime levels.
    * C. fell sharply.
    D. rose sharply.

15. The farm organizations of the 1920s:
    A. moved more toward a political alliance with urban leaders.
    B. opposed the concept of marketing associations.
    * C. saw farmers as profit-conscious businessmen.
    D. were generally sympathetic to the Populists' approach to agricultural reform.

16. The McNary-Haugen bill:
    * A. called for dumping surplus crops on the world market in order to raise domestic prices.
    B. failed to pass Congress in 1922 but passed in 1927 with the support of President Coolidge.
    C. effectively raised domestic commodity prices.
    D. is correctly represented by all the above statements.

17. In "yellow-dog" contracts, employers:
    A. agreed to submit all grievances to an arbitration panel whose decision was binding.
    * B. forced workers to agree to stay out of unions.
    C. agreed to hire only union workers.
    D. agreed to automatic wage increases in return for the workers' promise not to strike.

18. In the 1920s, labor unions:
    A. won a number of important victories in the Supreme Court.
    B. gained about 1.5 million members.
    * C. lost about 1.5 million members.
    D. were helped by the prosperity of the decade.

19. The Democrats lost the presidential election of 1928 because:
    A. most Americans would not vote for a former Methodist minister from Nebraska who had written two books on the evils of drinking.
    * B. Americans were pleased with the Republican prosperity of the 1920s.
    C. the Democratic candidate had offended Catholic and immigrant voters.
    D. the Socialist candidate split the reform vote.

20. President Herbert Hoover's progressive and humanitarian reforms included all the following *except*:
    A. supporting a plan for tax reductions in the lower-income brackets.
    B. rejecting "red hunts" or interference with the peaceful picketing of the White House.
    C. seeking financial assistance for all-black Howard University.
  * D. supporting a bill to provide federal financial assistance to lower-income families.

21. The uneven distribution of wealth in America helped cause the Depression because:
  * A. as production increased, demand declined.
    B. corporations no longer had sufficient capital to expand their productive capacities.
    C. many people no longer had extra money to invest in stocks.
    D. Americans with less spending power began buying cheaper imported goods rather than American-made goods.

22. Part of the reason for the stock market crash was:
    A. the high rate of deflation in the 1920s.
    B. the tax policies of the 1920s that hurt the wealthy, who might otherwise have bought more stocks.
  * C. the buying of great amounts of stock "on margin."
    D. the low tariff, which allowed imports to corner several important American markets.

23. All the following were governmental policies that contributed to the crash *except*:
  * A. increased taxes on upper levels of income.
    B. hostility toward labor unions (which worsened income balances).
    C. high tariffs.
    D. lax enforcement of antitrust laws.

24. How many people were out of work in early 1933?
    A. 130,000
    B. 1.3 million
  * C. 13 million
    D. 1.3 billion

25. Hoover's early efforts to end the Depression included:
    - A. cutbacks in public works, to shore up the public treasury.
    - B. a stricter credit policy by the Federal Reserve, to stop the flow of "easy money" available for speculation.
    - C. an increase in aid to farmers, to allow them to produce more.
    - * D. asking businessmen to maintain wages and avoid layoffs, in order to keep purchasing power strong.

26. In the elections of 1930:
    - A. Herbert Hoover was soundly defeated by Franklin D. Roosevelt.
    - B. Herbert Hoover won a second term as president, but by a very small margin.
    - C. Republicans won a majority in the House of Representatives.
    - * D. Democrats won a majority in the House of Representatives.

27. In 1931, just as economic indicators were beginning to rise:
    - A. New York's Chase Manhattan Bank closed, increasing investors' panic and setting off runs on other banks.
    - * B. Austria's largest bank closed, triggering a panic that swept through Europe and caused European investors to withdraw their American gold and dump their American securities.
    - C. a drought in the Midwest caused crop failures that raised food prices and increased panic.
    - D. the tax increase of 1928 took effect, suddenly lessening the purchasing power of the average consumer.

28. The Reconstruction Finance Corporation:
    - A. was created over Hoover's veto.
    - * B. offered emergency loans to banks, farm mortgage associations, building and loan societies, and other such businesses to prevent bankruptcies.
    - C. was criticized for its alleged favoritism to farmers and workers.
    - D. is correctly represented by all the above statements.

29. In the early years of the Depression, farmers:
    A. suffered less than most other groups.
    B. were hurt by the McNary-Haugen Act, which cut farm assistance nearly in half.
    C. supported Hoover's Emergency Relief and Construction Act, which provided loans to prevent agricultural bankruptcies.
    * D. often lost their farms as their income continued to fall.

30. The "Bonus Expeditionary Force":
    A. consisted of angry farmers who sometimes acted outside the law to prevent the foreclosure of mortgages on their farms.
    B. toured the country to create support for the Communist party.
    * C. marched on Washington in an attempt to get immediate payment of a veterans' bonus that Congress had voted in 1924.
    D. was a special division within the army created to help local authorities deal with disturbances.

Essay Questions

1. What had the progressivism of the prewar period turned into by the 1920s? What factors led to this transformation?

2. What did Warren G. Harding mean by "normalcy"? Is that a good term to describe the 1920s?

3. How might the decade of the 1920s be called "the decade of prosperity?

4. Discuss the various causes of the stock market crash, paying particular attention to government policies that helped bring on the crash.

5. Describe Herbert Hoover's attempts at recovery in the first three years of the Depression. Which of his policies were effective? What more might he have done?

Matching Questions

A)   secretary of the treasury
B)   movie director
C)   secretary of the interior
D)   cleared out "rioting" veterans from Washington in summer of 1932
E)   died in 1923
F)   wrote *American Individualism*
G)   Republican vice-presidential candidate in 1920
H)   Democratic presidential candidate in 1928
I)   Supreme Court chief justice
J)   Progressive party presidential candidate in 1924

G   1. Calvin Coolidge
B   2. D.W. Griffith
E   3. Warren G. Harding
C   4. Albert Fall
F   5. Herbert Hoover
J   6. Robert La Follette
D   7. Douglas MacArthur
A   8. Andrew Mellon
H   9. Al Smith
I   10. William H. Taft

Chapter 28

NEW DEAL AMERICA

This chapter covers FDR's election, the first Hundred Days, opposition to the New Deal from the left and the Supreme Court, the second Hundred Days, labor and the New Deal, the slump of 1937, economic policy and the New Deal, and the legacy of the New Deal.

Chapter Outline

I. From Hoover to FDR
- A. The parties in 1932
    1. Republicans
        - a. Renominated Herbert Hoover
        - b. Mood of defeat
    2. Democrats
        - a. Nominated FDR
        - b. FDR promised "a new deal for the American people"
- B. FDR's rise
    1. Early political career
    2. Platform
    3. Voters had confidence in FDR
- C. The election of 1932
- D. FDR takes office
    1. The long wait
        - a. Four months until inauguration
        - b. Hoover refused to allow FDR to begin policies until inauguration
        - c. Depression's panic spread
    2. FDR's inauguration
        - a. Speech stressed hope and promised change
        - b. "The analogue of war"

II. The first Hundred Days
- A. Strengthening America's finances
    1. The banking crisis
        - a. FDR declared four-day banking holiday
        - b. Emergency Banking Relief Act

        c. FDR's "fireside chats" assured banks' safety

        d. By March 15, banking crisis over

    2. Economy Act

    3. The end of Prohibition

    4. The problem of debt

        a. Farm Credit Administration

        b. Emergency Farm Mortgage Act and Farm Credit Act

        c. Home Owners' Loan Corporation

    5. Banking and investment reforms

        a. Federal Deposit Insurance Corporation

        b. Federal Securities Act

    6. Devaluing the currency

B. Relief Measures

    1. Civilian Conservation Corps

    2. Federal Emergency Relief Administration

    3. Civil Works Administration

C. Agricultural recovery through controlled production

    1. The Agricultural Adjustment Act

    2. Success of the programs

    3. The Dust Bowl and "Okies"

    4. Supreme Court, in *United States* v. *Butler*, ended AAA

    5. Soil Conservation and Domestic Allotment Act

    6. Second Agricultural Adjustment Act

D. Industrial recovery—the National Industrial Recovery Act

    1. Public Works Administration

    2. National Recovery Administration

    3. Codes of fair practice

    4. Criticism of the NRA

    5. NRA struck down by Supreme Court

    6. Legacy of the NRA

        a. Set new standards

        b. Spurred growth of unions

        c. Advanced trend of stabilization

E. The Tennessee Valley Authority

    1. Started as power and nitrate plants at Muscle Shoals, Alabama

    2. New objectives: overall regional planning

    3. Rural Electrification Administration helped spread electricity through rural areas

III. The human cost of Depression

    A. Continuing hardships

    B. Dust bowl migrants

  C. Minorities and the New Deal
   1. Effects of farm programs
   2. Mexican Americans
   3. Native Americans
  D. Court decisions and black voters

IV. Culture in the thirties
  A. Writers and "social significance"
   1. John Steinbeck
   2. Richard Wright
  B. Popular art and social documentary expression in the 1930s
  C. Popular culture during the Depression

V. Opposition to the New Deal
  A. Early support for Roosevelt's programs
  B. Conservative opposition
  C. Thunder on the left
   1. Huey Long
   2. Francis Townsend
   3. Charles Coughlin
   4. Pushed Roosevelt to "steal the thunder" of the left
  D. The Supreme Court and the New Deal
   1. Struck down NIRA (*Schechter Poultry Corporation* v. *United States*)
   2. Entire New Deal seemed in danger

VI. The Second New Deal
  A. National Labor Relations Act
  B. Social Security Act
  C. Revenue Act of 1935 (Wealth Tax Act)
  D. The Second New Deal and the left

VII. The election of 1936
  A. FDR's popularity
  B. Republicans nominated Alfred M. Landon
  C. Democrats create a new electoral coalition
  D. Landslide victory for FDR

VIII. FDR and the Supreme Court
  A. The Court's decisions seemed to endanger the New Deal
  B. FDR decided to enlarge the Court, to enable him to appoint pro–New Deal justices
  C. Court-packing scheme met with much opposition
  D. Court packing became unnecessary

IX. Labor in the New Deal
   A. Growth of unions
   B. Industrial unions
      1. Movement to organize workers in mass-production industries
      2. Craft unions in AFL opposed to industrial unions
      3. Formation of CIO
   C. The CIO
      1. Success in automobile industry
      2. Success in steel industry
      3. CIO had soon unionized much of industrial America

X. The slump of 1937
   A. Sharper than crash of 1929
   B. Reasons for slump
   C. Economic theories
      1. Less government spending and a balanced budget
      2. Renewed spending

XI. Economic policy and reform
   A. Recovering from the slump of 1937
   B. Wagner-Steagall Housing Act
   C. Bankhead-Jones Farm Tenant Act
   D. Other Acts
      1. Agricultural Adjustment Act
      2. Food, Drug and Cosmetics Act
      3. Fair Labor Standards Act

XII. The legacy of the New Deal
   A. FDR and the Democratic party
      1. Southern Democrats drifted toward a coalition with conservative Republicans
      2. The conservative opposition
      3. FDR's efforts to cleanse Democratic party
      4. In the election of 1938, the Democratic majorities in Congress began to slip
         a. Factions in Democratic party
         b. Growth of conservative opposition
   B. The Half Way Revolution
      1. Through the 1930s the power of the national government was vastly enlarged
      2. FDR had taken the road between the extremes of laissez-faire and socialism

Lecture Ideas

1. A general lecture on the New Deal will establish the rest of the 1930s material. Focus on Roosevelt's plans for getting America out of its worst depression in history. See Ronald Edforth's *The New Deal: America's Response to the Great Depression* (2000) and Anthony J. Badger's *The New Deal: The Depression Years, 1933–1940* (1989).

2. Divide the class up into various groups and have each research the life and career of Franklin D. Roosevelt. The class can look at his life as governor of New York, public service to his country, and all four terms of his presidency. See Kenneth Davis's three-volume collection *FDR* (1985, 1986, 1993), Arthur Schlesinger's *The Coming of the New Deal* (1959), and Richard Polenberg's *The Era of Franklin D. Roosevelt* (2000).

3. For a lecture on Roosevelt's court-packing scheme, William E. Leuchtenburg's essay on that topic in *Essays on the New Deal*, edited by Harold M. Hollingsworth and William F. Holmes (1969), and William Leuchtenburg's *The Supreme Court Reborn* (1995).

4. A lecture on the political challenges to FDR would also be helpful to the students. You could focus on Huey Long and Father Charles Coughlin. See Alan Brinkley's *Voices of Protest* (1982), David Warren's *Radio Priest* (1996), and William Hair's *The Kingfish and His Realm* (1991).

True/False Questions

T 1. During the 1932 presidential campaign, the Republican and Democratic candidates both promised generally to balance the budget.

T 2. The Twentieth Amendment moved the presidential inauguration date from March to January.

F 3. The HOLC addressed the problem of overcharging by doctors and others in the medical and health professions.

T 4. "Okies" were people who traveled west to escape the effects of the Dust Bowl or because they had been driven off the land by New Deal benefit programs.

T 5. By 1935, the NRA had become unpopular.

F   6. The Fair Labor Standards Act forbade racial discrimination in hiring.

T   7. The American Liberty League opposed New Deal measures as violations of personal and property rights.

T   8. FDR called the Social Security Act the "most significant achievement" of the New Deal.

F   9. Eleanor Roosevelt was a shy person who shunned attention, but she did much work behind the scenes to raise support for her husband's New Deal.

T   10. Despite the New Deal, full recovery from the Depression did not come until the crisis of World War II.

Multiple-Choice Questions

1. Franklin D. Roosevelt:
   * A. was permanently crippled after contracting polio.
   B. was twice elected governor of Georgia.
   C. was born into a family of sharecroppers.
   D. supported the continuation of Prohibition.

2. In the presidential election of 1932:
   * A. radical Socialist and Communist party candidates won nearly one million votes.
   B. Franklin D. Roosevelt's training as vice-president under Herbert Hoover helped him win the Democratic nomination.
   C. Republican Alfred Landon won the electoral votes of only six states.
   D. Franklin D. Roosevelt promised to continue the economic policies of Herbert Hoover.

3. Between the election in November 1932 and Roosevelt's inauguration in March 1933:
   A. leading economic indicators showed an upswing in the nation's economy.
   B. many banks that had been closed since 1929 reopened.
   C. President Hoover asked Roosevelt to consult with congressional leaders on "this most serious matter of national concern."
   * D. the panic of the Depression spread.

4. The main purpose of the Civilian Conservation Corps was to:
   A. train young men for the Army Corps of Engineers.
   * B. provide work relief for young men.
   C. give young women an opportunity to earn money for higher education.
   D. promote conservation practices by the general public.

5. The "Blue Eagle" was the symbol of compliance for the:
   A. AAA.
   B. FERA.
   * C. NRA.
   D. WPA.

6. The Federal Emergency Relief Administration:
   A. was created during the first Hundred Days.
   B. often gave financial assistance to the needy through the dole rather than through work.
   C. was actually administered through the states.
   * D. is correctly represented by all the above statements.

7. The goal of the Agricultural Adjustment Act of 1933 was to raise farm income mainly through:
   * A. cutbacks in production.
   B. intensive farming.
   C. marketing quotas.
   D. state and federal subsidies.

8. Among the objectives of the Tennessee Valley Authority were all the following *except*:
   A. the production of cheap electric power.
   * B. the development of air transportation.
   C. flood control.
   D. soil conservation and forestry.

9. "Codes of fair practice" were part of:
   A. FDIC.
   B. HOLC.
   * C. NRA.
   D. PWA.

10. Huey Long:
    * A. was from Louisiana.
    B. founded the National Union for Social Justice.
    C. challenged FDR for the Democratic presidential nomination in 1936.
    D. complained that the New Deal had gone too far by infringing on "the rights of persons and property."

11. In the case of *Schechter Poultry Corporation* v. *United States*, the Supreme Court:
    A. overturned the Farm Credit Act.
    * B. overturned the National Industrial Recovery Act.
    C. decided that Schechter was involved in interstate, not local, trade.
    D. upheld the constitutionality of the second Agricultural Adjustment Act.

12. The National Labor Relations Act:
    A. was upheld by the Supreme Court in *United States* v. *Butler*.
    B. gave jobs to several thousand unemployed miners.
    * C. was often called the Wagner Act.
    D. was struck down by the Supreme Court in 1935.

13. Which of the following statements about the Social Security Act is *not* true?
    A. It was, according to Roosevelt, the "supreme achievement" of the New Deal.
    B. It committed the national government to a broad range of welfare activities.
    C. It provided old-age pensions.
    * D. It was based on a progressive tax that took a larger percentage of higher incomes.

14. The Revenue Act of 1935 (sometimes called the Wealth Tax Act):
    A. provided for a regressive tax.
    B. increased federal revenue significantly and thus helped finance the New Deal.
    * C. raised taxes on incomes above $50,000.
    D. created a more equal distribution of wealth in America.

15. In the case of *Norris* v. *Alabama*, the Supreme Court:
    A. upheld the state's Democratic white primary.
    B. overturned a state law restricting the sale of petroleum products beyond certain quotas.

* C. ruled that the systematic exclusion of blacks from juries denied defendants equal protection of the law.
    D. dealt a major blow to FDR's New Deal.

16. Which of the following groups would have been least likely to support Roosevelt in the election of 1936?
    A. ethnic groups in northern cities
    B. labor unions
* C. wealthy businessmen
    D. blacks

17. In the presidential election of 1936:
    A. African Americans voted overwhelmingly Republican for the first time since Reconstruction.
    B. Republicans won most of the western farm vote and almost upset Roosevelt.
* C. Republicans hoped that third-party candidates might split the Democratic vote and throw the election to them.
    D. Socialist and Communist candidates together received over two million votes.

18. Roosevelt's court-packing scheme became unnecessary when:
    A. the Supreme Court ruled that the president, and not Congress, has authority to adjust the number of justices.
    B. the Supreme Court agreed to an extension of the number of justices.
    C. Congress removed cases involving the New Deal from the Supreme Court's jurisdiction.
* D. the Supreme Court began reversing previous judgments and upholding the New Deal.

19. The "sit-down strike" was used successfully in 1937 by:
    A. black workers.
    B. southern workers.
    C. steel workers.
* D. automobile workers.

20. Labor's "new direction" in the late 1930s was toward:
    A. decentralization of union organization.
* B. industrial unions.
    C. women in unions.
    D. the Republican party.

21. The 1937 economic slump was caused in part by:
    * A. a sharp decrease in government spending.
    B. a sharp rise in private spending.
    C. the huge government deficit.
    D. the repeal of the Revenue Act of 1935.

22. Keynesian economics called for:
    * A. more government spending in times of economic downswing.
    B. a balanced budget in times of economic downswing.
    C. a higher tariff wall.
    D. a return to the gold standard.

23. In the elections of 1938:
    A. Roosevelt was defeated in his bid for reelection.
    * B. Roosevelt's attempts to "purge" the Democratic party were largely unsuccessful.
    C. Republicans won control of the House and the Democrats kept a majority of only two in the Senate.
    D. Republicans won control of the Senate and Democrats kept a majority of only two in the House.

24. The Farm Security Administration:
    A. administered the Agricultural Adjustment Act of 1937 (the "Second AAA").
    * B. offered loans to marginal farmers (so they could avoid falling into tenancy) and to tenant farmers (so they could purchase their own farms).
    C. provided federal subsidies for the expansion of large farms.
    D. established educational programs to teach farmers new agricultural methods.

25. The conservative Democratic opposition to the New Deal in the late 1930s:
    * A. was heaviest in the South.
    B. succeeded in removing three of Roosevelt's cabinet members.
    C. supported plans to replace Roosevelt with Henry Wallace as the Democratic presidential candidate in 1936.
    D. supported plans to replace Roosevelt with Huey Long as the Democratic presidential candidate in 1936.

26. Charles E. Coughlin:
    * A. was a "radio priest" and founder of the National Union for Social Justice.
    B. headed the TVA.
    C. headed the BIA.
    D. wrote *Uncle Tom's Children*.

27. Muscle Shoals, Alabama, was:
    * A. where the TVA began.
    B. where FDR vacationed.
    C. where Huey Long was born.
    D. the home of Francis E. Townsend.

28. The Indian Reorganization Act:
    * A. attempted to reinvigorate traditional Indian cultures.
    B. broke up tribal lands and allocated them to individuals.
    C. had the support of western congressmen and assimilated Indians.
    D. is correctly represented by all the above statements.

29. The literary work that best captured the ordeal of the Depression was *The Grapes of Wrath* by:
    A. Lucy Mercer.
    B. Margaret Mitchell.
    C. Paul Muni.
    * D. John Steinbeck.

30. Richard Wright:
    A. led the conservative outcry against New Deal business regulation.
    B. starred in the original version of *Scarface*.
    * C. wrote *Native Son*, a story of racial prejudice.
    D. was the outspoken head of the Farm Security Administration.

Essay Questions

1. Describe the gains made by labor during the New Deal.

2. How did the "thunder on the left" shape New Deal policies?

3. Why did Roosevelt attempt to "pack" the Supreme Court? Did he achieve his goals?

4. How did New Deal reforms attempt to raise farm prices and stabilize industry?

5. How did the nation's perceptions of the role of government—its powers and responsibilities—change in the 1930s?

Matching Questions

A) Republican presidential candidate in 1932
B) Share Our Wealth program
C) Texas congressman, referred to New Dealers as "Red Dupes"
D) BIA commissioner
E) Republican presidential candidate in 1936
F) CIO leader
G) proposed to pay $200 a month to those over 60 who retired and promised to spend the money
H) wrote *The General Theory of Employment, Interest, and Money*
I) director of the TVA
J) headed the FERA and the WPA

D   1. John Collier
C   2. Martin Dies
A   3. Herbert Hoover
J   4. Harry L. Hopkins
H   5. John Maynard Keynes
E   6. Alfred M. Landon
F   7. John L. Lewis
I   8. David E. Lilienthal
B   9. Huey Long
G   10. Francis E. Townsend

Chapter 29

FROM ISOLATION TO GLOBAL WAR

This chapter covers American foreign policy between the wars, the portents of war in Europe and Asia, American neutrality, the war in Europe, American aid to Britain, and Japanese aggression leading to Pearl Harbor.

Chapter Outline

I. Isolationism vs. internationalism
 A. America seemed to favor isolationism
 B. America could not stay isolated
 C. America and the League of Nations

II. War debts and reparations
 A. Allied debt to America renegotiated to $11.5 billion
 B. Allies felt they should not pay
 C. German reparations
 D. Johnson Debt Default Act of 1934

III. Disarmament
 A. Concern for growth of Japanese power
 B. Strains in Japanese-American relations
  1. Japan's growth in the Pacific
  2. Japan's growth in China
 C. Washington Armaments Conference (1921)
  1. Five-Power Naval Treaty
   a. America, Britain, Japan, France, and Italy
   b. Tonnage limits, moratorium on capital ship-building, no further fortification of Pacific possessions
  2. Four-Power Treaty
   a. America, France, Britain, and Japan
   b. Each would respect others' Pacific possessions
  3. Nine-Power Treaty
   a. Five Powers plus China, Belgium, Portugal, and the Netherlands

        b. Agreed to support the Open-Door Policy and the territorial integrity of China

    4. Effect of treaties

IV. Attempts to outlaw war

    A. Growth of peace societies and programs

    B. Kellogg-Briand Pact (Pact of Paris)

V. The "Good Neighbor" Policy

    A. Policy of peace and noninvolvement in Latin America

    B. Examples

        1. U.S. paid Colombia $25 million for canal

        2. American forces pulled out of the Dominican Republic and Nicaragua

        3. Peacefully solved problem with Mexico of expropriation of American oil properties

        4. Clark memorandum

        5. Platt Amendment, with its provisions allowing intervention in Cuba, abrogated

VI. War clouds

    A. In the Far East

        1. Japanese seizure of Manchuria

        2. American reaction

    B. In Europe

        1. Italy

            a. Mussolini had wide appeal

            b. By 1925 Mussolini was dictator

        2. Germany

            a. Hitler and National Socialist (Nazi) Party

            b. Reichsführer in 1934

    C. America's reaction

        1. Isolationism

        2. Internationalism

            a. Trade Agreements Act

            b. Diplomatic recognition of Soviet Russia

    D. The war clouds spread

        1. Japan

            a. War with China

            b. Signed "Anti-Comintern Pact" with Germany and Italy

        2. Spain

            a. Civil War

            b. Franco established Fascist dictatorship

      3. Italy
         a. Conquest of Ethiopia
         b. Conquest of Albania
      4. Germany
         a. Hitler's early attacks and conquests
         b. When Hitler invaded Poland, Britain and France declared war on Germany

VII. American neutrality
    A. Nye Committee's "merchants of death"
    B. Neutrality Act of 1935
      1. Forbade sale of arms or munitions to belligerents
      2. Weakness of act soon became apparent
    C. America and the Spanish Civil War
      1. Roosevelt refused to intervene
      2. Neutrality laws extended to cover civil wars
    D. Neutrality Act of 1937
      1. Provisions
      2. In Chinese-Japanese confrontation, Roosevelt did not invoke act—a step away from isolationism
    E. Roosevelt's "quarantine" speech—another step from isolationism
    F. *Panay* incident
    G. Neutrality against Germany weakened
      1. After the German occupation of Czechoslovakia, Roosevelt no longer pretended to be impartial
      2. Neutrality Act of 1939
      3. American attitudes continued to vacillate

VIII. The storm in Europe
    A. *Blitzkrieg* (spring 1940)
      1. Denmark, Belgium, Norway, and the Netherlands
      2. Mussolini entered the war
      3. The fall of France
    B. American defense
      1. Increased defense budget
      2. National Defense Research Committee set up to coordinate military research
    C. Aid for Britain
      1. Battle of Britain ended threat of German invasion
      2. United States gave fifty "overage" destroyers to Britain in return for leases on naval and air bases
    D. First peacetime conscription
    E. Continued debate in America

IX. The election of 1940
   A. The candidates
      1. Republicans chose Wendell Willkie
      2. Democrats chose Roosevelt again
   B. The campaigns
      1. Roosevelt too busy to campaign
      2. Willkie attacked FDR's foreign policy
   C. Roosevelt won an unprecedented third term

X. The Lend-Lease Act
   A. Provisions
   B. Isolationists opposed to bill

XI. War continued to spread in Europe
   A. German victories and defeats
   B. The Atlantic Charter
   C. German attacks on American vessels
   D. American reaction
      1. Convoying ships
      2. End of neutrality

XII. The storm in the Pacific
   A. Japanese aggressions
      1. Movement into French Indochina
      2. Tripartite Pact with Germany and Italy
      3. Nonaggression pact with Russia
   B. America's reaction
      1. Restricted oil exports to Japan
      2. Organized the armed forces of the Philippines into the U.S. Army
   C. Japanese-American negotiations
   D. Japanese attack on Pearl Harbor
   E. The same day, Japan attacked the Philippines, Guam, Midway, Hong Kong, and the Malay Peninsula
   F. America entered the war

Lecture Ideas

1. A lecture on Franklin D. Roosevelt's foreign policy is the best way to introduce his diplomatic efforts. See Robert Dalleck's *Franklin D. Roosevelt and American Foreign Policy, 1932–1945* (1995) and Wayne S. Cole's *Roosevelt and the Isolationists* (1983).

2. The bombing of Pearl Harbor gives you the perfect opportunity to break the class up into two groups. One group will look at the bombing of Pearl Harbor as a surprise that caught the United States off guard and the other group will research the possibility that the government of the United States knew or should have known of the impending attack. See Gordon Prange's *At Dawn We Slept* (1981) and *Pearl Harbor: The Verdict of History* (1986), and Robert J. C. Burtow's *Tojo and the Coming of War* (1961).

True/False Questions

F   1. Having decided not to join the League of Nations, the United States refused to have anything to do with the organization in the 1920s and 1930s.

T   2. Most Allied countries defaulted on their war debts to the United States during the Great Depression.

T   3. The Nicaraguan National Guard, a legacy of American intervention, was used to support a dictatorship after the United States Marines left.

F   4. In his "quarantine speech" of October 1937, President Roosevelt called for the United States to isolate itself from world affairs.

F   5. American isolationism reached its peak late in 1941.

F   6. The first German submarine attack on an American ship was in 1938.

F   7. The war in Europe led many Democrats to support Thomas E. Dewey for the presidential nomination in 1940.

F   8. France was the main beneficiary of the Lend-Lease Act.

F   9. The *Greer,* the *Reuben James,* and the *Kearney* were American warships sunk by the Japanese at Pearl Harbor.

T   10. In the presidential election of 1940, both candidates supported all-out aid to Great Britain.

Multiple-Choice Questions

1. The biggest reason England and France had trouble repaying their war debts to the United States was:
   A. America's low tariff gave Europeans a cheap foreign market.
   B. the lack of American investments and loans abroad kept those nations starved for capital.
   * C. they could pay the United States only as they collected reparations from Germany.
   D. the Johnson Debt Default Act doubled the interest on unpaid balances.

2. A concern for the growing power of what nation led to the Washington Armaments Conference?
   A. England
   B. Germany
   * C. Japan
   D. Russia

3. The Lansing-Ishii Agreement:
   A. allowed the Japanese special tariff concessions in the Philippines.
   B. almost doubled the number of Japanese immigrants allowed into the United States.
   * C. acknowledged that Japan had "special interests" in China.
   D. limited the number of submarines Japan and the United States could have.

4. In the Five-Power Naval Treaty, the signatories agreed to all the following provisions *except* to:
   A. refrain from further fortification of their Pacific possessions.
   B. build no capital ships for ten years.
   C. limit naval tonnage.
   * D. assist one another in case of outside attack.

5. The Kellogg-Briand Pact:
   * A. outlawed war among signatories as an instrument of national policy.
   B. reduced the Allied war debt.
   C. limited the size of America's standing army.
   D. was defeated in the Senate.

6. American foreign policy in Latin America in the period between world wars included all the following *except*:
   A. withdrawing American marines from Nicaragua and Haiti.
   * B. rejecting the Pan-American Conference.
   C. accepting the Clark Memorandum.
   D. abrogating the Platt Amendment.

7. America's "Good Neighbor" Policy:
   A. allayed Canadian fears of American intervention.
   B. included American military and economic aid to the Allies.
   C. was demonstrated in 1926 when the United States sent marines to Nicaragua to help put down disorders.
   * D. included nonintervention in Latin America.

8. The National Socialist party was:
   * A. led by Adolph Hitler.
   B. led by an officer known as "Il Duce."
   C. strongest in Italy.
   D. strongest in Czechoslovakia and Hungary.

9. Benito Mussolini's rise to power in Italy:
   A. followed the death of President Hindenburg.
   B. followed Hitler's rise in Germany.
   C. followed his successful invasion of Ethiopia.
   * D. came about largely because he promised to restore order to a country torn by dissension.

10. A renewal of diplomatic relations between American and the Soviet Union came about:
   A. mainly because of the threat of Nazi Germany.
   B. under President Harding.
   * C. in 1933.
   D. despite President Franklin Roosevelt's objections.

11. In the 1938 agreement signed at Munich:
   A. Mussolini agreed not to invade Albania.
   * B. Britain and France agreed to let Hitler have the Sudetenland.
   C. Japan joined Germany and Italy in the "Anti-Comintern Pact."
   D. Hitler achieved the union of Austria and Germany.

12. Both Britain and France went to war:
    - A. to keep Germany from seizing Czechoslovakia.
    - B. when Mussolini conquered Ethiopia.
    - * C. when Hitler invaded Poland.
    - D. after Japan joined Italy and Germany in the "Anti-Comintern Pact."

13. The Nye Committee:
    - * A. investigated the role of bankers and munitions makers in America's entry into World War I.
    - B. recommended that Europeans appease Hitler by allowing him to annex Czechoslovakia.
    - C. compiled an official list of America's international obligations under existing treaties.
    - D. condemned the actions of the "merchants of death," those foreign mercenaries who had committed atrocities against European civilians during World War I.

14. The Neutrality Act of 1935:
    - A. was directed against Japanese action in China.
    - B. allowed the American navy to stop and search German ships on the high seas.
    - * C. forbade the sale of arms and munitions to warring nations.
    - D. stopped German and Italian military aid to Francisco Franco.

15. President Roosevelt was hesitant to intervene in the Spanish Civil War because:
    - * A. he wanted to keep the fight localized.
    - B. the Neutrality Act of 1938 forbade intervention.
    - C. Catholics favored the Spanish Republic.
    - D. Germany and Italy were supporting the Spanish Republic.

16. President Roosevelt's so-called "moral embargo":
    - * A. concerned shipments of arms to Spain.
    - B. concerned shipments of arms to China.
    - C. was violated by both England and France.
    - D. was defeated in Congress.

17. The proposed Ludlow Amendment:
    - A. demonstrated American support for intervention in the Far East.
    - B. would have required American firms to get congressional approval before selling war materials to any European belligerents.

C. demanded immediate payment of the German war reparations.
* D. would have required a public referendum for a declaration of war except in case of attack on American territory.

18. The Neutrality Act of 1939:
* A. allowed the United States to sell arms on a cash-and-carry basis to England and France.
B. failed to pass Congress by only four votes.
C. renewed America's isolationist stance toward the war in Europe.
D. was passed over Roosevelt's veto.

19. After the German occupation of Czechoslovakia in 1939, Roosevelt:
* A. no longer professed impartiality in the impending European struggle.
B. maintained the status quo pertaining to Europe.
C. asked the Germans for payment to the Czech people.
D. rescinded the Neutrality Acts.

20. In the late summer of 1940, President Roosevelt agreed to send fifty "overaged" destroyers to Britain in return for:
A. Republican promises not to ask for a peacetime draft.
B. congressional approval of a draft registration act.
C. a renegotiated payment schedule of the Allies' war debt from World War I.
* D. ninety-nine-year leases on a series of naval and air bases.

21. The America First Committee:
A. pushed for more aid to England and France in order to defend America.
* B. argued that a Nazi victory in Europe would pose no threat to American national security.
C. urged an immediate declaration of war on Germany.
D. drew most of its support from the East and West Coasts and the South.

22. In the presidential election of 1940:
A. the Republican candidate won.
B. most voters supported the isolationist candidate.
C. the Republican slogan was, "Don't change horses in the middle of the stream."
* D. the Democratic and Republican candidates agreed on most fundamental issues.

23. With the Lend-Lease Act:
    * A. the United States moved further away from isolationism.
    B. President Roosevelt was able to please both isolationists and internationalists.
    C. American aid to England was reduced by about one-half.
    D. England became the "arsenal of democracy."

24. Which of the following was *not* an isolationist in 1940–1941?
    A. William E. Borah
    B. Herbert Hoover
    C. Charles A. Lindbergh
    * D. Wendell Willkie

25. The Atlantic Charter included all the following principles *except*:
    A. freedom of the seas.
    B. economic cooperation.
    * C. the elimination of communism.
    D. self-determination for all peoples.

26. When Germany began attacking American ships in 1941:
    A. Congress declared war on Germany.
    * B. Congress in effect repealed the neutrality acts through new legislation lifting the ban on arms sales to belligerents.
    C. Roosevelt ordered ships to avoid combat zones.
    D. Roosevelt broke diplomatic relations with Germany.

27. In response to Japanese encroachments in Indochina in 1940 and 1941, Roosevelt:
    A. ordered the strategic bombing of Japanese military sites.
    B. sent 200,000 troops to China.
    * C. restricted oil exports to Japan.
    D. declared a naval blockade of Japan.

28. The United States said it would reopen trade with Japan only after that country:
    A. gave up its recently acquired territory in New Zealand.
    B. signed an agreement not to attack Russia.
    * C. withdrew completely from China and Indochina.
    D. paid England and Holland for the oil and other resources it had taken from their colonies.

29. One way in which the Japanese attack on Pearl Harbor was not a total success was that the Japanese:
   A. failed to disable the American planes lined up on the ground.
   * B. ignored shore installations and oil tanks.
   C. did not immediately follow up with assaults on the Philippines, Guam, Hong Kong, and other American and British possessions in the Pacific.
   D. withdrew their attack before significantly damaging any of the battleships in the harbor.

30. The congressional resolution for war:
   A. came just one week after the Japanese attack on Pearl Harbor.
   B. passed by a margin of seven to one.
   C. came just after Italy and Germany showed their support for Japan by declaring war on America.
   * D. reflected the mood of America, and American isolationism was cast aside.

Essay Questions

1. Describe the Atlantic Charter and explain its significance.

2. How were attempts at disarmament and outlawing war in the 1920s ineffective?

3. What was the "Good Neighbor" Policy? How did it reflect the general foreign-policy mood of the nation?

4. Describe the major steps in America's move away from neutrality between 1935 and 1941.

5. Discuss the negotiations between the United States and Japan in 1940 and 1941. How did the actions of each contribute to war?

Matching Questions

A) wrote 1928 document denying that the Monroe Doctrine justified U.S. intervention in Latin America
B) Republican who was named secretary of war in 1940
C) Democratic presidential candidate in 1940
D) American spokesman at Washington Armaments Conference
E) placed in charge of all U.S. military forces in the Far East
F) proposed to lower tariffs with reciprocal trade agreements
G) lost presidential election in 1940
H) with American president, drew up Atlantic Charter
I) voted against war with Japan
J) secretary of state under Coolidge, helped shape Pact of Paris

H	1. Winston Churchill
A	2. J. Ruben Clark
D	3. Charles Evans Hughes
F	4. Cordell Hull
J	5. Frank Kellogg
E	6. Douglas MacArthur
I	7. Jennette Rankin
C	8. Franklin Roosevelt
B	9. Henry L. Stimson
G	10. Wendell L. Willkie

Chapter 30

THE SECOND WORLD WAR

This chapter covers World War II, its effects on American society, and the Yalta agreements.

Chapter Outline

I. America's early battles
  A. Setbacks in the Pacific
    1. Collapse along the Pacific
    2. Surrender of the Philippines
    3. Japanese strategy
    4. American harassment
    5. Battle of the Coral Sea
  B. Battle of Midway
    1. American cryptanalysts had broken Japanese code
    2. Japan lost its four best aircraft carriers
    3. A turning point in the Pacific war
  C. Setbacks in the Atlantic
    1. Devastation from German submarines
    2. American response

II. Mobilization at home
  A. Mobilization of the armed forces
  B. Economic conversion
    1. Agencies for mobilization
      a. War Powers Acts
      b. War Production Board
      c. Reconstruction Finance Corporation
    2. Supplying strategic materials
    3. Gross National Product more than doubled
  C. Financing the war
    1. Taxation
      a. Revenue Act of 1942
      b. Taxes paid about 45 percent of wartime expenditures

    2. Borrowing from the public
       a. War bonds
       b. Financial institutions
  D. Impact of the war on the economy
    1. Rise in wages
    2. Price controls by Office of Price Administration
    3. Wages and farm prices were not controlled
    4. Stabilization Act of 1942
    5. Efforts of the War Labor Board
    6. Seizure of industries
    7. Prices rose only 31 percent by the end of the war
  E. Wartime domestic conservatism
    1. Elections of 1942 showed gains for Republicans
    2. Many New Deal agencies cut or abolished
    3. Actions against labor
       a. Smith-Connally War Labor Dispute Act
       b. State legislation
  F. Mobilization and the development of the West
    1. Population boom
    2. Economic growth

III.   Social effects of the war
  A. On women
    1. 200,000 women joined the armed forces
    2. 6,000,000 women entered the civilian work force
    3. Changed attitudes toward sex roles
  B. On blacks
    1. Blacks in armed forces—usually in segregated units
    2. Blacks in war industries
       a. A. Philip Randolph's March on Washington
       b. FEPC
       c. Revived migration from the South
    3. Challenges to other forms of discrimination
       a. The "Double V"
       b. *Smith* v. *Allwright* struck down Texas's white
         primary
    4. Detroit race riot
  C. Mexican workers
    1. *Bracero* program
    2. Ethnic tensions
  D. On Native Americans
    1. Support for war
    2. "Code talkers"

E. On Japanese-Americans
   1. Over 100,000 sent to War Relocation Camps
   2. Japanese-Americans in the war effort
   3. Federal compensation to internment survivors in 1983

IV. The war in Europe
   A. Decision to move against Germany first
      1. Nazis posed greater threat to Western Hemisphere
      2. Still, more Americans went to Pacific in 1942
   B. Aspects of joint conduct of war
      1. Declaration of the United Nations
         a. Affirmed the Atlantic Charter
         b. Pledged full resources
         c. Agreed not to seek a separate peace
      2. Strategy
         a. Americans wanted to strike directly across the English Channel
         b. British wanted to wait and build up forces
   C. The North Africa campaign
      1. Eisenhower's landing
      2. German surrender there
   D. Agreements at Casablanca
      1. Cross-channel invasion further postponed
      2. Atlantic antisubmarine campaign planned
      3. Agreement to end war only with "unconditional surrender" of all enemies
   E. The battle of the Atlantic
      1. Allied advantages
      2. Allied shipping records
   F. Sicily and Italy
      1. Invasion of Sicily
      2. Italian surrender
      3. German control of northern Italy
      4. The battle for Rome
   G. Strategic bombing of Europe
      1. Anglo-American cooperation
      2. Impact
   H. The Teheran Conference
      1. Included "Big Three" leaders—Roosevelt, Churchill, and Stalin
      2. Decisions
         a. Planning for the D-Day invasion and the Russian offensive
         b. Russia promised to enter war against Japan

    I. D-Day
        1. Eisenhower in command of Operation "Overlord"
        2. The invasion
        3. German reaction
        4. Slowing momentum of the drive on Germany

  V. The war in the Pacific
      A. Guadalcanal offensive
      B. MacArthur's leapfrogging in the West Pacific
      C. Nimitz in the Central Pacific
        1. The Gilberts
        2. The Marshalls
        3. Battle of the Philippine Sea
        4. Battle of Leyte Gulf
            a. Decision to use the Philippines for staging area
            b. MacArthur into the Philippines
            c. Japanese need Philippines for war resources
            d. The largest naval battle in history and loss of
               most of Japan's remaining sea power

  VI. The election of 1944
      A. Republicans nominate Thomas E. Dewey
      B. Democrats named Truman for vice-president
      C. Victory for Roosevelt

  VII. Closing on Germany
      A. German counteroffensive
      B. Allied moves against Germany

  VIII. The Yalta Conference
      A. Roosevelt's ideas
        1. Ensure that Russia join the war against Japan
        2. Form a world organization—the United Nations
      B. The division of Germany and Berlin
      C. Russia "given" eastern Europe
        1. Many of those countries lacked strong democratic
          traditions
        2. Russia wanted a buffer zone between it and Germany
      D. Yalta's legacy
        1. Soviet violations
        2. Secret agreements concerning the Far East

  IX. Collapse of the Third Reich
      A. Roosevelt's death
      B. Collapse of Germany

           1. Mussolini and Hitler dead

           2. Unconditional surrender

     C. Discovery of the Nazi Holocaust

X. Collapse of Japan

     A. Allied moves toward an invasion of Japan

           1. The Philippines

           2. Iwo Jima

           3. Okinawa

     B. The atomic bomb

           1. Development of the bomb

           2. Decision to use the bomb

              a. Target chosen

              b. Potsdam Declaration threatened bombing if Japan did not surrender immediately

           3. Devastation of the bomb

              a. At Hiroshima

              b. At Nagasaki

           4. Japanese surrender

              a. Emperor allowed to keep his throne under the authority of the Allied supreme commander

              b. Formal surrender signed on the *Missouri*

XI. The final ledger on the war

     A. Estimates of death and destruction

     B. Impact on America and Russia

Lecture Ideas

1. A good general overview of World War I will give your students the necessary background to understanding America's role in the war. Included in this lecture should be a discussion on the alliances, strategies, and military aspects of the fighting. See Murry Williamson and Alan R. Millett's *A War to Be Won: Fighting the Second World War* (2000), Gordon Wright's *The Ordeal of Total War* (1968), and John Keegan's *The Second World War* (1990).

2. America and the homefront in World War II give you a great topic to break the class up into groups and assign a topic regarding the domestic experience during the war. Groups should include, race relations and the black experience, the role of women, Native Americans, the economy, and the experiences of Japanese Americans. See John W. Jeffries's *Wartime America: The World War II Homefront* (1996), Michael Adams's *The Best War Ever: America and World War II* (1993),

Susan A. Hartmann's *The Homefront and Beyond* (1982), Roger Daniels's *Concentration Camps USA: Japanese Americans and World War II* (1981), Sherna Berger Gluck's *Rosie the Riveter Revisited* (1981), Karen Andersen's *Wartime Women* (1981), Richard M. Dalfiume's *Desegregation of the U.S. Armed Forces* (1969), Albert R. Buchanan's *Black Americans in World War II* (1977), David Kryder's *Divided Arsenal* (2000), Kenneth Townsend's *At the Crossroads* (2000), and Ronald Takaki's *Double Victory* (2000).

3. Obviously one of the greatest moments of the war was Truman's decision to drop the atomic bomb on Japan. A lecture on this decision is a must. See Gar Alperovitz's *The Decision to Drop the Atomic Bomb and Architecture of an American Myth* (1987), Herbert Feis's *Atomic Bomb and the End of World War II* (1996), Paul Boyer's *By the Bomb's Early Light: American Thought and Culture at the Dawn of the Atomic Age* (1985), and Ruth H. Howes's *Their Day in the Sun: Women of the Manhattan Project* (1999).

True/False Questions

T   1. By the end of World War II, over six million women had entered the workforce.

T   2. Black American soldiers usually served in segregated units in World War II.

F   3. In *Smith* v. *Allwright*, the Supreme Court upheld the conviction of a man accused of avoiding the draft.

T   4. "Nisei" were Americans of Japanese descent.

T   5. The U.S. military used Native Americans as "code talkers" during World War II.

F   6. The FEPC loaned money to defense industries.

T   7. In the Katyn Forest massacre of 1940, Russians killed over 14,000 Polish officers.

F   8. Adolph Hitler surrendered to the Allies on board the battleship *Missouri*.

T   9. Some six million Jews were killed in the Nazi Holocaust.

T   10. The Potsdam Declaration, issued just before the atomic bomb fell on Hiroshima, demanded that Japan surrender immediately or face "prompt and utter destruction."

Multiple-Choice Questions

1. In the first two months of American involvement in World War II:
    * A. news from the Pacific was "all bad," according to President Roosevelt.
    B. the United States scored impressive victories in Guam and the Gilbert Islands.
    C. Japanese on the Philippines surrendered to General Douglas MacArthur.
    D. the Japanese were finally repelled from China.

2. The Battle of Midway:
    * A. was the turning point of the war in the Pacific.
    B. was fought in the Coral Sea.
    C. was fought to a draw.
    D. cost the United States almost one-third of its remaining naval force.

3. The purpose of the War Production Board was to:
    * A. direct industrial conversion to war production.
    B. finance the building of war plants.
    C. oversee military scientific research and development.
    D. publish and distribute American propaganda.

4. Of the following, the biggest single source of government financing for America's war effort was:
    A. loans from financial institutions.
    B. the sale of public lands in the Northwest.
    * C. increased federal taxes.
    D. the printing of more paper money.

5. The Office of Price Administration:
    A. was designed to combat the serious wartime deflation.
    B. was designed to raise consumer prices.
    * C. rationed tires, sugar, coffee, gasoline, and other items.
    D. is correctly represented by all the above statements.

6. During the war, domestic politics was marked by:
   * A. a growing conservatism.
   B. continued concern for New Deal programs.
   C. the "liberalization" of southern Democrats.
   D. the decline of Republican power in Washington.

7. The area that experienced the fastest rate of urban growth during the war years was:
   * A. the Far West.
   B. the upper Midwest.
   C. New England.
   D. the South.

8. The *bracero* program:
   A. led to the forced evacuation of over 100,000 Japanese-Americans.
   B. was a reaction to the "zoot suit" riots.
   C. allowed most recent immigrants to join the American armed services after a thorough background check.
   * D. brought some 200,000 Mexican farmworkers into the western United States.

9. The "W" in WAC stood for:
   A. War.
   B. Western.
   * C. Women's.
   D. World.

10. In response to a proposed march on Washington in 1941, President Roosevelt issued an executive order:
    * A. prohibiting racial discrimination in defense work.
    B. desegregating the armed forces.
    C. forbidding "right-to-work" laws.
    D. allowing women into the military service.

11. The "Double V" was:
    A. the flying formation used for the strategic bombing of German targets.
    * B. a slogan that meant victory abroad over Hitler and victory at home over racial discrimination.
    C. a group of cryptanalysts (code breakers).
    D. the code name for the atomic bomb.

12. War Relocation Camps:
    A. were actually prisoner-of-war camps for captured Germans.
    * B. housed over 100,000 Japanese-Americans during the war.
    C. helped the families of American servicemen cope with the absence of husbands and fathers.
    D. was the German euphemism for Nazi concentration camps.

13. In the Declaration of the United Nations, anti-Axis governments:
    A. revoked the Atlantic Charter.
    B. agreed on a strategy against Hitler.
    C. named Gen. H. H. "Hap" Arnold to head the Allied naval force.
    * D. agreed not to seek a separate peace with common enemies.

14. The French Vichy government:
    * A. collaborated with the Germans.
    B. was headed by Charles De Gaulle.
    C. led the resistance to Gen. Erwin Rommel in North Africa.
    D. crumbled in 1939.

15. President Roosevelt and Winston Churchill finally agreed to strike first:
    A. across the English Channel.
    B. on the Eastern front.
    C. against Japan.
    * D. in North Africa.

16. Following the Allied victory in Sicily:
    A. Mussolini's forces held off the Allied force advancing on Italy for fifteen months.
    B. Mussolini committed suicide.
    * C. Italy joined the Allies.
    D. the Allies turned their attention to Egypt.

17. The meeting of Roosevelt, Churchill, and Stalin to plan an invasion of France and a Russian offensive took place in:
    * A. Teheran.
    B. Paris.
    C. Geneva.
    D. Casablanca.

18. Operation "Overlord" was the:
    A. top-secret work of American cryptanalysts (code breakers).
    * B. D-Day invasion at Normandy.
    C. Allied invasion of North Africa.
    D. joint American-Russian effort to free Poland.

19. The new strategy used in the Pacific in 1943 was:
    - A. attacking only the smallest Japanese naval vessels.
    - B. attacking the northern islands first, then moving southward.
    - * C. neutralizing the Japanese strongholds, leaving them to "die on the vine."
    - D. firebombing the islands to destroy all the foliage where Japanese could hide.

20. The Battle of Leyte Gulf:
    - * A. was the largest naval engagement in history.
    - B. caught Hitler by surprise.
    - C. was a victory for the Japanese.
    - D. began with a German submarine destroying the *Mongoose*, an American aircraft carrier, before it could get a single plane off the deck.

21. In the presidential election of 1944:
    - A. George Marshall was the Democratic candidate.
    - * B. Thomas Dewey was the Republican candidate.
    - C. the Republican candidate was reelected.
    - D. the Democrats argued that America needed younger men to replace the tired old leaders of the New Deal.

22. Following their quick sweep across France, the Allies:
    - * A. lost momentum in the fall of 1944.
    - B. just as quickly captured most of Germany.
    - C. were forced to retreat to their pre-1944 lines.
    - D. were surrounded and nearly defeated in Normandy.

23. The Yalta Conference:
    - A. was the only time that Allied leaders met with their Axis counterparts before the actual surrenders.
    - B. discussed wartime economic cooperation.
    - C. decided on the long-awaited cross-channel invasion against Germany.
    - * D. gave Russia control of eastern Germany.

24. To ensure that Russia joined the war against Japan, in 1945 Roosevelt:
    - A. threatened to use the atomic bomb on Russian targets.
    - B. gave Russia the secrets of the American atomic bomb.
    - * C. made certain secret agreements concerning Russian territorial demands.
    - D. promised to assume half of the Russian war debt.

25. President Roosevelt died:
    * A. less than a month before the surrender of Germany.
      B. less than a month after the surrender of Japan.
      C. while returning from the Yalta Conference.
      D. of leukemia.

26. V-E Day:
    * A. celebrated the defeat of Germany.
      B. celebrated the defeat of Japan.
      C. honored the exiled German scientists who had perfected the VE rocket for Allied use against their homeland.
      D. followed the Allied victory at Iwo Jima.

27. The Battle of Okinawa:
      A. was relatively bloodless.
    * B. was most significant for wearing down the remaining Japanese defenses.
      C. cost the life of American general Dwight Eisenhower.
      D. cost the life of American general "Tony" MacAuliffe.

28. The development of the atomic bomb that was dropped on Hiroshima:
      A. was opposed by most Americans.
    * B. was the responsibility of the Manhattan Project.
      C. was the responsibility of a group of scientists headed by Albert Einstein.
      D. began in the spring of 1945.

29. The Japanese surrender:
    * A. allowed the emperor to keep his throne under the authority of an Allied supreme commander.
      B. came just hours after an atomic bomb virtually destroyed the city of Hiroshima.
      C. saved thousands of lives, because Americans had a second atomic bomb they threatened to use.
      D. left only Russia for the Allies to defeat to end World War II.

30. The total cost of World War II:
      A. included military expenditures and property losses for all involved nations of perhaps $100 million.
    * B. included some 49 million military and civilian dead.
      C. was greater for the United States (in proportion to population) than for any other major power.
      D. is correctly described by all the above statements.

Essay Questions

1. Discuss America's industrial and economic mobilization for World War II.

2. What were the effects of the war on American women and African Americans?

3. What factors influenced the Allied victory in the Pacific?

4. Describe the agreements made during the war that shaped the postwar world. In your view, did Roosevelt "sell out" to the Russians?

5. Why did America drop the atomic bomb on Japan? Was the action justified?

Matching Questions

A) Democratic presidential candidate in 1944
B) headed Brotherhood of Sleeping Car Porters
C) headed Operation "Overlord"
D) American admiral
E) secretary of war
F) lost presidential election in 1944
G) elected vice-president in 1944
H) led coal miners on strike in 1943
I) said "People of the Philippines: I have returned"
J) directed construction of atomic bomb

F   1. Thomas Dewey
C   2. Dwight D. Eisenhower
H   3. John L. Lewis
I   4. Douglas MacArthur
D   5. Chester Nimitz
J   6. J. Robert Oppenheimer
B   7. A. Philip Randolph
A   8. Franklin D. Roosevelt
E   9. Henry L. Stimson
G   10. Harry Truman

Chapter 31

THE FAIR DEAL AND CONTAINMENT

This chapter covers domestic and foreign affairs in the Truman administration, including demobilization, the cold war, the Korean War, and the second Red Scare.

Chapter Outline

I. Demobilization under Truman
   A. Harry Truman
      1. Background and character
      2. Domestic proposals of 1945
   B. Demobilization
      1. Rapid reduction of armed forces
         a. By 1950, armed forces down to 600,000
         b. The baby-boom generation
      2. Demobilization did not bring depression
         a. Unemployment pay and other Social Security benefits
         b. Servicemen's Readjustment Act of 1944
         c. Pent-up demand for consumer goods
         d. Rise in business investment and the GNP
   C. The problem of inflation
      1. Demands for wage increases
      2. Strikes
         a. General Motors
         b. Steel Workers
         c. United Mine Workers
         d. Railroads
      3. Truman's response to strikes
         a. The gradual death of the Office of Price Administration
         b. Price controls ended after 1946

II. Truman's early domestic policies
    A. Significant legislative achievements
        1. Employment Act of 1946
            a. Dropped the Democratic party commitment to full employment
            b. Created the Council of Economic Advisors
        2. Control of atomic energy
            a. Question of military or civilian control
            b. Created the Atomic Energy Commission
    B. Congressional elections of 1946
        1. Discontent with Democrats
        2. Republicans won majorities in both houses of Congress
    C. Record of the Republican Congress
        1. Taft-Hartley Act
            a. Restrictions on labor
            b. Passed over Truman's veto
            c. Effect of act
        2. Tax reduction
            a. Truman felt that the government debt should be reduced
            b. Congress overrode Truman's veto of a $5-billion tax cut
        3. National Security Act
            a. Response to the congressional investigation of Pearl Harbor
            b. Created the National Military Establishment, the National Security Council, and the Central Intelligence Agency

III. Development of the cold war
    A. The United Nations
        1. Outline of the United Nations
        2. Ratification of the United Nations charter
    B. War-crimes trials
        1. Records of the trials
        2. Debate over the justice of the trials
    C. Differences with the Soviets
        1. Problems in eastern Europe
            a. Russian violations of the Yalta agreements
            b. Communist takeovers
        2. Postwar settlement treaties confirmed Soviet control of eastern Europe
        3. Proposals to control atomic energy

D. The policy of containment
  1. Formulated by George F. Kennan
  2. Possible crisis in Iran avoided
  3. The Truman Doctrine
     a. Communist influence in Turkey and Greece
     b. Financial aid "to support free peoples who are resisting attempted subjugation"
  4. The Marshall Plan
     a. War damage and dislocation in Europe invited Communist influence
     b. Economic aid to all European countries offered in the European recovery program
     c. European response
  5. Dividing Germany
     a. Merger of Allied zones
     b. Berlin blockade and airlift
     c. Creation of East and West Germany
  6. North Atlantic Treaty Organization (NATO)
     a. Members
     b. Pledged signers to treat an attack against one as an attack against all
     c. Counterpart in eastern Europe
  7. Establishment of Israel

IV. Domestic politics
  A. Civil rights in the 1940s
     1. Mob violence
     2. FEPC
     3. Jackie Robinson
  B. Division of the Democratic party
     1. Southern conservatives upset over Truman's civil rights stand
     2. Democratic left upset at Truman's firing of Henry Wallace
     3. Efforts to shore up the New Deal coalition
  C. The 1948 election
     1. Republicans nominated Thomas E. Dewey
     2. Democrats nominated Truman and included a strong civil rights plank
        a. Southern conservatives formed the States' Rights Democratic party ("Dixiecrats") and nominated J. Strom Thurmond
        b. The Democratic left formed the Progressive party and nominated Henry Wallace

        3. Election results
- a. Truman won in major upset
- b. Split in Democratic party helped Truman
- c. Democratic majorities in Congress
- d. A vindication of the New Deal

        4. Fair Deal proposals
- a. Truman won on higher minimum wage and extension of Social Security, rent controls, farm price supports, housing, and rural electrification
- b. Truman lost on civil rights bills, national health insurance, federal aid to education, and repeal of the Taft-Hartley Act

V. The cold war heats up
- A. Truman's foreign policy
- B. China
  1. History of the Communist movement in China
     - a. Rise of Mao Tse-tung
     - b. U.S. support for Chiang Kai-shek
  2. Nationalists forced to Formosa (Taiwan)
  3. U.S. sought to shore up friendly Asian regimes
- C. Problems of the Atomic Age
  1. Russia detonated its first atomic bomb
  2. Truman ordered construction of the hydrogen bomb
  3. Call for buildup of conventional forces to provide options to nuclear war

VI. The Korean War
- A. America's entry
  1. Korea from World War II to 1950
  2. North Korean forces invaded South Korea
  3. U. N. sanctioned aid to South Korea
  4. Truman ordered American military forces to Korea under U. N. auspices
- B. America in the Korean War
  1. Gen. Douglas MacArthur commanded U. N. forces
  2. Chiefly an American affair
  3. Congress never voted a declaration of war
- C. Military developments
  1. Decision to invade the North
  2. Chinese Communists entered the war
- D. Dismissal of MacArthur
  1. Different views of the Korean War
  2. MacArthur openly criticized Truman

        3. MacArthur dismissed
        4. Public reaction
          a. Initially in favor of MacArthur
          b. Senate investigation justified Truman
   E. End of the war
        1. Snags in negotiations
        2. Truce signed
        3. Cost of the war

VII. Another Red Scare
   A. Evidences of espionage
   B. Truman's loyalty program
   C. The Hiss case
        1. Whittaker Chambers, former Soviet agent, accused
          Hiss of passing secret documents
        2. Hiss convicted of perjury
   D. The Rosenbergs
        1. Charged with giving atomic bomb secrets to the
          Soviet Union
        2. Executed
   E. Joseph McCarthy's witch-hunt
        1. Rise of McCarthy
        2. His anti-Communist tactics
        3. Assessment of McCarthy
   F. McCarran Internal Security Act
        1. Passed over Truman's veto
        2. Attempt to control Communist activities

VIII. Assessment of the cold war

Lecture Ideas

1. An overview of the cold war is essential. Discuss the origins and the realities of this postwar development in American diplomatic history. See Melvyn Leffler's *A Preponderance of Power* (1992), John L. Gaddis's *We Now Know* (1997), Bernard Weisberger's *Cold War, Cold Peace* (1984), and Warren I. Cohen's *America in the Age of Soviet Power, 1945–1991* (1993).

2. Divide the class up into groups and have them look at the events that led up to the Korean War. A good starting place would be to examine the cold war, the development of the United Nations, postwar Asia, and so on. See Stanley Sandler's *The Korean War: No Victor, No Vanquished* (1999), Paul G. Pierpaoli's *Truman and Korea: The Political*

Culture of the Early Cold War (1999), and Stanley Weintraub's
McArthur's War: Korea and the Undoing of an American Hero (2000).

3. An overview of Truman's Fair Deal will enable the students to gain
   a good perspective on the postwar economy. A critical look at
   Truman's Fair Deal is Barton J. Bernstein's "America in War and
   Peace: The Test of Liberalism," in *Towards a New Past*, edited by
   Bernstein (1968).

4. You should deliver at least one lecture on McCarthyism. See Robert
   Griffith's "American Politics and the Origins of 'McCarthyism,'" in
   The Specter, edited by Griffith and Athan Theoharis (1974). Griffith
   places McCarthyism within the larger anti-Communist movement of
   the time. Also see Richard Fried's *Nightmare in Red* (1990), Stanley
   Kutler's *The American Inquisition* (1982), and Ellen Schrecker's *The
   Age of McCarthyism* (1994).

True/False Questions

T   1. Harry Truman was born and raised in Missouri.

T   2. The Servicemen's Readjustment Act was also known as
the "GI Bill of Rights."

T   3. Within a few months of the end of World War II, there
were strikes or other labor disputes in the automobile,
steel, and coal industries.

F   4. J. Strom Thurmond was from New York.

T   5. "Operation Dixie" was a unionization drive in the South.

T   6. In the civil war that broke out in Greece after World War II,
the United States assisted the British-supported government.

F   7. In the presidential election of 1948, Republicans saw little
hope for victory.

F   8. The "Fair Deal" was President Truman's name for his
approach to foreign policy in the early days of the cold war.

F   9. In the early months of the Korean War, U. N. forces
encountered little resistance until they reached the Chinese
border.

T   10. Whittaker Chambers accused Alger Hiss of supplying U.S.
secret documents to the Soviets.

Multiple-Choice Questions

1. The domestic program that Harry Truman sent to Congress in September 1945:
   A. was a setback for labor.
   * B. proposed to continue and enlarge the New Deal.
   C. addressed only the problem of demobilization.
   D. proposed to reverse most of his predecessor's policies.

2. Harry Truman:
   A. replaced much of Roosevelt's cabinet soon after becoming president.
   B. was seen at first as simply a "caretaker" president.
   C. had been involved in the clothing business, among other things, before entering politics.
   * D. is correctly represented by all the above statements.

3. Among the factors that cushioned the economic impact of demobilization after World War II were all the following *except*:
   A. unemployment pay and other Social Security benefits.
   B. the "GI Bill of Rights."
   * C. reductions in business investments.
   D. the pent-up demand for consumer goods.

4. By 1950:
   A. international tensions had decreased.
   B. the birth rate had dropped.
   * C. the army had fallen to 600,000 men.
   D. All the above statements are true.

5. When trainmen and locomotive engineers staged a strike shortly after the end of the war, President Truman:
   A. threatened to nationalize the railroads.
   * B. threatened to draft strikers into the armed forces.
   C. suggested a pay raise of two cents an hour.
   D. argued that the federal government could not interfere in what was fundamentally a private business matter.

6. The main economic problem faced by Truman in his first term was:
   * A. inflation.
   B. falling prices.
   C. a dwindling money supply.
   D. tight credit.

7. The Taft-Hartley Act:
    A. was passed with Truman's support.
    B. set up a Council of Economic Advisors.
    C. ended discrimination on the basis of race in hiring for defense-related jobs.
  * D. was generally a setback for labor.

8. The National Security Act:
    A. was passed over President Truman's veto.
  * B. set up the CIA and the National Security Council.
    C. set up the FBI and the House Un-American Activities Committee.
    D. set up the OSS and the Atomic Energy Commission.

9. James F. Byrne:
    A. was called "the Father of the Computer."
    B. was convicted of passing atomic secrets to Communist China.
    C. headed the Office of Price Administration under Truman.
  * D. was Truman's first secretary of state.

10. Which of the following was *not* a permanent member of the Security Council of the United Nations?
    A. Britain
    B. France
  * C. Japan
    D. Russia

11. In its first application of the Truman Doctrine, Congress approved economic aid to:
    A. Czechoslovakia.
    B. Turkey and Yugoslavia.
    C. Albania.
  * D. Greece and Turkey.

12. The Marshall Plan of economic aid:
    A. was "to support free peoples who are resisting attempted subjugation by armed minorities or by outside pressures."
    B. set up the Committee of National Liberation.
  * C. was "directed not against country or doctrine, but against hunger, poverty, desperation, and chaos."
    D. prevented a Soviet takeover of Czechoslovakia.

13. East Germany was controlled after World War II by the:
    A. United States, France, and Great Britain.
    B. United States, France, and Italy.
    C. United States, the Soviet Union, and Great Britain.
    * D. Soviet Union.

14. In response to a Soviet blockade of West Berlin, Truman:
    A. used armed convoys to supply the city.
    * B. used a massive airlift to supply the city.
    C. conceded Berlin to the Russians in order to save West Germany.
    D. conceded Berlin to the Russians in order to save East Germany.

15. The North Atlantic Treaty:
    A. pledged signers to "consult immediately" in case of attack.
    * B. was originally signed by twelve nations.
    C. was a response to the Communist invasion of South Korea.
    D. was also known as the Nuclear Non-Proliferation Treaty.

16. When Jewish leaders proclaimed the independent state of Israel in 1948, the United States:
    A. refused to recognize the new state until democratic elections had been held.
    B. broke diplomatic relations with most of the Arab states.
    * C. recognized the new state within minutes.
    D. offered military and financial aid to the Arab states.

17. In the area of civil rights, President Truman:
    * A. issued an Executive Order banning racial segregation in the armed forces.
    B. allowed racial segregation in the hiring of federal employees to continue.
    C. refused to address the problem of racial violence.
    D. pushed through Congress a voting rights act that effectively ended barriers to black voting.

18. The person usually credited with formulating the doctrine of containment was:
    A. James F. Byrnes.
    B. Harry Hopkins.
    * C. George F. Kennan.
    D. George C. Marshall.

19. In the election of 1948:
    A. liberal Republicans bolted their party and named Strom Thurmond the candidate of the new States' Rights Republican party.
    B. "Dixiecrats" carried all of the former Confederate states.
    C. Republicans finished third in the presidential race.
    * D. Democrats won majorities in both houses of Congress in addition to winning the White House.

20. Following the election of 1948, Truman was able to push through Congress:
    A. a civil rights bill, federal aid to education, and national health insurance.
    * B. farm price supports, a public housing program, and more money for the TVA and rural electrification.
    C. a repeal of the Taft-Hartley Act.
    D. all the above.

21. Who said "There is no substitute for victory" in 1951?
    A. Joseph McCarthy
    * B. Douglas MacArthur
    C. Harry Truman
    D. Harry Hopkins

22. In the "China tangle," Chiang Kai-shek fought against:
    A. the Chinese Nationalists.
    B. the Kuomintang.
    * C. Mao Tse-tung.
    D. Ho Chi Minh.

23. The top-secret document prepared by the National Security Council in 1950:
    A. was a plan for military aid to the French-supported regime of Bao Dai in Vietnam.
    B. was a response to the Soviet takeover of Czechoslovakia.
    * C. called for rebuilding America's conventional military forces.
    D. addressed the problem of Communists in South Korea.

24. The United States entered the Korean War:
    A. against the wishes of President Truman.
    * B. without a declaration of war by Congress.
    C. without sanction by the United Nations.
    D. because of its interest in the oil deposits off the southern tip of the Korean peninsula.

25. Truman removed General Douglas MacArthur:
    A. because of popular demand.
    B. because MacArthur did not want to fight an all-out war in Korea and China.
    C. after a Senate investigative committee found MacArthur had held secret negotiations with Chinese officials.
    * D. because MacArthur openly criticized the president for not wanting to fight Red China.

26. The war in Korea:
    A. began in 1946, when Mao Tse-tung's forces refused to leave South Korea.
    B. was responsible for almost a million American casualties.
    * C. began in 1950, when North Korean forces invaded South Korea.
    D. lasted just eight months.

27. Julius and Ethel Rosenberg:
    A. were convicted of perjury in a case involving purported espionage activities.
    B. accused Whittaker Chambers of passing secret documents to Soviet agents.
    * C. were executed for supposedly giving the Russians the secret to the atomic bomb.
    D. sued Richard M. Nixon for slander.

28. Joseph McCarthy:
    * A. accused George C. Marshall of disloyalty.
    B. was Truman's vice-president.
    C. pronounced Richard Nixon's charges of communism in the state department "a fraud and a hoax."
    D. was the first director of the Atomic Energy Commission.

29. The McCarran Internal Security Act of 1950:
    * A. was passed over Truman's veto.
    B. was upheld by the Supreme Court's "clear and present danger" doctrine.
    C. forced over 2000 civil service employees to resign.
    D. led to the arrest of Alger Hiss.

30. By the end of the Truman years, the United States had:
    A. returned to its isolationist stance.
    B. repudiated almost all its peacetime alliances.
    * C. become committed to a major and permanent national military establishment.
    D. repudiated the Monroe Doctrine.

Essay Questions

1. Describe the social and economic effects of demobilization.

2. Trace the major developments in the cold war from 1945 to 1948.

3. Why did Truman win the presidential election of 1948? Why was his victory considered a major upset?

4. What did Truman mean by a "Fair Deal"? How did it compare to FDR's New Deal?

5. Describe the Red Scare that followed the end of World War II. What factors caused it? What were its major results?

Matching Questions

A) wrote influential article on cold war policy in *Foreign Affairs*
B) fired as secretary of commerce in 1946
C) "Dixiecrat" presidential candidate in 1948
D) convicted in 1950 of perjury in an espionage case
E) Republican presidential candidate in 1948
F) gave civil rights speech at 1948 Democratic convention
G) said, "Once war is forced upon us, there is no alternative than to apply every available means to bring it to a swift end"
H) senator from Wisconsin
I) secretary of state in 1947
J) led U.N. forces in Korea after April 1951

E   1. Thomas E. Dewey
D   2. Alger Hiss
F   3. Hubert Humphrey
A   4. George F. Kennan
I   5. George C. Marshall
G   6. Douglas MacArthur
H   7. Joseph R. McCarthy
J   8. Matthew B. Ridgway
C   9. J. Strom Thurmond
B   10. Henry A. Wallace

Chapter 32

THROUGH THE PICTURE WINDOW: SOCIETY AND CULTURE, 1945–1960

This chapter discusses the growth of the postwar economy, suburban migration, and other factors that led to the so-called corporate life, or conformity, of the 1950s. Various reactions to the corporate life by social critics, artists, and writers are also covered.

Chapter Outline

I. People of plenty
    A. The postwar economy
        1. Growth of the economy
            a. GNP doubled from 1945 to 1960
            b. Perpetual economic growth now seen as possible and desirable
        2. Reasons for growth
            a. Military spending
            b. Automation
            c. Consumer demand
            d. "Baby boom"
        3. The GI Bill of Rights
            a. Servicemen's Readjustment Act of 1944
            b. GI Bill democratized higher education
    B. Consumer culture
        1. Increased production
            a. Variety
            b. The television
        2. Increased purchasing
            a. Dispersion through society
            b. Role of advertising
            c. Credit
            d. Shopping centers
    C. Suburban frontier
        1. Urban growth
            a. Most population growth was urban and suburban

        b. Rise of "Sunbelt"
        c. Suburbia
    2. Reasons for suburban growth
        a. Levittown and mass production
        b. Low-cost loans
        c. Automobiles and highways
        d. Racial considerations
    3. The great black migration

II. A conforming culture
    A. Corporate life
        1. Growth of the middle class
        2. Growth of big business
    B. Women's "place"
        1. Conformity emphasized
        2. The cult of feminine domesticity
    C. Religious revival
        1. Americans as joiners
        2. Increase in church membership
        3. Other reasons for religious revival
            a. Patriotism
            b. The message of the popular religion
    D. Neo-orthodoxy
        1. Criticism of popular religion
        2. Reinhold Niebuhr

III. The lonely crowd
    A. Social criticism
        1. Galbraith's *The Affluent Society*
        2. Keats's *The Crack in the Picture Window*
        3. Riesman's *The Lonely Crowd*
        4. Mills's *White Collar Society*
    B. Youth culture
        1. Delinquency
        2. Rock 'n' roll
    C. Alienation on the stage
        1. Miller's *Death of a Salesman*
        2. Other plays
    D. The novel
        1. Jones's *From Here to Eternity*
        2. Ellison's *Invisible Man*
    E. Painting
        1. Edward Hopper
        2. Jackson Pollock
    F. The Beats

1. Leading figures
   a. Allen Ginsberg
   b. Jack Kerouac
2. Their philosophy and works

Lecture Ideas

1. Divide the class up into groups and have them research the various aspects of American society in the 1950s. Topics should include the consumer culture, race relations, and various cultural themes. See John Diggins's *The Proud Decade* (1988), William E. Leuchtenburg's *A Troubled Feast* (1983), George Lipsitz's *Time Passages* (1990), and David Halberstam's *The Fifties* (1993).

2. For an interesting lecture on how the science-fiction movies of the 1950s reflected the conformity and anti-communism of the decade, see the last chapter in Nora Sayre's *Running Time: Films of the Cold War* (1982).

3. For a lecture on one of America's most famous and interesting suburban communities, see Herbert J. Gans's *The Levittowners* (1967) or, much briefer, Alexander O. Boulton's "The Buy of the Century" (*American Heritage*, July/Aug. 1993). For suburbs in general, see Scott Donaldson's *The Suburban Myth* (1969), Kenneth T. Jackson's *The Crabgrass Frontier: The Suburbanization of the United States* (1985), and Rosalyn F. Baxadall and Elizabeth Ewen's *Picture Windows: How the Suburbs Happened* (2000).

4. For a discussion of the development and early years of the credit card— and how it has changed our spending habits—see Nancy Shepherdson's "Credit Card America" (*American Heritage*, Nov. 1991).

5. An overview lecture on the American family in this era will help set a discussion for the change in the family in coming chapters. See Stephanie Coontz's *The Way We Never Were* (1992) and Elaine Tyler May's *Homeward Bound: American Families in the Cold War* (1988).

True/False Questions

T   1. Rural areas experienced practically no population growth in the 1950s and 1960s.

T   2. The GI Bill of Rights provided financial assistance for home loans and college expenses.

T   3. Many adults, having experienced the Depression and wartime rationing, had to be "taught" to consume more in the 1950s.

T   4. The years during and after World War II witnessed tremendous growth in big business.

F   5. The postwar era witnessed tremendous economic depression and failing social contentment.

T   6. The phrase "one nation under God" was added to the Pledge of Allegiance in the 1950s.

T   7. "Fire-and-brimstone" sermons declined in the 1950s.

F   8. During the 1950s, the black population of Chicago declined by half as a result of the "great migration."

F   9. Will Herberg's slogan was "Be liked and you will never want."

F   10. The Beats took their name because of their pervasive sense that society had beaten them, or triumphed over their spirits.

Multiple-Choice Questions

1. Between 1945 and 1960, the gross national product (GNP):
   - A. stayed roughly the same, in constant dollars.
   - B. actually declined, in constant dollars.
   - * C. nearly doubled.
   - D. quadrupled.

2. During the 1950s:
   - A. American leaders realized that sustained economic growth was not necessary for national well-being.
   - B. the gap in living standards between the United States and the rest of the world decreased.
   - C. President Eisenhower warned that another economic collapse was possible.
   - * D. leading economists of the postwar era agreed that perpetual economic growth was possible.

3. Which of the following was *not* a major stimulant to the post-1945 economy?
   - A. military spending
   - B. the virtual American monopoly over international trade

      * C. the movement of women into the workforce
         D. the unleashing of pent-up consumer demand

4. The baby boom:
    A. peaked in 1957.
    B. was a large part of a 30-percent growth in American population between 1945 and 1960.
    C. paralleled a similar boom in consumer demand.
  * D. is correctly represented by all the above statements.

5. The fastest-growing new periodical in the 1950s was:
    A. *Jet.*
    B. *Mother Earth.*
  * C. *TV Guide.*
    D. *Working Woman.*

6. Which of the following decreased in the postwar years?
    A. the number of shopping centers
    B. consumer debt
    C. ownership of television sets
  * D. the portion of income that Americans saved (rather than spent)

7. All the following factors promoted the growth of suburbs *except*:
    A. low-cost government loans.
    B. expanded road and highway construction.
  * C. laws forbidding residential segregation by races.
    D. increased automobile production.

8. Automobile production in the postwar years:
    A. declined as war needs fell off.
    B. remained relatively low.
    C. remained high despite the government's hesitancy to provide improved roads until the late 1960s.
  * D. increased.

9. Which of the following statements about the postwar years is *not* true?
    A. Suburbs grew six times faster than central cities.
  * B. The so-called Sunbelt became the most densely populated area.
    C. Blacks migrated in record number from the rural South to the cities of the North and Midwest.
    D. Church membership increased from less than 50 percent to over 65 percent of the population.

10. Which of the following statements about the original Levittown
    is *not* true?
    A. Homeowners were required to mow their lawns once a
       week.
    B. Blacks were not allowed to buy homes there.
    C. Each house had identical floor plans and accessories.
    * D. Children were not allowed until after 1963.

11. According to Life magazine, the proper role for a woman in the
    1950s was:
    * A. being a good mother and wife.
    B. working.
    C. being active in government and civic affairs.
    D. fighting for women's rights.

12. The prevailing tone of the popular religious revival of the
    1950s was:
    A. personal guilt.
    * B. upbeat and soothing.
    C. social ills, such as poverty and racial segregation.
    D. Calvinism.

13. According to Reinhold Niebuhr:
    A. "each age finds its own [artistic] technique."
    B. parents should foster in their children qualities that
       enhance their chances in the "personality market."
    C. advertisers should take an active role in creating consumer
       demand.
    * D. the popular religion of the 1950s was woefully inadequate
       to cure the ills of society.

14. Which of the following did *not* promote the upbeat and soothing
    popular religion of the 1950s?
    A. Dwight Eisenhower
    * B. Will Herberg
    C. Norman Vincent Peale
    D. Fulton J. Sheen

15. Which book argued that sustained economic growth would not
    in itself solve America's chronic social problems?
    A. *The Failure of America*
    * B. *The Affluent Society*
    C. *The Waste Makers*
    D. *The Other America*

16. *The Crack in the Picture Window*:
    * A. argued that suburbanites were living in a "homogeneous, postwar Hell."
    B. urged people to turn to God as the only hope for America in the 1950s.
    C. led many women to leave the workforce in order to raise their children properly.
    D. is correctly represented by all the above statements.

17. The "other-directed" personality:
    A. had a core set of fixed principles.
    B. was self-assured and self-reliant.
    * C. valued popularity more than independence.
    D. is correctly represented by all the above statements.

18. *The Lonely Crowd* was written by:
    A. Marynia Farnham.
    B. John Keats.
    C. Joseph Wood Krutch.
    * D. David Riesman.

19. The "corporate character" of American life, as described in this chapter:
    A. led to an "inner-directed" personality type.
    * B. was an increasingly regimented conformity.
    C. concerned primarily the increasing role of business in American society.
    D. led people to shy away from social organizations.

20. Alan Freed:
    A. hosted a syndicated religious TV show, "Life Is Worth Living."
    B. compared suburban houses to "little boxes made of ticky-tacky."
    C. died in the plane crash that killed Buddy Holly.
    * D. coined the phrase "rock 'n' roll."

21. According to David Riesman, Dr. Spock's book on child care:
    A. stressed the value of teaching children independence.
    B. emphasized feeding schedules and how to change a diaper rather than social values.
    * C. encouraged parents to develop the "gregarious" talents of their children.
    D. had low sales in the 1950s because parents were more interested in their own well-being than their children's.

22. Willy Loman:
    A. was one of the most popular evangelists of the 1950s.
    B. wrote *What's Right with America Today* to counter the social critics of the 1950s.
    C. was chairman of General Motors in the 1950s.
    * D. was a character in *Death of a Salesman*.

23. *The Robe* and *Exodus*:
    * A. were best-sellers in the 1950s.
    B. described, respectively, a white woman and a black family in the conforming society of the 1950s.
    C. were praised by critics for their unsettling impact.
    D. are correctly represented by all the above statements.

24. The author of *Rabbit, Run* is:
    A. James Baldwin.
    B. Joseph Heller.
    * C. John Updike.
    D. H. G. Wells.

25. *Invisible Man*, the novel that developed the theme of loneliness from the black perspective, was written by:
    A. James Baldwin.
    B. John Cheever.
    * C. Ralph Ellison.
    D. H. G. Wells.

26. The American painter whose work depicted isolated melancholy and anonymous individuals was:
    * A. Edward Hopper.
    B. Franz Kline.
    C. Mark Rothko.
    D. Norman Rockwell.

27. A major proponent of the technique of "action painting"—the artist trying "literally to be in the painting"—was:
    A. Gregory Corso.
    B. Joyce Carol Oates.
    * C. Jackson Pollock.
    D. John Updike.

28. The Beats:
    * A. were, like the abstract expressionists, motivated by a desire to liberate self-expression.
    B. originated in San Francisco.
    C. were ironically themselves conformists, for they each subsumed their own unique personalities to the "Beat" philosophy.
    D. are correctly represented by all the above statements.

29. All the following were Beats *except*:
    A. Gregory Corso.
    B. Allen Ginsberg.
    C. Jack Kerouac.
    * D. George Meany.

30. Allen Ginsberg wrote:
    A. *Dangling Man.*
    B. *From Here to Eternity.*
    C. *Leaves of Grass.*
    * D. *Howl.*

Essay Questions

1. Describe the growth in the postwar American economy. What factors might account for this growth?

2. What were the main reasons for suburban growth in this period? How did it affect American society?

3. How did the image of women reflect the "corporate life" of the 1950s?

4. How did the religious revival and neo-orthodoxy fit into the culture of the 1950s?

5. Show briefly how playwrights, novelists, painters, and the Beats reacted to the "corporate life."

Matching Questions

A) wrote *The Organization Man*
B) wrote *The Affluent Society*
C) wrote *On the Road*
D) U.S. president in the 1950s
E) wrote *The Crack in the Picture Window*
F) wrote *Howl*
G) abstract expressionist artist
H) suburban home builder
I) wrote *The Power of Positive Thinking*
J) wrote *Death of a Salesman*

D   1. Dwight Eisenhower
B   2. John Kenneth Galbraith
F   3. Allen Ginsburg
E   4. John Keats
C   5. Jack Kerouac
H   6. William Levitt
J   7. Arthur Miller
I   8. Norman Vincent Peale
G   9. Jackson Pollock
A   10. William A. Whyte, Jr.

Chapter 33

CONFLICT AND DEADLOCK: THE EISENHOWER YEARS

This chapter covers Eisenhower's rise to the presidency and his domestic and foreign policies, including developments in civil rights and the cold war.

Chapter Outline

I. Eisenhower's rise to the presidency
   A. "Time for a change" from the Truman administration
   B. Republicans in 1952
      1. Robert A. Taft inspired little enthusiasm and had made enemies
      2. Dwight D. Eisenhower had stood outside and above politics, and won nomination
   C. Democrats in 1952
      1. Truman decided not to run again
      2. Nomination went to Adlai Stevenson
   D. The election of 1952
      1. Eisenhower won landslide victory
      2. Victory for Republicans
         a. In South
         b. In New Deal coalition
      3. Except for presidency, Democrats fared well in 1952
   E. Eisenhower's career before 1952

II. Eisenhower's "dynamic conservatism"
   A. Cutbacks in New Deal programs
   B. Endurance of the New Deal
      1. Extended the coverage of the Social Security Act
      2. Farm-related programs
      3. Public works
         a. St. Lawrence Seaway
         b. Federal Aid Highway Act of 1956

III. The Korean peace talks
    A. Continuing deadlock in early 1953
    B. Aerial bombardment and "secret" threats used to obtain agreement
    C. Negotiations moved quickly to armistice

IV. The end of McCarthyism
    A. McCarthy still strong after 1952
    B. Attack on the United States Army
    C. Televised hearings led to McCarthy's downfall
    D. Eisenhower's concern for internal security
        1. Executive order allowed firing of "security risk" government workers
        2. J. Robert Oppenheimer's security clearance removed
    E. The Warren Court and the Red Scare

V. Foreign policy in Eisenhower's first term
    A. John Foster Dulles
        1. Dulles's career
        2. Dulles's foreign policy
            a. Containment was needlessly defensive
            b. Liberation
        3. Role of the Central Intelligence Agency
    B. Dulles and containment
        1. No significant departure from containment
        2. "Massive retaliation"
        3. "Brinksmanship"
    C. Indochina
        1. European colonies in Asia
            a. Independence for British colonies
            b. United States aided Dutch and French efforts to regain colonies from local control
            c. Ho Chi Minh's efforts for Indochinese independence
        2. First Indochina War
            a. Conflict between Ho and Bao Dai
            b. Increased American aid for French and Bao Dai
            c. Eisenhower's "domino theory"
            d. French defeat at Dien Bien Phu
        3. The Geneva Accords
            a. Proposed to unify Vietnam after elections in 1956
            b. American response—the establishment of the Southeast Asia Treaty Organization (SEATO)
        4. Rise of Ngo Dinh Diem
            a. Installed as Vietnamese premier by the French

        b. Diem's corrupt and oppressive regime

        c. Refused to sanction elections in 1956

        d. Vietcong, an opposition guerrilla movement with Communist support, emerged in 1960 as the National Liberation Front

    D. Red China

        1. Red Chinese began artillery shelling of Quemoy and Matsu

        2. Navy "leaked" word that the U.S. was considering destroying Red Chinese military strength

        3. Attacks ceased

VI. The election of 1956

    A. Democrats

        1. Chose Stevenson again

        2. Platform

    B. Victory for Eisenhower

VII. Foreign crises in the election year

    A. The Middle East

        1. Failure of the Middle East Treaty Organization

        2. Suez Canal

            a. Egyptian government ordered the British out of Egypt

            b. Israel, France, and Britain began military attacks on Egypt

            c. America sided with Nassar

    B. Communist repression in Hungary

        1. Hungary withdrew from the Warsaw Pact

        2. Russian troops forced Hungary back into the Communist fold and executed Imre Nagy

VIII. Domestic affairs in Eisenhower's second administration

    A. The beginning of the space race

        1. Russia launched *Sputnik* I (October 1957)

        2. Americans suddenly noted apparent "missile gap"

            a. Enlarged defense spending

            b. Created NASA

            c. National Defense Education Act of 1958 authorized federal grants for training in sciences

IX. Problems abroad

    A. Lebanon

        1. The Eisenhower Doctrine

        2. Leftist coup in Iraq threw out the pro-Western government

          3. Lebanon received American military aid
          4. American marines left Beirut when the situation stabilized

   B. East Asia
          1. Red Chinese renewed bombardment of Nationalists
          2. Eisenhower's proposed cease-fire was partially accepted by Red China

   C. West Berlin
          1. Khrushchev raised possibility of another blockade
          2. Khrushchev stressed "peaceful coexistence"

   D. The "U-2 summit"
          1. Russians shot down American U-2 spy plane
          2. Eisenhower's response
          3. Khrushchev left the summit meeting

   E. Cuba
          1. In his fight against the dictator Batista, Castro had American support
          2. Castro crushed the opposition, became a dictator himself, and welcomed Communist aid
          3. Eisenhower's reaction

X. Civil rights in the 1950s
   A. Eisenhower's ambiguous stance
   B. The *Brown* decision (1954)
          1. "'Separate but equal' has no place"
          2. Reactions
              a. Eisenhower's reluctance
              b. Token integration
              c. Massive resistance

   C. Montgomery bus boycott
          1. Rosa Parks arrested for refusing to give up her seat on a bus to a white man
          2. Martin Luther King, Jr., organized a bus boycott
          3. Federal courts ruled against "separate but equal"
          4. Southern Christian Leadership Conference formed

   D. Legislation
          1. Civil Rights Act of 1957
          2. Civil Rights Act of 1960

   E. Little Rock
          1. Arkansas Gov. Orval Faubus prevented black students from registering for high school
          2. Eisenhower ordered military protection for students

        3. Faubus closed the high schools in Little Rock

        4. By 1960 massive resistance confined to Deep South

  XI. Assessing Eisenhower's presidency

Lecture Ideas

1. Divide the class into two groups and have them review and report on the presidency of Dwight D. Eisenhower. The groups can look at the campaigns, his background, how he handled his foreign policy, his relationship to the New Deal, and the struggles he had within the Republican Party over conservatism versus moderation. See Geoffrey Perret's *Eisenhower* (1999), Stephen Ambrose's *Eisenhower*, 2 vols. (1983, 1984), Fred I. Greenstein's *The Hidden-Hand Presidency* (1982), Richard Melanson and David Mayers's *Reevaluating* (1986), and Robert Devine's *Eisenhower and the Cold War* (1981).

2. A good overview on the origins of the Vietnam War is essential. By giving the background to the conflict, students will better appreciate how the situation there evolved. See Andrew Rotter's *The Path to Vietnam* (1987), David L. Anderson's *Trapped by Success* (1991), and Loren Baritz's *Backfire* (1985).

3. Harvard Sitkoff's *The Struggle for Black Equality, 1954–1992* (1993) would be a good source for a lecture on the early years of the modern civil rights movement (and for later years in the following chapters). Additionally, see Aldon Morris's *The Origins of the Civil Rights Movement* (1984), Robert Weisbrot's *Freedom Bound: A History of America's Civil Rights Movement* (1990), and Scott DeVeaux's *The Birth of BeBop* (1998).

True/False Questions

T   1. Many people perceived Dwight Eisenhower as a generally inactive president who rose above politics.

T   2. When Red China began attacking islands held by Chiang Kai-shek's Nationalists, the administration "leaked" word that it was considering destroying Red China's military strength.

T   3. J. Robert Oppenheimer, the "father of the atomic bomb," was branded a "security risk" in 1953.

F   4. As president, Eisenhower relaxed many of the stringent government security measures of the Truman years.

T   5. In 1954 the United States helped topple the government of Guatemala.

F   6. Martin Luther King, Jr.'s eloquence hid the fact that his formal education ended with the fifth grade.

T   7. When Fidel Castro accepted Communist support, the CIA began training Cuban refugees to overthrow him.

T   8. President Eisenhower supported the desegregation of public services in Washington, D.C., as well as navy yards and veterans' hospitals.

T   9. The Civil Rights Acts of 1957 and 1960 concerned black voting rights.

T   10. The National Defense Education Act, which authorized federal grants for training in mathematics and science, was a response to the Soviet launching of Sputnik.

Multiple-Choice Questions

1. The Twenty-second Amendment, the first ratified after World War II:
    A. ended the poll tax as a requirement for voting.
    B. allowed eighteen-year-olds to vote in national elections.
    C. granted statehood to Alaska and Hawaii.
  * D. limited presidents to two terms.

2. In the election of 1952:
    A. women voters overwhelmingly supported Taft.
    B. Democrats for the first time since 1860 carried every state in the Northeast.
  * C. Eisenhower won five states in the periphery of the South.
    D. Democrats were able to keep their New Deal coalition intact.

3. Dwight D. Eisenhower grew up in:
  * A. Kansas.
    B. Massachusetts.
    C. Mississippi.
    D. Virginia.

4. Eisenhower's "domestic conservatism" included all the following *except*:
   A. budget cutting.
   * B. cutting support for Interstate Highways.
   C. ending wage and price controls.
   D. reducing farm subsidies.

5. Eisenhower's administration extended the reach of the New Deal through all the following *except*:
   A. extending coverage of the Social Security Act.
   B. increasing the federal minimum wage.
   C. increasing federal expenditures for public health.
   * D. increasing federal expenditures for low-income housing.

6. In order to end the deadlock in the Korean peace talks, Eisenhower:
   * A. hinted that the United States might use atomic weapons.
   B. agreed to return all prisoners.
   C. threatened to cut off shipments of food and medicine to South Korea.
   D. suggested that the talks be held in Moscow.

7. Joseph McCarthy:
   A. died of a sudden heart attack at the peak of his popularity.
   * B. was "condemned" by the Senate for contempt of that body.
   C. won the Democratic nomination for president in 1956.
   D. became convinced that there were communists in the United States Army when he served as chief American negotiator in the peace talks to end the Korean War.

8. The Warren Court:
   * A. limited internal security measures.
   B. took the position that the states, rather than the federal government, were responsible for internal security.
   C. consistently upheld state laws requiring racial segregation.
   D. followed Eisenhower's conservatism in social and political matters.

9. The term "brinksmanship" is most associated with:
   A. Winston Churchill.
   * B. John Foster Dulles.
   C. Harry Truman.
   D. Earl Warren.

10. Ngo Dinh Diem:
    - A. was a Communist.
    - B. was the French-supported leader of North Vietnam.
    - * C. received American assistance during Eisenhower's administration.
    - D. is correctly represented by all the above statements.

11. Ho Chi Minh:
    - A. was a Communist.
    - B. was a Vietnamese nationalist.
    - C. received American aid to fight the Japanese during World War II.
    - * D. is correctly represented by all the above statements.

12. Concerning the uprisings in French Indochina, the Truman and Eisenhower administrations:
    - * A. sided with the French.
    - B. sided with the Vietnamese.
    - C. sided with the Chinese.
    - D. tried to remain strictly neutral.

13. The Geneva Accords:
    - A. followed the French victory at Dien Bien Phu.
    - B. left the French in control of North Vietnam.
    - * C. called for elections to reunify Vietnam in 1956.
    - D. were signed by the Americans, but by no other major power.

14. The "A" in SEATO stood for:
    - A. Alliance.
    - B. American.
    - C. Anti-nuclear.
    - * D. Asia.

15. In order to put down a national uprising near the end of 1956, Russian tanks rolled into:
    - A. Czechoslovakia.
    - * B. Hungary.
    - C. Romania.
    - D. Yugoslavia.

16. In the election of 1956:
    A. Eisenhower's liberal policies almost cost him the Republican nomination.
    * B. Eisenhower became the first Republican since Reconstruction to win a Deep South state.
    C. Democrats campaigned mainly on the civil rights issue.
    D. Democrats won the White House and majorities in both houses of Congress.

17. When Israeli forces invaded Egypt in October 1956, the United States:
    * A. supported the Egyptians.
    B. supported the Israelis.
    C. tried to remain strictly neutral.
    D. opposed the Soviet position.

18. Americans suddenly became concerned about the apparent "missile gap" between the United States and the Soviet Union in 1957:
    A. when the CIA discovered the size of the Russian military budget.
    B. as a direct result of heavy cuts in defense spending.
    * C. when Russia launched *Sputnik* I.
    D. when Russia exploded its first hydrogen bomb.

19. The first manned flight in orbit was led by:
    A. John Glenn.
    * B. Alan B. Shepard, Jr.
    C. Neil Armstorng.
    D. Sherman Adams.

20. Just before the Manila Conference in 1954, the islands of Quemoy and Matsu were controlled by:
    A. China.
    B. Japan.
    C. Laos.
    * D. Taiwan.

21. The Eisenhower Doctrine promised financial and economic aid against Communist aggression in what area?
    * A. the Middle East
    B. East Asia
    C. Berlin
    D. Hungary

22. The 1960 Russian-American summit meeting in Paris failed:
    A. when Eisenhower refused to give Russia permission to inspect American military installations.
    B. after Russia offered military aid to the rebel government in Hungary.
  * C. because of the U-2 spy-plane incident.
    D. when Russian troops invaded Iraq just one week before the proposed meeting.

23. Fidel Castro's revolution:
    A. replaced the democratic government in Cuba with a dictatorship.
    B. angered many Russians who had wanted Cuba as a Communist foothold in the Western Hemisphere.
  * C. initially had the support of many Americans.
    D. ushered in a golden age of Cuban-American trade relations.

24. During the Eisenhower administration, most advances in civil rights came from:
  * A. the judicial branch.
    B. the executive branch.
    C. northern senators.
    D. southern senators.

25. The name of Rosa Parks is usually identified with the:
    A. Citizens' Councils.
    B. Civil Rights Act of 1957.
  * C. Montgomery bus boycott.
    D. school desegregation cases.

26. In the *Brown* decision, the Supreme Court:
    A. ruled in favor of the Topeka Board of Education.
    B. outlawed segregation in public schools by a split five-to-four decision.
    C. agreed with Eisenhower's sentiments toward civil rights.
  * D. cited sociological and psychological findings in support of its decision.

27. "Massive Resistance" was a slogan and policy associated with which of the following?
    A. Thurgood Marshall
    B. the NAACP
  * C. Harry F. Byrd
    D. Martin Luther King, Jr.

28. The "Southern Manifesto":
    A. supported the *Brown* decision.
    * B. opposed the *Brown* decision.
    C. was written by Martin Luther King, Jr.
    D. was written by Dexter Morehouse.

29. When black students tried to enter Little Rock's Central High School in 1957:
    * A. the governor called out the National Guard to block them.
    B. the governor called out a thousand paratroopers to protect them.
    C. President Eisenhower refused to intervene in what he said was "purely a state concern."
    D. Martin Luther King, Jr., organized a massive boycott of school buses to draw attention to continued segregation in public schools.

30. In his Farewell Address, Eisenhower warned against:
    A. increased unemployment.
    * B. the growing military-industrial complex.
    C. moral laxity in foreign affairs.
    D. an overemphasis on looking to the future.

Essay Questions

1. Compare the achievements of Eisenhower's "dynamic conservatism" to those of the New Deal.

2. How did America become involved in Indochina? How did that involvement escalate during Eisenhower's administration?

3. Discuss the civil rights movement in the 1950s. What civil rights did blacks achieve in that decade?

4. Describe the major trends in American foreign policy in the 1950s.

5. Why did Eisenhower's popularity decline between 1956 and 1958?

Matching Questions

A)   Supreme Court chief justice
B)   failed to win Republican presidential nomination in 1952
C)   Democratic presidential candidate in 1956
D)   said "I don't believe you can change the hearts of men with laws or decisions"
E)   White House chief of staff who resigned in a scandal
F)   army counsel in the televised McCarthy hearings
G)   U-2 spy-plane pilot
H)   NAACP lawyer
I)   Arkansas governor
J)   secretary of state in 1950s

E   1. Sherman Adams
J   2. John Foster Dulles
D   3. Dwight Eisenhower
I   4. Orval Faubus
H   5. Thurgood Marshall
G   6. Francis Gary Powers
C   7. Adlai Stevenson
B   8. Robert A. Taft
A   9. Earl Warren
F   10. Joseph Welch

Chapter 34

NEW FRONTIERS: POLITICS AND SOCIAL CHANGE IN THE 1960s

This chapter covers the administrations of Kennedy and Johnson, including social and economic developments, the civil rights revolution, and developments in Vietnam.

Chapter Outline

I. Kennedy's rise
  A. The election of 1960
    1. Backgrounds of the candidates
    2. The campaign
      a. Kennedy's Catholicism not a problem
      b. Televised debates favored Kennedy
      c. The civil rights issue
    3. Results
  B. Kennedy's administration
    1. Cabinet appointments emphasized youth
    2. The "Kennedy style"

II. The Kennedy record
  A. Congress Democratic but conservative
  B. Legislative successes
    1. Foreign aid
    2. Trade Expansion Act
    3. Domestic social legislation
  C. The Warren Court on civil liberties
  D. Civil rights under Kennedy
    1. Kennedy at first hesitant to act
    2. Sit-ins
      a. Based on King's "militant nonviolence" philosophy
      b. Creation of SNCC
    3. Freedom riders
      a. Organized by Congress on Racial Equality
      b. Tested the ban on segregated buses and trains

       4. Integration of the University of Mississippi
       5. Demonstration in Birmingham
          a. Police Commissioner Eugene "Bull" Connor
          b. King's "Letter from Birmingham City Jail"
          c. Impact on civil rights movement
       6. March on Washington
          a. High point of movement
          b. King's "I Have a Dream" speech

III. Foreign frontiers
    A. Bay of Pigs disaster
       1. 1,500 anti-Castro Cubans prepared by CIA
       2. Failure of invasion
    B. Berlin Wall
       1. Khrushchev threatened to limit access to Berlin
       2. Kennedy asked Congress for more defense funds
       3. Soviets constructed Berlin Wall
    C. Cuban missile crisis
       1. Discovery of missiles in Cuba
       2. Kennedy's reaction
          a. Choice of a blockade or an air strike
          b. Kennedy announced decision for blockade one week after discovery of the missiles
       3. Soviet response
          a. Soviet ships did not try to cross blockade
          b. Two messages from Khrushchev
       4. Aftereffects
          a. Lowered tensions
          b. Sale of wheat
          c. Washington-Moscow "hot line"
          d. Removal of obsolete missiles
          e. Nuclear test ban treaty
    D. Vietnam
       1. Neutrality for Laos
       2. Kennedy's reluctance to escalate
       3. Premier Ngo Dinh Diem
          a. Lack of economic and social reform
          b. Opposition to Diem
          c. Overthrow of Diem and later military regimes

IV. The end of Kennedy's administration
    A. Assassination in Dallas
    B. Lee Harvey Oswald
    C. Jack Ruby
    D. Chief Justice Earl Warren

V. Lyndon Johnson and the Great Society
   A. Johnson's background and style
      1. Comparisons to other leaders
      2. Admiration for FDR
      3. "The last frontiersman"
      4. Mastery of politics and Congress
      5. Broke the congressional logjam that had blocked Kennedy's programs
   B. The war on poverty
      1. Michael Harrington's *The Other America*
      2. Economic Opportunity Bill
   C. The election of 1964
      1. Republicans
         a. Sought "a choice, not an echo"
         b. Nominated Barry Goldwater
         c. Goldwater's weaknesses
      2. Johnson's appeal for consensus
      3. Landslide victory for Johnson
   D. Landmark legislation
      1. Health insurance
         a. Medicare for the aged
         b. Medicaid for the indigent
      2. Federal aid to education
      3. Appalachian redevelopment
      4. Housing and urban development
      5. Immigration Act
   E. Assessment of legislation

VI. From civil rights to Black Power
   A. Civil rights legislation
      1. Civil Rights Act of 1964
      2. Voting Rights Act of 1965
         a. The march to Montgomery
         b. Provisions of the act
   B. Rise of the Black Power movement
      1. Riots in 1965 and 1966
      2. Condition of urban blacks
      3. Philosophy of the Black Power movement
      4. Malcolm X and other leaders
      5. Assessment of the Black Power movement
         a. Minority of blacks supported it
         b. Effects on civil rights movement
            (1) Helped African Americans take pride in their racial heritage

        (2)   Forced King and others to focus attention on plight of inner-city blacks

VII. The tragedy of Vietnam
    A. Efforts to avoid defeat
        1. Escalation
        2. The cost of the war
    B. The Tonkin Gulf Resolution
        1. Official sanction for escalation
        2. Response to attack on American destroyers
        3. Johnson interpreted to be congressional approval for war
    C. Escalation in 1965
        1. Attack at Pleiku
        2. "Operation Rolling Thunder"
        3. Combat troops to Vietnam
    D. The context for policy
        1. Consistent with earlier foreign policy goals
        2. Goal of American involvement
        3. Erosion of support
    E. The turning point
        1. The Tet Offensive
        2. Further erosion of support
        3. Presidential primaries became referendums on Johnson's Vietnam policy
        4. Johnson announced that he would not seek another term

VIII. The crescendo of the sixties
    A. Tragedies of 1968
        1. Assassination of Martin Luther King, Jr.
        2. Assassination of Robert Kennedy
    B. The election of 1968
        1. Democrats
            a. Nominated Hubert Humphrey
            b. Party in disarray
        2. Republicans
            a. Quiet convention in Miami
            b. Nominated Richard Nixon
            c. Represented stability and order
        3. George Wallace
            a. Candidate of the American Independent party

        b. Could have thrown the election into the House
          of Representatives
    4. Results
        a. Narrow victory for Nixon
        b. Wallace received 10 million votes

Lecture Ideas

1. For a lecture on the continuing story of the American involvement in Vietnam, see George C. Herring's *America's Longest War* (2nd ed., 1986). Also see Marilyn B. Young's *The Vietnam Wars, 1945–1990* (1991) and Larry Berman's *No Peace, No Honor: Nixon, Kissinger, and Betrayal in Vietnam* (2001). Neil L. Jamieson's *Understanding Vietnam* (1993) offers a number of insights on Vietnamese perspectives on the war.

2. Divide the class up into two groups and have them research and analyze the Cuban missile crisis. One group could look into how America discovered the missiles and the other group can report on the crisis from that point. See Mark White's *Cuba: Kennedy, Khrushchev, Castro and the 1962 Crisis* (1977) and Robert F. Kennedy's *Thirteen Days* (1969).

3. A lecture on the year 1968 sets the tone for the height of the protest movement in the 1960s. Evaluate the culture, economics, war, and politics of that year to show the change in American society that took place throughout the decade. See John C. McWilliams's *The 1960s Cultural Revolution* (2000). Maurice Isserman and Michael Kazin's *America Divided: The Civil War of the 1960s* (2000), Irwin Unger and Debi Unger's *Turning Point: 1968* (1988), David Farber's *Chicago '68* (1988), and Alexander Bloom's *Long Time Gone: Sixties America Then and Now* (2001).

4. To show how race relations and conditions for blacks changed in the South after the civil rights gains of the mid-1960s, see John Shelton Reed's "Up from Segregation" (*Virginia Quarterly Review*, Summer 1984), Robert Westbrot's *Freedom Bound: A History of America's Civil Rights Movement* (1990), and Robert C. Smith's *Racism in the Post-Civil Rights Era* (1995).

5. Perhaps the best source of information on the domestic policies of the Kennedy and Johnson years is Allen J. Matusow's *The Unraveling of America* (1984). Thomas Brown's *JFK: History of an Image* (1988) would be good for a lecture evaluating Kennedy's achievements.

True/False Questions

F   1. Volunteers in Service to America was a group of Republican young people who campaigned for Nixon and other conservative candidates in 1960.

T   2. Hubert Humphrey was Lyndon Johnson's running mate in the presidential race of 1964.

F   3. Jack Ruby was charged with assassinating President John F. Kennedy, but doubts about his guilt linger.

T   4. Lyndon Johnson's domestic program was called the Great Society.

T   5. Barry Goldwater said "extremism in the defense of liberty is no vice."

F   6. President Johnson was not as adept at handling Congress as President Kennedy had been.

F   7. The Black Panthers organization was formed in 1961.

F   8. Congress narrowly defeated President Johnson's request in 1964 for authorization to "take all necessary measures" to prevent further aggression in Vietnam.

T   9. The Vietcong were the rebel army in South Vietnam.

T   10. The Tet Offensive marked a turning point in public support for the war in Vietnam.

Multiple-Choice Questions

1. Which of the following statements about Richard Nixon is *not* true?
   A. He was Eisenhower's vice-president.
   B. He was from California.
   C. He was a nationally known Republican by the early 1950s.
   * D. He was Catholic.

2. Which of the following was assassinated in 1965?
   * A. Malcolm X
   B. John F. Kennedy
   C. Robert F. Kennedy
   D. Martin Luther King, Jr.

3. Which of the following statements about John F. Kennedy is
   not true?
   A. He was the author of *Profiles in Courage*, a book about
      political leaders who "made the tough decisions."
   B. His family was wealthy.
   * C. He was an outspoken critic of McCarthy.
   D. He gained support after his television debate with
      Nixon.

4. Robert F. Kennedy served as President Kennedy's:
   A. secretary of defense.
   B. secretary of state.
   * C. attorney general.
   D. chairman of the National Security Council.

5. President Kennedy's cabinet appointments:
   * A. emphasized youth.
   B. were mostly politicians who had been helpful to the
      Democratic party.
   C. included the first black secretary of the treasury.
   D. are correctly described by all the above statements.

6. One of the biggest legislative accomplishments of the Kennedy
   administration came in the field of:
   * A. tariff reduction.
   B. civil rights for blacks.
   C. federal aid to education.
   D. health insurance for the aged.

7. In *Miranda* v. *Arizona*, the Supreme Court:
   A. outlawed residential segregation by race.
   B. ruled that school prayer was unconstitutional.
   * C. confirmed the obligation of police to inform arrested
      suspects of their rights before questioning.
   D. ordered the release of a conscientious objector who
      refused to fight in Vietnam for moral reasons.

8. The "N" in SNCC stands for:
   A. National.
   B. Negro.
   * C. Nonviolent.
   D. North.

9. The philosophy of "militant nonviolence" was best seen in the work of:
    A. Eldridge Cleaver.
   * B. Martin Luther King, Jr.
    C. H. Rap Brown.
    D. Huey P. Newton.

10. The author of "Letter from Birmingham City Jail" was:
    A. Ross Barnett.
    B. Eugene Connor.
   * C. Martin Luther King, Jr.
    D. James Meredith.

11. The 1963 March on Washington:
    A. ended when Jesse Jackson and other civil rights leaders were arrested for parading without a permit.
    B. was the setting of Jesse Jackson's "I Have a Dream" speech.
   * C. was the largest civil rights demonstration in American history.
    D. is correctly represented by all the above statements.

12. The Bay of Pigs incident:
    A. freed 154 American prisoners-of-war still being held by the North Koreans.
    B. was a limited success.
   * C. resulted in the capture of 1100 men.
    D. forced Cuba to grant certain trade concessions.

13. Faced with the presence of Soviet missiles in Cuba, President Kennedy:
    A. ordered a "surgical" air strike.
    B. waited to see what the Russians would do.
   * C. ordered a naval blockade of Cuba.
    D. broke off diplomatic relations with Cuba.

14. Following the Cuban missile crisis, several steps were taken that eased Russian-American tensions. These included all the following *except*:
    A. a treaty that banned nuclear testing in the atmosphere.
    B. installation of a "hot line" between Moscow and Washington.
   * C. the halting of construction on the Berlin Wall for several years.
    D. the removal of obsolete missiles from Turkey, Italy, and Britain.

15. Concerning Vietnam, President Kennedy:
    A. continued to support the Pathet Lao.
    * B. increased the number of American "advisers" there.
    C. asked Congress to send American combat troops to force the surrender of Diem's pro-Communist regime.
    D. reduced the number of American troops there by half.

16. Lyndon Johnson was from:
    A. Arizona.
    B. Georgia.
    C. Pennsylvania.
    * D. Texas.

17. *The Other America* described the problem of:
    * A. poverty.
    B. racial discrimination.
    C. Cuban refugees.
    D. Native Americans.

18. In the early 1960s, conservative Republicans felt that in the previous two decades their party had:
    A. been too isolationist in foreign policy and too limited in domestic policy.
    * B. merely echoed the Democratic party.
    C. strayed too far from the principles of Franklin Roosevelt.
    D. been too ideological.

19. In the election of 1964:
    A. Republicans increased their majorities in Congress.
    * B. Lyndon Johnson won by a landslide.
    C. the race issue helped Johnson win the states of the Deep South.
    D. Barry Goldwater campaigned on a platform of "peace in Vietnam and civil rights at home."

20. The health insurance bill passed by Congress in 1965:
    * A. created Medicaid to help cover medical payments for the indigent.
    B. was opposed by the American Medical Association.
    C. was vetoed by Johnson because Congress refused to raise taxes to pay for it.
    D. was ruled unconstitutional by the Supreme Court two years later.

21. The Civil Rights Act of 1964 did all the following *except*:
    * A. require that African Americans be given preference over equally qualified white applicants in most employment situations.
    B. outlaw discrimination in restaurants, hotels, and other public accommodations.
    C. require that literacy tests for voting be administered in writing.
    D. require federally assisted programs and private employers to eliminate discrimination.

22. The Watts riots:
    A. led to passage the following year of the Voting Rights Act.
    * B. signaled a new phase in the civil rights movement.
    C. began with the assassination of Martin Luther King, Jr.
    D. is correctly represented by all the above statements.

23. The Immigration Act of 1965:
    A. favored immigrants from southern and eastern Europe.
    B. favored immigrants from northern and western Europe.
    * C. treated all nationalities equally.
    D. resulted in a tremendous surge of European immigration to the United States.

24. The Tonkin Gulf Resolution:
    A. was the declaration by the United Nations that condemned Communist aggression in South Vietnam.
    * B. authorized the president to take whatever means were necessary to defend American forces and prevent further Communist aggression.
    C. was the result of a South Vietnamese attack on a camp of American military advisers.
    D. was vetoed by Johnson.

25. Operation "Rolling Thunder" was the:
    A. code name for Lyndon Johnson's presidential campaign of 1964.
    B. code name for Barry Goldwater's presidential campaign of 1964.
    C. first major "search-and-destroy" operation carried out by American troops in Vietnam.
    * D. first sustained bombing of North Vietnam.

26. The 1968 Republican convention:
    A. was held in Los Angeles.
    B. was held in Chicago.
    C. was marred by riots and antiwar demonstrations.
    * D. nominated Spiro Agnew as its vice-presidential candidate.

27. America's goal in Vietnam was to:
    A. provoke Red China to enter the war.
    * B. keep the North Vietnamese and Viet Cong from winning.
    C. force the Communists from North Vietnam.
    D. reopen vital Asian trade routes.

28. Who came in a close second in the 1968 New Hampshire Democratic primary?
    A. Hubert Humphrey
    B. John F. Kennedy
    C. Robert F. Kennedy
    * D. Eugene McCarthy

29. The presidential candidate of the American Independent party in 1968 was:
    A. Eugene McCarthy.
    B. Clark Clifford.
    * C. George Wallace.
    D. Curtis LeMay.

30. In the election of 1968:
    A. Richard Nixon won by the largest landslide since 1924.
    B. Democrats won the Deep South states.
    C. most of Richard Nixon's support came from the Northeast.
    * D. Hubert Humphrey was the Democratic candidate for president.

Essay Questions

1. Compare the philosophies and styles of Martin Luther King, Jr., and the leaders of the Black Power movement.

2. What were the main domestic achievements of the New Frontier and the Great Society? Which accomplished more? Why?

3. Describe the major trends in the cold war in the 1960s.

4. "American military intervention in Vietnam was . . . a logical culmination of the assumptions widely shared by the foreign policy establishment and leaders of both political parties since the early days of the cold war." Explain this statement.

5. Describe the candidates, issues, and results of the presidential elections of 1960, 1964, and 1968.

Matching Questions

A) Chief Justice of U.S. Supreme Court
B) won California's Democratic primary in 1968
C) first black student at the University of Mississippi
D) Birmingham police commissioner
E) won Arizona in 1964 presidential race
F) wrote *The Other America*
G) elected vice-president in 1960
H) secretary of state
I) American army commander in Vietnam
J) became major spokesman for Black Muslim movement

D	1. Eugene Connor
E	2. Barry Goldwater
F	3. Michael Harrington
G	4. Lyndon Johnson
B	5. Robert F. Kennedy
J	6. Malcolm Little
C	7. James H. Meredith
H	8. Dean Rusk
A	9. Earl Warren
I	10. William C. Westmoreland

Chapter 35

REBELLION AND REACTION IN THE 1960s AND 1970s

This chapter describes the youth revolt of the late 1960s, including the New Left and the counterculture, and traces the gains made by women and ethnic minorities. It covers Nixon's foreign and domestic affairs, stressing Vietnam, stagflation, and Watergate. It also discusses the domestic and foreign policies of the Ford and Carter administrations.

Chapter Outline

I. Attacks on traditional institutions
   A. Youth revolt
      1. The maturing baby-boom generation
      2. The beginnings of the youth revolt
   B. The New Left
      1. Students for a Democratic Society
         a. Founded by Tom Hayden and Al Haber
         b. The Port Huron statement
      2. Free Speech Movement
         a. Origins at Berkeley
         b. Program and tactics
      3. Role of Vietnam war in radicalizing youth
      4. Increased college protests
      5. The 1968 Democratic convention
      6. The breakup of the New Left
   C. The counterculture
      1. Origins and philosophy
      2. Communal living
      3. Rock music concerts
      4. Downfall of the counterculture
   D. Feminism
      1. Betty Friedan's *The Feminine Mystique*
      2. National Organization for Women
      3. Legal gains
      4. Divisions within the movement
      5. Changes in traditional sex roles

     E. Sexual Revolution and the Pill
1. Freedom of expression
2. Development of the pill
     F. Minorities
1. Hispanics
     a. "Chicanos"
     b. United Farm Workers
     c. Growth of Hispanic population
     d. Political power
2. Native Americans
     a. Conditions that fostered concern
     b. The American Indian Movement
3. Gay rights
     a. The Stonewall riots
     b. Internal divisions and conservative backlash

II. Nixon and Vietnam
     A. Gradual withdrawal
1. Immediate withdrawal of troops rejected
2. Nixon's Vietnam policy
     a. American demands at the Paris peace talks
     b. Quell domestic unrest by gradual withdrawal of troops
     c. Expanded air war
     B. Divisions at home
1. Decline in military morale
2. My Lai massacre
3. Nixon's Cambodian "incursion"
     a. Kent State
     b. Many Americans supported National Guard
4. Publication of *Pentagon Papers*
     C. War without end
1. Peace talks
     a. Shifts in American negotiating position
     b. "Christmas bombings"
     c. Peace agreement signed
2. Effects of American withdrawal
3. The legacy of Vietnam

III. Nixon and Middle America
     A. Domestic affairs
1. Civil rights
     a. Nixon's stance
     b. Supreme Court decisions

      2. Nixon's efforts to shape the Court
         a. The Warren Court characterized
      3. Social programs
         a. Nixon's domestic program characterized
         b. Social legislation of the Democratic Congress
   B. Economic malaise
      1. Effects
      2. Causes
         a. Holdover problems from Johnson's administration
         b. International competition
         c. Oil embargo
         d. Increasing work force
      3. Efforts to cure stagflation
   C. Environmental protection
      1. Creation of Environmental Protection Agency
      2. Increased understanding of limited nature of resources
      3. Few people willing to sacrifice

IV. Nixon triumphant
   A. China
      1. Official recognition
      2. Effects
   B. Détente
      1. Nixon's visit to China
      2. SALT agreement
      3. Wheat deal
   C. Shuttle diplomacy
      1. Problems in Middle East
      2. Kissinger's role in seeking peace
   D. 1972 election
      1. Republicans nominate Nixon
      2. Democrats nominate McGovern
      3. Landslide victory for Nixon

V. Watergate
   A. Uncovering the cover-up
      1. Previous incidents of "dirty tricks"
      2. Developments in the Senate committee hearings
      3. Nixon's resignation
   B. Effects of Watergate
      1. Cynicism over Ford's pardoning of Nixon
      2. Legislative responses to Watergate

VI. An unelected president
    A. The Ford years
        1. Conservative domestic philosophy
            a. Role of the federal government
            b. The economy
        2. Foreign policy
            a. Arms talks
            b. Middle East
            c. Cambodian Communists and the *Mayaguez* incident
    B. The 1976 election
        1. Republicans nominated Ford
        2. Democrats nominated Carter
        3. Carter won
            a. New Deal coalition
            b. Low voter turnout

VII. The Carter interregnum
    A. Policy stalemate
        1. The Carter style
        2. Liberal successes
        3. Energy policy
            a. The energy bill
            b. Fuel shortage
        4. The Panama Canal Treaty
    B. The Camp David accords
        1. Provisions
        2. Effect
    C. Mounting troubles
        1. The economy
        2. SALT II
        3. Soviet invasion of Afghanistan
    D. Iran
        1. Background to the problem
        2. Hostages taken
        3. Carter unable to gain their release

Lecture Ideas

1. One of the defining moments of the Nixon administration was the Watergate affair. Divide the class up into groups and assign each a particular aspect of this event. Include the motivation for conducting such an operation, the operation itself, and, of course, the coverup and its aftermath. See Michael Schudson's *Watergate in American*

History (1992), Leonard Garment's *In Search of Deep Throat: The Greatest Political Mystery of Our Time* (2000), Arthur M. Schlesinger Jr.'s *The Imperial Presidency* (1973), Stanley Kutler's *Abuse of Power* (1997), and Anthony Summers's *The Arrogance of Power: The Secret World of Richard Nixon* (2000).

2. For a lecture on the feminism of the 1970s, see the pertinent sections of William H. Chafe's *Women and Equality* (1977). Marcia Cohen's *The Sisterhood* (1988) contains an interesting account of Betty Friedan and *The Feminine Mystique* and would be useful for a discussion of how that book changed the women's movement. *Rites of Passage*, edited by Joan Hoff-Wilson (1986), is more detailed on the failure of the ERA. Also see Kathleen C. Berkeley's *The Women's Liberation Movement in America* (1999), Jo Freeman's *The Politics of Women's Liberation* (1979), and Winfred D. Wandersee's *On the Move: American Women in the 1970's* (1998).

3. An overview lecture of American society in the 1970s will enable your students to gain an understanding of future events in American society. Focusing in on the Ford and Carter years would be helpful as you probably covered the Nixon years in earlier lectures. See David Frum's *How We Got Here* (2000), Peter N. Carroll's *It Seemed Like Nothing Happened* (1983), and Bruce Shulman's *The Seventies: The Great Shift in American Culture, Society, and Politics* (2001).

4. William E. Leuchtenburg's *In the Shadow of FDR* (2nd ed., 1992) would be a useful source for a discussion of Jimmy Carter (and later presidents—the most recent edition of the book takes the comparison down to Clinton).

True/False Questions

F   1. The New Left came together in opposition to Richard Nixon's policies.

F   2. "Chicano" was originally a term for any immigrant in Chicago.

T   3. In 1960, unemployment among Native Americans was ten times the national average, their life expectancy was twenty years lower, and their suicide rate was a hundred times greater.

T   4. "New Federalism" was one of the names of Richard Nixon's domestic program.

F   5. Richard Nixon was impeached for Watergate-related offenses.

T   6. President Ford vetoed more bills than any previous president.

F   7. The Camp David Accords were agreements between Iran and Iraq.

F   8. President Carter's greatest achievement in domestic reform was the comprehensive energy program he successfully pushed through Congress.

T   9. Economic problems during Carter's administration included high unemployment, high inflation, and high interest rates.

T   10. The American hostages in Iran were held for over a year.

Multiple-Choice Questions

1. "We are the people of this generation, bred in at least moderate comfort, housed in universities, looking uncomfortably to the world we inherit." This statement was:
    A. written by Jerry Rubin.
    B. written by Clark Kerr.
    * C. the manifesto of the Students for a Democratic Society.
    D. called "the hippie's creed."

2. The Weathermen:
    A. made up the pacifist faction of the SDS.
    * B. followed the strategy of revolutionary terrorism.
    C. were led by Elliot Richardson.
    D. broke from the SDS over the issue of civil rights.

3. The Stonewall riots helped forge a new sense of solidarity among:
    A. African Americans.
    * B. gays.
    C. Native Americans.
    D. women.

4. The "I" in AIM stands for:
    A. immediate.
    * B. Indian.
    C. Indochina.
    D. intercontinental.

5. The author of *The Feminine Mystique*:
    A. was Alice Paul.
    B. was Jane Fonda.
    C. focused on the many gains women had made in the twentieth century.
    * D. protested against the supposed blissful domesticity of American women after World War II.

6. Victories for the women's movement in the 1970s included all the following *except*:
    A. affirmative action.
    B. *Roe* v. *Wade*.
    * C. ratification of the Equal Rights Amendment.
    D. increased economic and political influence.

7. The United Farm Workers:
    A. was especially concerned with black tenant farmers in the South.
    * B. was especially concerned with Hispanic migrant workers.
    C. led a national boycott of beef.
    D. sponsored a national campaign to increase beef consumption.

8. The "silent majority" referred to:
    * A. conservative working- and middle-class citizens.
    B. women.
    C. the coalition of ethnic minorities, the aged, women, and the poor.
    D. the nation's youth, defined by Abbie Hoffman to be anyone under thirty.

9. Nixon's Vietnam policy included all the following *except*:
    A. demands at the Paris peace talks for the withdrawal of Communist forces from South Vietnam.
    * B. continued buildup of American armed forces in Vietnam.
    C. reduction of domestic unrest over the war.
    D. expansion of the air war in Vietnam.

10. The student demonstrations at Kent State University that resulted in the deaths of four students were a response to:
    A. news of the My Lai massacre.
    B. passage of the Gulf of Tonkin resolution.
    C. Nixon's announcement of his planned "Vietnamization" of the war.
    * D. the "incursion" into Cambodia.

11. The so-called *Pentagon Papers*:
    - A. were published in defiance of a Supreme Court decision prohibiting such publication.
    - B. quieted many critics of the Vietnam War.
    - C. broke the story of the My Lai massacre.
    - * D. revealed that Congress and the American people had not been told the full story of the Tonkin Gulf incident.

12. When the United States signed an agreement ending the war in Vietnam:
    - * A. the North Vietnamese kept troops in South Vietnam.
    - B. the war-torn country of Vietnam was finally reunited.
    - C. South Vietnam agreed to a Communist government.
    - D. peace came to the region for almost a dozen years, until the Communist takeover in Cambodia.

13. Nixon's policies on civil rights:
    - * A. were foiled, in part, by the Supreme Court's decision in the *Swann* case.
    - B. had the support of liberal congressmen.
    - C. included strong efforts to desegregate the nation's public schools.
    - D. included support for a renewed Voting Rights Act.

14. The Twenty-sixth Amendment:
    - A. prohibited the president from sending troops out of the country for more than 60 days without the consent of Congress.
    - B. set in motion the affirmative action program.
    - * C. gave eighteen-year-olds the right to vote.
    - D. repealed the Twentieth Amendment.

15. The economic malaise during Nixon's administration was caused by all the following *except*:
    - * A. a rapid contraction of the money supply.
    - B. increased government spending through the 1960s without a major tax increase.
    - C. the stiff competition American goods faced on the international market.
    - D. the oil shortage.

16. The "Saturday Night Massacre":
    - A. resulted in the deaths of 12 Native American demonstrators.
    - B. resulted in the destruction of three Vietnamese villages and the killing of over 100 "suspected" Viet Cong.

    C. was the name given the police assault on student demonstrators at Columbia University.

*   D. involved the firing of Archibald Cox, special prosecutor for the Watergate case.

17. Nixon's triumph concerning China was:

*   A. American diplomatic recognition of the People's Republic of China.

    B. American diplomatic recognition of Taiwan.

    C. the successful conclusion of negotiations for nuclear arms reduction.

    D. the signing of a mutual defense treaty.

18. The SALT agreement:

    A. ended the arms race.

    B. greatly limited the development of new weapons systems.

*   C. set limits on certain types of nuclear weapons.

    D. prohibited either side from producing or possessing intercontinental ballistic missiles.

19. In the presidential election of 1972:

*   A. Nixon won by the largest majority ever for a Republican candidate.

    B. the Democrats won only the states of the Deep South and New England.

    C. George Wallace won ten electoral votes as the nominee of the American Independent party.

    D. all the above statements are true.

20. In response to the Watergate revelations, Congress passed several pieces of legislation designed to curb executive power. This legislation included all the following *except*:

    A. the War Powers Act.

    B. an act that set new limits on campaign contributions and expenditures.

    C. a strengthening of the Freedom of Information Act.

*   D. the Presidential Pardon Act.

21. In foreign policy, President Ford:

    A. was advised mainly by Dean Rusk.

*   B. laid the foundation for SALT II.

    C. negotiated the Camp David agreements.

    D. called for an international trade embargo of Iran.

22. Jimmy Carter:
    A. was governor of Virginia.
    B. was only the second Catholic to be elected president.
  * C. was a peanut farmer and former naval officer.
    D. is correctly represented by all the above statements.

23. In the presidential election of 1976:
  * A. Jimmy Carter won most of the black vote in the South.
    B. Jimmy Carter beat Ronald Reagan by a small margin.
    C. Ronald Reagan won every southern state except Virginia.
    D. voter turnout was over 60 percent, reflecting a greatly increased political awareness following the Watergate affair.

24. As president, Jimmy Carter:
    A. opposed significant environmental legislation.
    B. showed a sustained increase in popularity after entering the White House.
  * C. created new cabinet-level departments of energy and education.
    D. appointed the first woman to the Supreme Court.

25. *Silent Spring*:
  * A. was written by Rachel Carson.
    B. described the "crisis of confidence" in the late 1970s and need for "a rebirth of the American spirit."
    C. described the "silent despair" in the months after the Woodstock music festival.
    D. was written by Eugene McCarthy.

26. President Carter said American foreign policy should be based on:
    A. anti-communism.
    B. maintaining American superiority around the world.
    C. economic self-interest.
  * D. the defense of human rights.

27. The Panama Canal treaties:
    A. were rejected by the Senate.
    B. passed the Senate but were rejected by President Carter.
  * C. barely passed the Senate, despite President Carter's support.
    D. angered liberals, who said Carter was selling out his principles for popular support.

28. President Carter's "crowning foreign policy achievement" was the:
    A. negotiation of free-trade agreements with communist nations.
    * B. arrangement of a peace agreement between Israel and Egypt.
    C. restoration of diplomatic relations with Taiwan.
    D. restoration of diplomatic relations with Cuba.

29. Faced with the Soviet invasion of Afghanistan, President Carter did all the following *except*:
    A. suspend shipments of grain to Russia.
    B. shelve the SALT II agreements.
    C. urge an international boycott of the 1980 Olympics in Moscow.
    * D. persuade Congress to pass a law reducing the number of Russians who could emigrate to the United States.

30. When President Carter sent American commandos to rescue the American hostages in Iran:
    A. Henry Kissinger resigned as secretary of state.
    * B. helicopter failures forced the mission's abortion.
    C. the shah of Iran threatened to kill the hostages if there was another such mission.
    D. All the above are true.

Essay Questions

1. Discuss the various aspects of President Nixon's Vietnam policy. How was Nixon's policy different from those of his predecessors?

2. Describe the domestic policy of the Nixon administration.

3. What economic problems did Presidents Ford and Carter face? How did they try to solve these problems, and how successful were they?

4. What were the main foreign policy achievements of the Carter administration? Where did Carter fail?

5. Describe the gains made by women and ethnic minorities in the 1960s and early 1970s. In each case, what accounted for the gains?

Matching Questions

A)   shot and left paralyzed in 1972
B)   secretary of state in 1975
C)   founded NOW
D)   led Senate investigation committee on Watergate
E)   convicted for My Lai massacre
F)   gave testimony before Senate committee that linked Nixon directly to Watergate cover-up
G)   wrote *Silent Spring*
H)   resigned as vice-president in 1973
I)   lost presidential election of 1976
J)   led United Farm Workers

H	1. Spiro Agnew
E	2. William Calley
G	3. Rachel Carson
J	4. Cesar Chavez
F	5. John Dean
D	6. Samuel J. Ervin, Jr.
I	7. Gerald Ford
C	8. Betty Friedan
B	9. Henry Kissinger
A	10. George Wallace

Chapter 36

A CONSERVATIVE INSURGENCY

This chapter examines domestic and foreign policy under the Reagan and Bush administrations.

Chapter Outline

I. The Reagan revolution
   A. The making of a president
     1. Reagan's background
     2. Influence of FDR
     3. Conservative transformation
     4. Reagan's attraction
     5. Record as California governor
   B. The move to Reagan
     1. Factors favoring Reagan
       a. Demographic
         (1) Population aging
         (2) Growth of "Sunbelt"
       b. Rise of new fundamentalism
         (1) Increased popularity
         (2) Political agenda
     2. The 1980 election
       a. Results
       b. Voter apathy

II. Reagan's first term
   A. Reaganomics
     1. Background to "supply-side" economics
     2. Reagan's early economic program
     3. Economic program passed by Congress
       a. Economic Recovery Tax Act
       b. Deficit increased
   B. Reagan's domestic policy
     1. Budget cuts
       a. Social programs cut
       b. Sagging bond and stock markets

           c. Tax increases
        2. New priorities
           a. Deregulation of public lands
           b. "Teflon Presidency"
           c. Reagan's stance on labor
           d. Reagan's stance on women
           e. Reagan's stance on civil rights
    C. Reagan's foreign policy
        1. The defense buildup
        2. The Americas
           a. El Salvador
           b. Nicaragua
        3. The Middle East
           a. Reasons for tensions
           b. America's position
           c. Tragedy in Lebanon
        4. Grenada

III. Reagan's second term
    A. The election of 1984
        1. Republicans
        2. Democrats
        3. Election results
    B. Tax reform
    C. Arms control and the Geneva summit
    D. The Iran-Contra affair
        1. Background
        2. Tower Commission
        3. Effects
    E. Central America
        1. Nicaragua
        2. El Salvador and Panama
    F. Debt and the stock market crash
    G. The poor, the homeless, and AIDS victims
    H. A historic treaty
        1. The INF Treaty
        2. Lessening of tensions with the Soviets
    I. The Reagan legacy
    J. The 1988 election
        1. Michael Dukakis
        2. George Bush
        3. The campaign
        4. Election results

IV. The Bush years
    A. Tone of the Bush administration
    B. The national debt
    C. The drug problem
    D. The end of the cold war
        1. Events in the Soviet Union
        2. Other democratic movements
    E. Panama
        1. The problem of Manuel Noriega
        2. Invasion of Panama and capture of Noriega
    F. The Gulf War
        1. Background
        2. Actions by United Nations and United States
        3. Operation Desert Shield
        4. Operation Desert Storm
        5. Aftermath of war

Lecture Ideas

1. An overview of the Reagan domestic agenda would be a good start-
ing point for this chapter. Divide the class into groups and have each
study a report on a particular aspect of Reagan's domestic initiatives—
economic, social, cultural. See John Karagac's *Between Promise and
Policy: Ronald Reagan and Conservative Reformism* (2000), John Sloan's
The Reagan Effect: Economics and Presidential Leadership (1999), Gary
Willis's *Reagan's America* (1987), David Stockman's *The Triumph of
Politics: How the Reagan Revolution Failed* (1986), Michael Schaller's
Reckoning with Reagan: America and its Presidents in the 1980s (1992),
and B. B. Kymlicka nd Jean V. Matthews's *The Reagan Presidency: An
Incomplete Revolution* (1990).

2. Michael Harrington, the writer and social activist who opened the
eyes of many Americans to the problem of poverty in 1962 with *The
Other America*, describes a new class of poor in *The New American
Poverty* (1984). Harrington's work would be a good source for a
lecture on this continuing problem in American society.

3. An overview of American foreign policy in the 1980s will give
students a good background into the diplomatic policies of
Presidents Reagan and Bush. Be sure to emphasize United States'
Central American policy. See Francis Fitzgerald's *Way Out There in
the Blue: Reagan, Star Wars, and the End of the Cold War* (2000), Beth
Fischer's *The Reagan Reversal: Foreign Policy and the End of the Cold
War* (1997), Caspar W. Weinberger's *Fighting for Peace: Seven Critical
Years in the Pentagon* (1990), Walter LeFeber's *Inevitable Revolution*

(1993), and Kenneth Coleman and George Herring's *Central American Crisis* (1985).

4. A good source for a lecture on the Gulf War is Lester H. Bruce's *America and the Iraqi Crisis, 1990–1992: Origins and Aftermath* (1993). Also see Colin Gordon's "Lessons of History? Past and Present in the Gulf War" (*Radical History Review*, Winter 1993), an article that makes several interesting analogies between the Gulf War and the conflict in Korea and refutes the more commonly heard analogies to Vietnam and the Munich Agreement. Also see Micah L. Sifry and Christopher Cerf, eds., *The Gulf War Reader* (1991) and Richard Hallon's *Storm Over Iraq* (1992).

5. John Steele Gordon's "Understanding the S&L Mess" (*American Heritage*, Feb./March 1991) would be a useful source for a lecture on the savings and loan crisis; Gordon's article is especially good at placing the crisis in historical perspective. See also Connie Bruck's *The Predators Ball* (1988) and L. William Seidman's *Full Faith and Credit: The Great S & L Debacle and Other Washington Sagas* (1993).

True/False Questions

T   1. Despite Ronald Reagan's poor church attendance and his divorce and remarriage, the Religious Right supported him over Jimmy Carter in 1980.

T   2. "Boll weevils" were southern conservative Democrats in Congress who supported Republican measures.

T   3. The "Sunbelt" includes the southern and western states.

T   4. The "Laffer curve" addressed the connection revenue and tax rates.

T   5. The Strategic Defense Initiative was also know as "Star Wars."

F   6. The Iran-Contra affair involved the illegal sales of arms to the Contra rebels in Iran.

F   7. Ronald Reagan made AIDS research a top priority of his administration.

T   8. The biggest domestic problem facing the Bush administration was the national debt.

F   9. President Bush ordered the invasion of Grenada, a small Pacific island, after its unstable government threatened to nationalize American-owned businesses located there.

F   10. By 2000 the AIDS epidemic had disappeared.

Multiple-Choice Questions

1. Ronald Reagan:
   A. turned to politics after a successful career as a lawyer.
 * B. had at one time supported FDR's New Deal.
   C. pushed for a stronger defense during his three terms in the U.S. Senate.
   D. resigned from Nixon's cabinet during the Senate Watergate hearings.

2. The 1980 Census reported that:
   A. the U.S. population was getting younger.
 * B. Americans were moving to the traditionally conservative South and West.
   C. nearly one-third of Americans lived in urban areas.
   D. All the above statements are true.

3. The Moral Majority stood for all the following *except*:
   A. outlawing abortions.
   B. teaching creationism in the schools.
 * C. bettering relations with the Soviet Union.
   D. allowing prayer in public schools.

4. In the race for president in 1980, Ronald Reagan:
   A. swept to an easy victory.
   B. just barely won the election.
 * C. won the popular vote.
   D. was selected by the House of Representatives.

5. In the presidential election of 1980:
 * A. Ronald Reagan, the Republican candidate, won an overwhelming majority of the popular vote.
   B. Walter Mondale, the Democratic candidate, carried just six states.
   C. George Wallace, an independent candidate, won two southern states.
   D. All the above statements are true.

6. Most of the nonvoters in the 1980 election were:
    A. conservatives in the Northeast.
  * B. working-class urban Democrats.
    C. southern blacks.
    D. Republicans in western states.

7. Who said, "Government is not the solution to the problem; government is the problem"?
    A. Bill Clinton
    B. Jesse Jackson
    C. Walter Mondale
  * D. Ronald Reagan

8. President Reagan's economic policy most closely resembled that of:
  * A. Andrew Mellon.
    B. Franklin D. Roosevelt.
    C. John F. Kennedy.
    D. Dwight D. Eisenhower.

9. John Anderson:
    A. was President Reagan's secretary of the interior.
    B. was President Reagan's secretary of state.
    C. was President Bush's secretary of state.
  * D. ran as an independent candidate in the 1980 presidential election.

10. "Reaganomics":
  * A. was Reagan's version of supply-side economics.
    B. was a simplified version of the Keynesian doctrine that the problems of the economy were mainly on the demand side.
    C. called for more government intrusion into the workplace.
    D. called for more taxes in order to increase government spending and to curtail runaway consumer spending.

11. As president, Reagan:
    A. supported the Equal Rights Amendment.
  * B. cut funds for civil rights enforcement.
    C. opposed the firing of striking air traffic controllers.
    D. All the above statements are true.

12. In Nicaragua, Reagan supported:
    A. followers of President José Napoleon Duarte.
  * B. the Contras.
    C. the Sandinistas.
    D. the PLO.

13. American troops were sent to Lebanon:
    A. to retaliate for an air strike against Israel.
    B. to prepare for the invasion of Grenada.
    * C. as "peacekeepers."
    D. over Reagan's veto.

14. Over 240 American marines were killed in 1983 when a truck loaded with dynamite blew up at their quarters in:
    A. Jerusalem.
    * B. Beirut.
    C. San Salvador.
    D. Teheran.

15. David Stockman was:
    * A. budget director under Reagan.
    B. chief of staff under Reagan.
    C. Speaker of the House in the mid-1980s.
    D. Senate minority leader in the mid-1980s.

16. Geraldine Ferraro was:
    A. fired from her position as chief of toxic waste cleanup at the EPA for favoritism to polluters.
    B. killed in the explosion of the space shuttle *Challenger*.
    * C. the Democratic vice-presidential candidate in 1984.
    D. Ronald Reagan's press secretary.

17. In the 1984 presidential election, Walter Mondale:
    A. chose Gary Hart as his running mate.
    B. promised he would not raise taxes.
    C. lost the endorsements of major labor, women's, and black organizations.
    * D. won only Minnesota and the District of Columbia.

18. The Tax Reform Act passed in 1986:
    A. increased tax shelters for businesses.
    B. raised the maximum income tax rate to 50 percent.
    C. was vetoed by Reagan.
    * D. reduced the number of tax brackets.

19. Reagan ordered the "rescue mission" in Grenada because:
    A. it served his Latin American strategy.
    * B. of appeals from neighboring islands.
    C. the Soviets asked the Untied States to remove the Cubans.
    D. the United Nations requested the United States do it.

20. The Wall Street crash of October 19, 1987:
    A. was the worst one-day drop in history.
    B. was caused in part by the size of the national debt and the high trade deficit.
    C. occurred partly because foreign investors were less willing to invest in the United States.
    * D. is correctly represented by all the above statements.

21. The INF treaty:
    * A. eliminated intermediate-range nuclear missiles.
    B. was between England, France, and the United States.
    C. doubled the amount of wheat sold annually to the Soviet Union.
    D. concerned whaling off the coast of Norway.

22. The term "Teflon Presidency":
    A. was coined by Gary Hart.
    B. was coined by Richard Nixon.
    * C. refers to Ronald Reagan.
    D. refers to George Bush

23. In the 1988 presidential campaign, Michael Dukakis:
    A. promised to continue the Reagan agenda.
    * B. won ten states and the District of Columbia.
    C. was the first Democratic candidate since the 1930s to win a majority of the southern states.
    D. All the above statements are true.

24. Who said, "Read my lips: no new taxes"?
    * A. George Bush
    B. Michael Dukakis
    C. Jesse Jackson
    D. Ronald Reagan

25. During the Reagan years, the national debt:
    A. decreased slightly because of massive cuts in social programs.
    B. stayed the same, despite massive cuts in social programs.
    * C. nearly tripled.
    D. rose by a factor of ten to over $500 million.

26. President Bush's position on Iraq was strengthened by:
    A. Israel's agreement to attack Iraq first.
    * B. U.N. Resolution 678.

        C. Desert Storm's operation becoming Desert Shield.
        D. U.S. production of SCUD missiles.

27. Oliver North was convicted on charges arising from:
        A. the illegal sale of public lands in the West.
        B. the savings and loan crisis.
        C. campaign fraud in the 1988 election.
  * D. the Iran-Contra affair.

28. In the Persian Gulf War, the United States:
        A. helped free Kuwait from Iraqi control.
        B. was one of 28 nations allied for Operation Desert Storm.
        C. called for a cease-fire after just six weeks of fighting.
  * D. All the above statements are true.

29. Manuel Noriega:
        A. was a CIA informant in Panama.
        B. was head of the Panamanian Defense Forces.
        C. was captured after a U.S. military invasion of Panama.
  * D. is correctly represented by all the above statements.

30. Who was known as the "Great Communicator"?
        A. George Bush
        B. Jimmy Carter
  * C. Ronald Reagan
        D. Caspar Weinberger

Essay Questions

1. Describe and illustrate the main features of Reaganomics.

2. What factors contributed to Republican political success in the 1980s?

3. What was America's role in world affairs during the Reagan and Bush years?

4. Ronald Reagan practiced "the politics of symbolism," according to one scholar. Is this an accurate assessment of Reagan's presidential career?

5. Were the Reagan and Bush administrations more successful at handling domestic or foreign problems? Explain.

Matching Questions

A) finished third in 1980 presidential race
B) Republican vice-presidential candidate in 1980
C) led the Moral Majority
D) governor of California
E) appointed "drug czar"
F) main actor in Iran-Contra affair
G) Supreme Court justice
H) Microsoft founder
I) secretary of the interior who resigned
J) said "[My opponent] will raise taxes, and so will I. He won't tell you. I just did."

A	1. John Anderson
E	2. William J. Bennett
B	3. George Bush
C	4. Jerry Falwell
H	5. Bill Gates
J	6. Walter Mondale
F	7. Oliver North
G	8. Sandra Day O'Connor
D	9. Ronald Reagan
I	10. James Watt

Chapter 37

TRIUMPH AND TRAGEDY:
AMERICA AT THE TURN OF THE CENTURY

This chapter describes recent demographic trends and covers the Clinton administration and the Bush administration.

Chapter Outline

I. America's changing face
   A. Age, gender, and race
      1. The Baby Boomers mature
      2. Growth of Sunbelt and urban areas
      3. Women and the workforce
      4. Decline of the "traditional family unit"
      5. Black Americans and poverty
   B. The new immigrants
      1. Changes in America's ethnic mix
      2. Rate of increase in immigration
      3. Origins of immigrants
      4. Immigrants and American culture
      5. Nativist response

II. The computer revolution
   A. An overview of the computer revolution
   B. Transformation of computers in the 1950s and 1960s
   C. Microchip and "personal computer" development

III. A new breed of cultural conservatives
   A. More ideological and partisan
   B. Attacks on liberalism
   C. The Religious Right
      1. Christian Coalition
      2. Political effect

IV. Bush to Clinton
   A. Decline in Bush's popularity
      1. Foreign affairs

       2. Economic recession
         a. Effects on business and workers
         b. Cure remained elusive
       3. The Clarence Thomas affair
         a. Thomas's background
         b. Charges of sexual misconduct
         c. Confirmation hearings
         d. Galvanized women's movement
       4. Broke "No new taxes" pledge
       5. Social issues threatened to split Republicans
    B. Meanwhile, Democrats presented solid centrist image
       1. Clinton's background
         a. Early years
         b. Positions on issues
         c. "Slick Willie"
       2. Election of 1994
         a. The Clinton-Gore team
         b. The Perot wild card
         c. Results

V. Domestic policy in Clinton's first term
    A. Controversy over gays in the military
    B. Family and Medical Leave Act
    C. Clinton's economic program
       1. Republicans blocked stimulus package
       2. Deficit-reduction package barely passed
    D. NAFTA
       1. Background and controversy
       2. Barely passed
    E. Health-care reform
       1. Background
       2. Clinton's plan
       3. Hillary Clinton chaired task force
       4. Vested interests opposed
       5. Democrats dropped fight for universal medical coverage
    F. Handguns and the crime bill
       1. Brady Bill put waiting period on handgun purchases
       2. Crime bill passed
    G. Mistrust of government and the militia movement
       1. Examples of the militia movement
       2. Examples
         a. Waco
         b. Oklahoma City

VI. Republican insurgency
   A. Republican landslide in midterm elections of 1994
   B. Democrats resented Clinton's "waffling"
   C. Republicans' "Contract with America"
      1. Rise of Newton Leroy Gingrich
      2. Fate of individual provisions
      3. "Gingrich revolution" fizzled out
   D. Legislative breakthrough
      1. Increase in minimum wage
      2. Personal Responsibility and Work Opportunity Act
   E. Election of 1996
      1. Bob Dole and Jack Kemp for Republicans
      2. Clinton/Gore for Democrats
      3. The campaign
      4. Democratic victory

VII. Economic and social trends of the 1990s
   A. The "new economy"
   B. The white-collar sweatshop
   C. Status of affirmative action began to shift
   D. Scandals
      1. Whitewater
      2. The Lewinsky affair

VIII. Foreign policy challenges
   A. Haiti
   B. The Middle East
   C. The Balkans

IX. The election of 2000
   A. Democrats nominate Albert Gore, Jr.
   B. Republicans nominate George W. Bush
   C. Election results
   D. Outcome determined by a decision of the Supreme Court

X. George W. Bush's presidency
   A. Cabinet appointments
   B. Economic conditions and policies
      1. 2001 recession
      2. Tax cuts
   C. Global terrorism
   D. September 11, 2001
   E. Bush declares war on terrorism
   F. Terrorism at home
   G. Middle East turmoil
   H. A return to normality

Lecture Ideas

1. An overview of the Clinton administration is a good way to divide the class and assign the various aspects of his presidency. See *The Postmodern Presidency: Bill Clinton's Legacy in U.S. Politics* edited by Steven E. Schier (2000), Lauren Berlant and Lisa Duggan, eds., *Our Monica, Ourselves: The Clinton Affair and the National Interest* (2001), William C. Hyland's *Clinton's World: Remaking American Foreign Policy* (1999), Jeffrey Toobin's *A Vast Conspiracy* (1999), theda Skocpol's *Boomerang: Clinton's Health Security Effort and the Turn Against Government in U.S. Politics* (1996), and Haynes Johnson's *The Best of Times: America in the Clinton Years* (2001).

2. A lecture on the election of 2000 will give students a good insight into the state of politics in the twenty-first century. It will also give you an opportunity to discuss the electoral college and the role of the Supreme Court. See Jeffrey Toobin's *Too Close to Call* (2001) and Roger Simon's *Divided We Stand: How Al Gore Beat George Bush and Lost the Presidency* (2001).

True/False Questions

T   1. During the 1970s and 1980s, women entered the workforce in increasingly larger numbers.

F   2. Most of the nation's population growth in the 1980s occurred in the Northeast.

F   3. George W. Bush won the popular vote in the 2000 presidential election.

T   4. By 1990, for the first time in the nation's history the majority of immigrants came not from Europe but from other parts of the world.

T   5. The "Brady Bill" required a brief waiting period before buying a handgun.

T   6. The African-American judge appointed to the Supreme Court by President Bush had questioned affirmative action programs and the use of busing to achieve desegregated schools.

F   7. According to Janet Reno, the proposed Equal Rights Amendment represented "a socialist, anti-family, political movement that encourages women to leave their husbands, kill their children, practice witchcraft, destroy capitalism, and become lesbians."

F   8. During the 1992 presidential campaign, critics called William J. Bennett "Slick Willie" for his inconsistent position on controversial issues.

T   9. Al Gore was elected vice-president in 1992.

F   10. President Clinton, trying to persuade Congress to reject a free trade bill, said that if the bill passed, the country would hear a "giant sucking sound" of American jobs being drawn to Mexico.

Multiple-Choice Questions

1. The presidential election of 2000 saw:
    A. George W. Bush win the popular vote.
    B. Albert Gore, Jr. lose to Ralph Nader.
    * C. the Supreme Court rule 5 to 4 in *Bush* v. *Gore*.
    D. the first woman nominated for vice-president.

2. During the 1980s, each of the following gained in population *except*:
    A. California.
    * B. the District of Columbia.
    C. Florida.
    D. Texas.

3. In 1990, the leading cause of death among black males between the ages of fifteen and twenty-four was:
    A. AIDS.
    B. automobile accident.
    * C. homicide.
    D. drug overdose.

4. The top item on George W. Bush's wish list after his inauguration in 2001 was:
    A. the downfall of Iraq.
    * B. a tax cut.
    C. appointment of Supreme Court Justices.
    D. faith-based initiatives.

5. The purpose of California's Proposition 187 was to:
   * A. deny illegal immigrants access to public schools, nonemergency health care, and other social services.
   B. lower the state sales tax.
   C. lower the property taxes.
   D. limit the number of military base closings.

6. The Christian Coalition:
   * A. was organized by Pat Robertson.
   B. worked closely with Democratic leaders to bring about social reform.
   C. supported gay rights as a way of "bringing Christ's Kingdom to Earth."
   D. is correctly represented by all the above statements.

7. In the immediate aftermath of the Gulf War, President Bush's approval rating:
   * A. topped 90 percent.
   B. stayed about the same.
   C. fell slightly.
   D. fell tremendously.

8. The economic recession of the early 1990s:
   A. was unusual in that it brought about high inflation with low unemployment.
   B. was the third national economic setback in six years.
   * C. resulted in a decline in the average standard of living.
   D. politically hurt Democrats more than Republicans.

9. Clarence Thomas was:
   * A. nominated to replace Thurgood Marshall, the first black Supreme Court justice.
   B. a liberal lawyer who worked for affirmative-action programs.
   B. forced to resign his Senate seat following allegations of sexual impropriety.
   D. the first white president of the Congress for Racial Equality (CORE).

10. Fourteen months after making the pledge of "No new taxes," President Bush angered many:
    * A. Republicans by promoting a tax increase bill.
    B. Democrats by vetoing a tax reduction bill.

    C. Republicans by promoting a tax reduction bill.

    D. Democrats by vetoing a tax increase bill.

11. Bill Clinton was was governor of:
* A. Arkansas.
    B. California.
    C. Georgia.
    D. Ohio.

12. As his vice-presidential running mate, Bill Clinton chose:
    A. Patrick Buchanan.
* B. Albert Gore, Jr.
    C. Dan Quayle.
    D. Pat Robertson.

13. In the 1992 presidential campaign, which candidate was accused of having manipulated the ROTC program during the Vietnam War to avoid the draft?
    A. George Bush
* B. Bill Clinton
    C. Bob Dole
    D. Jack Kemp

14. Anita Hill:
    A. was appointed to the Supreme Court by President Clinton.
    B. accused Bill Clinton of sexual harassment.
* C. became the rallying point for a new surge in the women's movement.
    D. was appointed attorney general in 1993.

15. Concerning homosexuals in the military, President Clinton:
    A. kept his campaign promise to end all discrimination.
    B. kept his campaign promise not to interfere with existing regulations.
* C. adopted a "Don't ask, don't tell" policy.
    D. said it was up to Congress, not the president, to formulate policy.

16. President Clinton's deficit-reduction program of 1993:
    A. was defeated by a Democratic filibuster.
    B. included raising taxes of middle-class families while lowering taxes for those in the upper brackets.
* C. passed Congress by the narrowest of margins.
    D. easily passed the Democratic-controlled Congress.

17. The "N" in NAFTA stands for:
    A. National.
    B. Negro.
    C. New.
    * D. North.

18. President Clinton's health care reform plan:
    A. was narrowly approved by Congress in the summer of 1994.
    * B. was attacked by drug companies and insurance interests.
    C. was sponsored in Congress by Republican James McDougal.
    D. is correctly represented by all the above statements.

19. On April 19, 1995, 168 people were killed when a truck bomb exploded outside a federal office building in:
    A. Ruby Ridge, Idaho.
    B. New York City.
    * C. Oklahoma City.
    D. Waco,Texas.

20. The Branch Davidians:
    A. occupied a fortress compound in Albany, Georgia.
    * B. were led by David Koresh.
    C. surrendered to the FBI after a 50-day siege.
    D. are correctly represented by all the above statements.

21. In foreign policy, President Clinton most closely resembled:
    A. Calvin Coolidge.
    B. FDR.
    C. Theodore Roosevelt.
    * D. Woodrow Wilson.

22. In Haiti, President Clinton supported:
    * A. Jean-Bertrand Aristide.
    B. Benjamin Netanyahu.
    C. the Contras.
    D. the Sandinistas.

23. In the midterm elections of 1994:
    * A. Republicans won both houses of Congress.
    B. Democrats won both houses of Congress.
    C. every Republican congressional incumbent was defeated.
    D. Democrats won a net gain of 11 governorships and 15 state legislatures.

24. The "Contract with America" included all the following *except*:
    A. a balanced-budget amendment.
    B. welfare reform.

* C. health-care reform.
   D. congressional term limits.

25. The welfare reform measure passed in the late summer of 1996:
   * A. was sponsored by Republicans and opposed by liberal Democrats.
     B. added over $50 billion to various welfare programs.
     C. took control of welfare programs from the states and gave it to the federal government.
     D. was opposed by President Clinton as an "unconscionable" effort to "end welfare as we know it."

26. In 1996, the Republican candidate for president was:
     A. George Bush.
   * B. Bob Dole.
     C. Ross Perot.
     D. Ronald Reagan.

27. In the mid-1990s, the Supreme Court:
     A. approved the gerrymandering of congressional districts to create black or Hispanic majorities.
   * B. generally became more conservative.
     C. included three female and two black justices.
     D. finally overturned *Plessy* v. *Ferguson*.

28. The "Whitewater" case:
     A. led to the conviction of Oliver North.
     B. increased congressional support for free trade.
     C. led to the indictment of Clinton's secretary of state.
   * D. involved a failed investment by the Clintons in an Arkansas resort project.

29. The Supreme Court case of *Adarand Constructors* v. *Peña* concerned:
     A. prayer in the public schools.
     B. gun control.
     C. abortion rights.
   * D. affirmative-action programs.

30. Concerned with Middle East diplomacy, the Bush administration:
   * A. initially withdrew from active involvement.
     B. was actively involved from his first day in office.
     C. sent Colin Powell to negotiate a peace settlement in early 2001.
     D. made this issue their number one priority.

Essay Questions

1. Did American foreign policy change significantly when Bill Clinton became president?

2. Briefly assess Clinton's achievements in domestic policy.

3. What factors might account for the Republican gains in the 1994 elections?

4. How accurate is the term "cultural politics" in describing the United States in the 1990s?

5. Describe the new patterns of immigration to the United States. What might account for this?

Matching Questions

A) resigned Senate seat (and role of majority leader) in 1996
B) Republican presidential candidate in 1992
C) attorney general
D) independent counsel
E) finished third in 1992 presidential election
F) authored the "Contract with America"
G) chaired health care plan task force
H) Federal Reserve Board chairman
I) author of "Bowling Alone: The Decline of Social Capital"
J) Democratic presidential candidate in 1992

B   1. George Bush
G   2. Hillary Clinton
J   3. William Jefferson Clinton
A   4. Bob Dole
F   5. Newt Gingrich
H   6. Alan Greenspan
E   7. H. Ross Perot
I   8. Robert Putnam
C   9. Janet Reno
D   10. Kenneth Starr

Appendix

SAMPLE FINAL EXAMINATIONS

The following sample final examinations may be of use to instructors using the Tindall and Shi text. These four samples (two covering American history through Reconstruction, two from Reconstruction to the present) are designed as three-hour exams. Instructors should use these samples only as guides; they are based on the textbook and cannot reflect the emphasis or additional information that an instructor adds in lectures. Instructors are therefore encouraged to modify these tests to suit their particular courses.

Instructors can, of course, make up a final examination consisting entirely of multiple-choice questions selected from the chapter tests, and in large classes this may be the only practical course. The exams that follow, however, are meant to allow students to show their mastery of the material by synthesizing facts, analyzing a large body of knowledge, and discerning trends over a long period of time. At this stage in a course, students should be prepared to use the facts they have learned to write historical essays.

Instructors may wish to remind students that, unless a narrative is specifically requested in an essay, they should concentrate instead on explanation—that is, they should analyze rather than retell the story. Instructors may find it difficult to grade the writing (as opposed to the content) of an essay and may have no ready answer when a student complains that "this is a history class, not an English class." Nonetheless, students should be encouraged to write coherent, organized essays. (You may wish to suggest that your students purchase and read a copy of Strunk and White's *Elements of Style* or another good style manual.) In the "short answer" sections, organization and careful thought are again needed, perhaps even more so than in the longer essays. Finally, the "identifications" are useful for testing more specific knowledge, but even here students should be reminded that facts do not exist in isolation. Suggest that students include a short sentence explaining the significance of each particular term or person.

American History Final Examination—To Reconstruction

Example 1

Part I. *Essay.* Answer any one (1) of the following.

     50 points.

    1. "From colonial times onward, American history has been marked more by division than by unity." Is this statement true for the period from 1763 to 1870? What factors have united Americans? What factors were more divisive?

    2. When did the Civil War become "inevitable"? Here are a few possibilities:

        November 1860 (election)

        1846 (Wilmot Proviso)

        early 1830s (Second Awakening)

        1793 (cotton gin)

        1776 (Declaration of Independence)

        1630 (Massachusetts Bay founded)

    For each of these, write a brief paragraph telling how these might be said to have "caused" the Civil War.

Part II. *Presidents.* Place the following U.S. presidents in proper chronological order.

    20 points (2 points each)

John Adams	Andrew Johnson
John Quincy Adams	Abraham Lincoln
Ulysses S. Grant	James Madison
Andrew Jackson	James K. Polk
Thomas Jefferson	Zachary Taylor

Part III. *Matching.* On a page in your examination book, write the numbers 1 to 15 down the left side. Then, write the letter for the best match. You will not use all the letters.

30 points (2 points each).

1. Catharine Beecher
2. John C. Calhoun
3. Jefferson Davis
4. Stephen Douglas
5. Jonathan Edwards
6. William Lloyd Garrison
7. Alexander Hamilton
8. William H. Harrison
9. Thomas Jefferson
10. James Madison
11. Nat Turner
12. Horace Mann
13. John Marshall
14. Harriet Beecher Stowe
15. Theodore Dwight Weld

A. kicked out of Massachusetts Bay
B. early leader in Jamestown
C. Great Awakening preacher
D. protested Mexican War, wrote "Civil Disobedience"
E. proposed Kansas-Nebraska Act
F. wrote *Uncle Tom's Cabin*
G. governor of Dominion of New England
H. wrote the Declaration of Independence
I. led Union troops on destructive march through the South
J. wrote *American Slavery as It Is*
K. "Great Compromiser"
L. nationalist Supreme Court justice
M. wrote *South Carolina Protest and Exposition*
N. "spot resolutions"
O. killed at Battle of Quebec
P. president during War of 1812
Q. wrote *Treatise on Domestic Economy*
R. preacher in Second Awakening
S. president of the Confederate States of America
T. edited *The Liberator*
U. Washington's secretary of the treasury
V. organized the Sons of Liberty
W. wrote *Common Sense*
X. president who died in 1841
Y. public-education reformer
Z. caned (beat) Charles Sumner

American History Final Examination—To Reconstruction

Example 2

Part I. *Essay.* Answer any one (1) of the following.

> 40 points.

1. The history of the United States through Reconstruction saw three political-party systems (Federalist/Republican, Democrat/Whig, Republican/Democrat). Describe them, explaining how, why, and when they came about and, where appropriate, what ended them.

2. "By the eve of the Civil War, America had grown into two distinct societies, North and South." Accept this statement as a given. Describe the two societies and discuss the main factors that contributed to separate sectional identities.

Part II. *Short answer.* Write full paragraphs on three (3) of the following.

> 30 points (10 points each).

1. At what point did it become clear that England, and not Spain, France, the Netherlands, or some other country, would control most of North America? Why?

2. Assess the social effects of the American Revolution.

3. Describe the Compromise of 1850. How was it designed to ease sectional tensions? What were its effects?

4. What advantages did the North have at the outbreak of the Civil War? What advantages did the South have?

5. Describe the plans of Reconstruction proposed by Abraham Lincoln, Andrew Johnson, and the Radicals. What philosophies motivated these plans?

Part III. *Identifications*. Identify and briefly show the historical significance of six (6) of the following.

30 points (5 points each).

Roger Williams
indentured servants
John Marshall
Wilmot Proviso
Shays's Rebellion
Jay's Treaty
Seneca Falls Convention
Anaconda strategy

American History Final Examination—Reconstruction to the Present

Example 1

Part I. *Essay.* Answer any one (1) of the following.

> 50 points.

1. Maybe history repeats itself, maybe not. In any case, American history seems to go in cycles. For example, the Gilded Age, the 1920s, the 1950s, and the late 1970s–1980s were, in several important ways, similar. Describe the similarities among these periods.

2. Compare the racial philosophies of W. E. B. Du Bois, Marcus Garvey, Martin Luther King, Jr., Malcolm X, and Booker T. Washington. (You do not have to discuss them in that order.) Your answer should place each person and philosophy into historical context.

Part II. *Identifications.* Identify and briefly show the historical significance of five (5) of the following.

> 20 points (4 points each).

> Dawes Severalty Act
> Atlantic Charter
> court-packing plan
> subtreasury plan
> "Teflon Presidency"
> Roosevelt Corollary

Part III. *Matching.* On a page in your examination book, write the numbers 1 to 15 down the left side. Then, write the letter for the best match. You will not use all the letters.

30 points (2 points each).

1. Dwight D. Eisenhower
2. Betty Friedan
3. James Garfield
4. Samuel Gompers
5. Helen Hunt Jackson
6. Lyndon Johnson
7. George F. Kennan
8. John F. Kennedy
9. Huey Long
10. Sandra Day O'Connor
11. John D. Rockefeller
12. John T. Scopes
13. Upton Sinclair
14. Booker T. Washington
15. Woodrow Wilson

A. convicted of teaching evolution in 1925
B. resigned as vice-president in 1973
C. president when Medicare and Medicaid were established
D. secretary of the treasury in 1920s
E. Democratic vice-presidential candidate in 1984
F. headed Committee on Public Information
G. named Supreme Court justice in 1981
H. wrote *The Feminine Mystique*
I. "I Have a Dream" speech
J. assassinated in 1881
K. "Father of Containment"
L. president of the Homestead Works
M. wrote *The Jungle*
N. "Gospel of Wealth"
O. founded Standard Oil
P. wrote rags-to-riches novels
Q. originated the Atlanta Compromise
R. wrote *The Influence of Sea Power upon History*
S. New Nationalism
T. popularized "Share Our Wealth" plan of 1930s
U. American Federation of Labor leader
V. wrote *Century of Dishonor*
W. known as "Deadwood Dick"
X. New Frontier
Y. dynamic conservatism
Z. Fourteen Points

American History Final Examination—Reconstruction to the Present

Example 2

Part I. *Essay.* Answer any one (1) of the following.

> 40 points.

1. American foreign policy has had a strong influence on the domestic scene—that is, American involvement overseas has affected various things here at home (such as labor patterns and politics, to name just two). The reverse is also true: domestic conditions have often shaped foreign policy. Write an essay demonstrating the close relationship between American foreign and domestic policy.

2. One theme of this course has been the growth of American government, from laissez-faire attitudes of the Gilded Age to the big government of the 1990s. Trace the main steps in the development of big government from 1877 to 1991.

Part II. *Short answer.* Write full paragraphs on four (4) of the following.

> 40 points (10 points each).

1. What were the main provisions of the platform of the Populist party?

2. What factors contributed to the growth of industry in late-nineteenth-century America?

3. What were the arguments for and against America's annexation of the Philippines?

4. What were the main themes of progressivism?

5. Describe the cultural paradox of the 1920s.

6. Explain the main features of Reaganomics.

Part III. *Identifications.* Identify and briefly show the historical significance of five (5) of the following.

20 points (4 points each).

Dawes Severalty Act
counterculture
Upton Sinclair
Betty Friedan
Operation "Overlord"
Horatio Alger